"Félix-Jäger and Shin have laid ⟨...⟩ t, and sagacious terms. This bool ⟨...⟩ ts of concise scholarship, and provokes theological imaginations. The book not only brilliantly treats the beauty, goodness, and truth in and of Pentecostal theology, it also transports the reader into the perichoretic beauty, goodness, and truth of a scholarship touched by grace."

—**Nimi Wariboko**, author of *Transcripts of the Sacred in Nigeria: Beautiful, Monstrous, Ridiculous*

"A bold and refreshing approach to a topic that can at times become a well-worn and tired subject. Félix-Jäger and Shin take seriously the differences a pneumatological perspective brings to the construction of a Christian worldview. The result is a provocative proposal that is both helpful for understanding one of the largest demographics among global Christianity (Pentecostals) and prescribing a way forward for anyone interested in an alternative to a traditional propositional approach. This timely work is sure to become a landmark in the field."

—**Lisa P. Stephenson**, Lee University

"*Renewing Christian Worldview* does just that: it reinvigorates the worldview discussion, albeit from a Pentecostal perspective. Félix-Jäger and Shin here provide a frame for engaging voices and perspectives from the global South as part of the necessary next steps both in the ongoing maturation of the Pentecostal academy and for further considerations of the transcendentals by theologians across world Christianity."

—**Amos Yong**, Fuller Theological Seminary

"This book is an achievement on many different levels. It represents a 'coming of age' of renewal traditions in the authors' ability to offer a form of sophisticated, world-regarding catechesis. It would have been a game-changer for me as a young person, when I had critical questions about life that neither my public school nor my church youth group was helping me answer. I felt lost so many times, openly wondering if my church tradition could keep up with the longings I had to make sense of the world and my place within it. This book could have helped me then, and I am convinced it will significantly help many people today. If read widely, this book could be part of a generational turning point."

—**Daniel Castelo**, Duke Divinity School

"Félix-Jäger and Shin have given us a constructive account of renewal theology, engaging a deep bench of philosophical and theological scholars. The authors' Spirit-filled worldview creates new vistas into truth, beauty, and goodness with deference to the Pentecostal and charismatic traditions. Though some will find points of friction here, the holistic approach appears to be the view with which all Pentecostal/charismatic theologies will have to contend. An invigorating read!"

—**Dru Johnson**, The King's College, New York City

"One of the greatest threats to the God-given fullness of human life is reductionism. When we attempt to make the unknowable known using reason and intellect alone, we unintentionally reduce the Infinite to the finite mind. Félix-Jäger and Shin have invited us to a renewed worldview through the integration of experience, emotion, and mind with beauty, goodness, and truth. This is a must-read for our time!"

—**Tammy Dunahoo**, Portland Seminary of George Fox University

"A fresh and innovative look at the nature and power of beauty, goodness, and truth—centered in the Spirit's work in and through creation—for personal and cultural renewal. Félix-Jäger and Shin expertly argue that a richer vision of reality, rooted in the Pentecostal imagination, can lead to a fresh movement of the Spirit in education, apologetics, and church ministry. This book is jampacked with wisdom and insight and is a must-read for anyone interested in worldview, apologetics, culture, and theology."

—**Paul M. Gould**, Palm Beach Atlantic University

"Félix-Jäger and Shin are two of the brightest emerging philosophical minds in the Pentecostal world. In *Renewing Christian Worldview*, they guide and form their readers in the beautiful, the good, and the true. This is the book we have needed for some time, full of the riches of the Christian tradition. In itself, this text is a philosophical education with and for the nearly one-fifth of the world's Christians in the charismatic-pentecostal tradition—and for many beyond."

—**L. William Oliverio Jr.**, Northwest University College of Ministry; co-editor-in-chief of *Pneuma: The Journal of the Society for Pentecostal Studies*

"Félix-Jäger and Shin deliver a thoroughgoing, renewalist Christian worldview, which flows from the central narrative and experience of Pentecost and is rooted in the affections and practices of Spirit-filled believers. In the process, the authors provide a robust philosophical and theological exploration of beauty, goodness, and truth as a resource for thinking about the Christian worldview in the Spirit. This will make an excellent textbook or supplemental reading for Christian worldview courses in need of Pentecostal/Charismatic perspectives."

—**Sammy Alfaro**, Grand Canyon University

RENEWING
CHRISTIAN
WORLDVIEW

RENEWING CHRISTIAN WORLDVIEW

A HOLISTIC APPROACH FOR SPIRIT-FILLED CHRISTIANS

✦ ✦ ✦

STEVEN FÉLIX-JÄGER AND YOON SHIN

Baker Academic

a division of Baker Publishing Group
Grand Rapids, Michigan

Published by Baker Academic
a division of Baker Publishing Group
Grand Rapids, Michigan
www.bakeracademic.com

Printed in the United States of America

Library of Congress Cataloging-in-Publication Data
Names: Félix-Jäger, Steven, author. | Shin, Yoon, author.
Title: Renewing Christian worldview : a holistic approach for spirit-filled Christians / Steven Félix-Jäger and Yoon Shin.
Description: Grand Rapids, Michigan : Baker Academic, a division of Baker Publishing Group, [2023]
Identifiers: LCCN 2022061923 | ISBN 9781540965912 (paperback) | ISBN 9781540966797 (casebound) | ISBN 9781493442737 (ebook) | ISBN 9781493442744 (pdf)
Subjects: LCSH: Pentecostalism. | Christianity—Philosophy. | Aesthetics—Religious aspects—Pentecostal churches. | Religious ethics. | Knowledge, Theory of.
Classification: LCC BR1644 .F45 2023 | DDC 230/.046—dc23/eng/20230221
LC record available at https://lccn.loc.gov/2022061923

Baker Publishing Group publications use paper produced from sustainable forestry practices and post-consumer waste whenever possible.

23   24   25   26   27   28   29   7   6   5   4   3   2   1

From Steven:
To my Pentecostal sisters and brothers around the world
that I've had the privilege of dialoguing with.
It's my honor to help you grow in your faith
as you've helped me grow in mine.
And to Connie and Mila, my personal support system.

From Yoon:
To my parents, who live sanctified Spirit-filled lives;
my parents-in-law, who faithfully serve as Pentecostal missionaries;
and my wife and children, who model the fruit of the Spirit.

CONTENTS

INTRODUCTION

Seeking Renewal amid Competing Worldviews

Key Words

Pentecostalism: *A global renewal movement within the Christian faith.*

Religious experience: *A mystical and unexplainable (or hard to explain) encounter in which one feels a loss of control and attributes the power to God.*

Renewal tradition: *Every Christian tradition that accentuates the Spirit's renewing presence and work in the lives of believers.*

Renewal worldview: *A fundamental orientation of the narrated body that implicitly and often subconsciously imagines and understands reality.*

Triperspectival: *The integration of three (tri) perspectives, as in a renewal worldview that integrates the emotional (soul), the active (body), and the mental (mind).*

Have you ever tried to mix oil and water? You can't do it! The oil molecules resist and push away from the water molecules, and because oil is less dense than water, it clumps together and rises to the top. If we take this as an analogy, we might see emotive and expressive faith traditions like Pentecostalism as the oil that doesn't mix with the water of cool, clear-eyed philosophy. But the Christian life is holistic, affecting the body, emotions, and mind. Jesus knows this when he tells us to "love the Lord your God with all your heart, and with all your soul, and with all your mind" (Matt. 22:37). Many Pentecostals are known for loving God well with heart and soul (oil) but not so much for loving God well with mind (water). But striving to love God with our *whole* being and thus to live holistically as Christians requires asking how we as renewal

Christians can think clearly about what it means to be a Christian today. All Christians are called, after all, to critically examine the faith so that we are always "ready to make [our] defense to anyone who demands from [us] an accounting for the hope that is in [us]" (1 Pet. 3:15). Consequently, we want to encourage Pentecostals and charismatics to understand the Christian faith both as the substance of Spirit-filled living *and* as a knowledge tradition, especially in light of its global and divergent reality.

It is our hope that this book helps you envision a renewal perspective on why Christianity is beautiful, good, true, and relevant to all aspects of life. Matters of beauty, goodness, and truth are what concern us most, and if we're serious about living holistically in the Spirit, we must feel, act, *and* think through what our experiences with God mean and how they shape our views and postures on what's most important to us. We believe that the Spirit experientially guides us toward beauty, goodness, and truth—ultimately toward God's own self as Beauty, Goodness, and Truth as such (what are known as the "transcendentals")—and this is what makes for a renewed Christian worldview. This book interacts with the history of philosophy and contrasts alternative visions within the Christian tradition in order to trace the historical and theoretical lineage of the renewal worldview. Also, to put flesh on the bones of the theories we'll put forward, this book offers practical, real-world applications of the renewal worldview. This introductory chapter clarifies terms, defining pivotal expressions such as "Pentecostalism," "worldview," and "renewal," and explains what is meant by the pursuit of beauty, goodness, and truth. We also explain the "triperspectival" method we're using to comprehend the Spirit's renewing work in the formation of a renewal worldview, before ending with an overview of the book.

A Renewal Perspective on Beauty, Goodness, and Truth

In our technologically advanced, global milieu, we are now able to see ways of life that, in centuries past, we could never have known even existed. Through a tablet screen we can peer into cultures around the world in real time! With these abilities we have become acutely aware of just how different people are around the world. Cultural expressions like art, music, dance, ceremonies, architectural forms, fashion, food, and customs vary greatly from region to region and between subcultures within regions. Furthermore, religious expressions, even if the traditions are denominationally the same, vary greatly around the world. Given this vast diversity within and outside religions, we can say that there isn't a *single* Pentecostal perspective. In fact, some scholars are beginning to define Pentecostalism in the plural, acknowledging the full range of "pentecostalisms."[1] This is in part due to the recent, rapid growth of Pentecostalism around the world,[2] and it is partly due to the difficulties of finding a single defining structure that captures the substance of every expression of Pentecostalism. Because of these difficulties, our attempts at crafting a systematic approach for clear Pentecostal thought will not be airtight or definitive but will unavoidably be fraught with exceptions. Nevertheless, if we want to get anywhere in the discussion, we have to start somewhere.

Conceding these limitations, we understand **Pentecostalism** as a global renewal movement within the Christian faith. While Pentecostalism includes classical Pentecostal denominations, as a global movement it also stretches beyond denominational borders. By "renewal" we do not mean just any sort of doctrinal restoration but one that is deeply connected to the Acts 2 narrative of the universal outpouring of the Holy Spirit. The Spirit is the source of *this* type of renewal, so when we refer to the **renewal tradition**, we mean every Christian tradition that accentuates the Spirit's renewing presence and work in the lives of believers. Speaking denominationally, "renewal" thus refers collectively to classical Pentecostal, charismatic, and neo-Pentecostal expressions of the Christian faith, such as the Assemblies of God, Catholics and Protestants who practice the gifts of the Holy Spirit, and independent or small networks of Pentecostal churches, respectively. Given these delimited connotations, we will use the terms "renewal" and "Pentecostal" interchangeably throughout this text, so readers shouldn't identify "Pentecostal" with only classically identifiable denominations. Importantly, since we're working with broad strokes of Pentecostalism, our generalizations will inevitably miss conflicts between specific traditions.

Since we have to start somewhere, we'll concentrate on three wide-ranging aspects of Pentecostalism that *seem* universally conventional: (1) Pentecostalism as a *global* Christian tradition, (2) Pentecostalism's focus on the *renewing work of the Holy Spirit,* and (3) Pentecostalism as *experiential* and holistic, like most forms of global Christianity.

---

1. See Keith Warrington, *Pentecostal Theology: A Theology of Encounter* (London: T&T Clark, 2008), 12; Allan Anderson, *An Introduction to Pentecostalism* (Cambridge: Cambridge University Press, 2004), 10; and Veli-Matti Kärkkäinen, "Pentecostals, and Pentecostal Theology in the Third Millennium," in *The Spirit in the World: Emerging Pentecostal Theologies in Global Contexts*, ed. Veli-Matti Kärkkäinen (Grand Rapids: Eerdmans, 2009), xvi.

2. Pentecostalism has been identified as one of the fastest-growing religious movements in the world. See "Spirit and Power—a 10-Country Survey of Pentecostals," Pew Research Center, October 5, 2006, http://www.pewforum.org/2006/10/05/spirit-and-power; Philip Jenkins, *The Next Christendom: The Coming Global Christianity* (New York: Oxford University Press, 2011); and Amos Yong, *The Spirit Poured Out on All Flesh: Pentecostalism and the Possibility of Global Theology* (Grand Rapids: Baker Academic, 2005), 19.

Christianity has always been a global faith. Because of Christianity's deep European roots throughout the Middle Ages, we tend to forget that Israel, as part of the Middle East, is actually located on the Asian continent! In fact, Israel is placed right at the nexus of Asia, Europe, and Africa, and every major Christian community in the first century sprang up on each of these continents before spreading out even farther through missionary zeal. Alexandria in Northern Africa, for instance, was considered a major intellectual hub of early Christianity. Saint Thomas is said to have established an Indian church in the second half of the first century.[3] Perhaps Israel was divinely and strategically chosen for the very purpose of becoming a wide-reaching, global faith. Even with its global origins, however, Christianity later became known as a predominantly Western religion.

Christianity's epicenter shifted from a transnational locale to a predominantely European one during the Middle Ages. The 800 CE christening of Charlemagne as the God-ordained emperor of the Holy Roman Empire all but sanctioned Christianity's European centrality for the next millennium. Recently, however, things have changed substantially as Christianity has grown exponentially in non-Western countries throughout the twentieth and twenty-first centuries. In 1900, for instance, 80 percent of Christians around the world lived in North America and Europe, but in recent decades just 40 percent live in North America or Europe with a majority now found in the global South. What's more, in 1970, Pentecostals comprised only 5 percent of the population; today, 25 percent of Christians identify as Pentecostal or charismatic.[4] Pentecostalism's message of Spirit-empowerment,[5] coupled with late modern globalization—the process of worldwide integration and expansion—has bolstered the resurgence of what is known as "world Christianity," and world Christianity is increasingly Pentecostal.[6] In fact, according to Philip Jenkins, out of all Anglo-European countries in the twenty-first century, only the US is projected to see growth in Christian populations, and this is mainly due to immigration.[7] Pentecostal immigrants are contributing significantly to this growth. Christianity in the US is thus the beneficiary of the global expansion of Pentecostalism. Furthermore, while the 1906–9 Azusa Street Revival in Los

---

3. Xavier Kochuparampil, "The St. Thomas Christians of India: Ecumenical and Missiological Challenges," *Exchange* 25, no. 3 (September 1996): 243.

4. Wes Granberg-Michaelson, "Think Christianity Is Dying? No, Christianity Is Shifting Dramatically," *Washington Post*, May 20, 2015, https://www.washingtonpost.com/news/acts-of-faith/wp/2015/05/20/think-christianity-is-dying-no-christianity-is-shifting-dramatically/.

5. Yong, *Spirit Poured Out*, 39.

6. Nimi Wariboko and L. William Oliverio, "The Society for Pentecostal Studies at 50 Years: Ways Forward for Global Pentecostalism," *Pneuma* 42 (2020): 327.

7. Jenkins, *Next Christendom*, 116–22.

Angeles has become the poster child for Pentecostal origins, other Pentecostal or Pentecostal-like revivals around the world materialized concurrently with Azusa Street, such as the Welsh Revival of 1904–5, the Mukti Revival of 1905 (India), and the Pyongyang Revival of 1907 (North Korea). We must not overlook or downplay the fact that Pentecostalism is truly a global renewal phenomenon.

The renewing work of the Holy Spirit is Pentecostalism's primary theological and practical focus. Every Christian tradition affirms, in some way, that the life-giving Spirit of God renews believers spiritually. Pentecostalism, however, makes renewal its central focus by emphasizing Spirit-related doctrines such as Spirit baptism and spiritual gifts as paramount for any Pentecostal theology. Furthermore, Pentecostal theology emphasizes the Spirit's presence and work in *every* other doctrine. For instance, Pentecostals focus on the Spirit's inspiration and illumination of Scripture (bibliology), on the Spirit's progressive roles in salvation (soteriology), on the Spirit's commissioning and empowering of the church (ecclesiology), and on Christian hope as the eschatological Spirit breaks into our present (eschatology). Importantly, Pentecostals believe that the Spirit's renewal is tangible and holistic, not merely spiritual or individualistic. A good life is available here and now for those who live in the Spirit. This notion has both aesthetic and ethical ramifications that will be explored in parts 1 and 2 of this book.

Even with a distinctively pneumatological outlook, however, Pentecostals reason practically. The Pentecostal focus on renewal is one that emerges not from a systematic theological method but from a lived, holistic experience of renewed life. In fact, as Walter Hollenweger, an early chronicler of Pentecostal theology, has noted, Pentecostals do not develop mere academic theologies of the Spirit but focus on the practical functions of the Spirit as if the work of the Spirit is presupposed in the Christian life. Historically, Pentecostals have been stronger at facilitating the experience of the Spirit than at articulating a theological interpretation of those experiences.[8] But when those experiences *are* interpreted, they are typically viewed through the backdrop of the Acts 2 narrative of Pentecost. Pentecostals view the events of Pentecost as the beginning of their story. In other words, the Pentecostal's experience of the Spirit is the same quality of experience that filled and empowered the 120 believers in the upper room. We can understand **religious experiences** as mystical and unexplainable (or hard to explain) encounters in which one feels a loss of control and attributes the power to God. This sort of experience is what theologian Keith Warrington calls the "unifying heartbeat" of Pentecostalism.[9]

---

8. Walter Hollenweger, *Pentecostalism: Origins and Developments Worldwide* (Peabody, MA: Hendrickson, 1997), 218.

9. Warrington, *Pentecostal Theology*, 20.

Not only does experience precede intellectual interpretation; it is typically valued more highly than "mentalist" approaches.[10] The language of "letting go" and "surrendering" to what the Spirit is doing is commonplace throughout Pentecostalism. Pentecostals, therefore, champion the old adage that renewal is "better caught than taught!" Therefore, because Pentecostalism is global, focused on the renewing work of the Spirit, and because it is experiential, it seems appropriate to talk about Pentecostalism's experiential spirituality as conventional for the faith.

To recap, the renewal tradition of Pentecostalism is global, experiential, and Spirit-focused. It is not primarily a doctrinal movement but an experiential spirituality that informs its beliefs. But what does this have to do with worldviews? Everything! It's not that Pentecostalism will revolutionize or drastically change the concept of worldview, but it can highlight important areas that are traditionally less emphasized by worldview studies—namely, areas that are not about *thinking* or *believing*. While thinking and believing are important elements of a worldview, they are only parts of a worldview and perhaps not even the most important parts.

Defining Christian Worldview

In his magisterial book on worldview, David Naugle provides a historical survey of the concept's development. In the Christian development of the concept, the Reformed tradition has used the concept of worldview throughout their theology and philosophy.[11] The Reformed influence also impacted apologetics, the field of defending and promoting the truth of the faith, and its ways of targeting worldview transformation. Evangelicals, who have been among the most ardent promotors of apologetics and the exclusivity of truth, also began to write about the importance of worldview.[12] A renewal approach to worldview highlights certain aspects of worldview that are less emphasized (or even opposed) by other worldview descriptions. A renewal worldview is

10. A more proper term is "noetic"—that is, about the mind or beliefs. Mentalism, on the other hand, is a specific theory about what justifies beliefs. For ease of understanding, we use the term "mental" in its more ordinary sense.

11. See David K. Naugle, *Worldview: The History of a Concept* (Grand Rapids: Eerdmans, 2002), 4–32. The Reformed tradition springs from the Protestant Reformation that began in 1517 and led to various streams. The Reformed tradition traces its roots to the stream started by the theologian John Calvin.

12. "Evangelicalism" is a contested term, but we will use David Bebbington's popular definition for brevity's sake. Bebbington describes Evangelicals as those committed to a high view of Scripture, a central focus on Jesus's sacrifice on the cross for salvation, the need for spiritual conversion, and a lifestyle geared toward changing the world. See David Bebbington, *The Evangelical Quadrilateral*, vol. 1, *Characterizing the British Gospel Movement* (Waco: Baylor University Press, 2021).

holistic, whereas much of the worldview literature revolves around propositional beliefs and arguments. This is partly because many Reformed and Evangelical traditions are doctrinal movements. Proving one's membership in the guild requires affirming their particular confessions. The reach of this confessionalism has been far and wide in church history, and its influence is evident in every church website that lists "What We Believe" prominently in the "About Us" section. This ritualized way of being Christian creates an innately strong pull toward propositional beliefs, even if the affective and narrative aspects of worldview are acknowledged. Renewal traditions, however, strongly emphasize the emotional, participatory, and experiential elements of their spirituality. Before we get too deep in our discussion of what sets apart a renewal worldview, let's review how Reformed and Evangelical Christians define worldview.

Many worldview proponents have emphasized its mental aspect, in which beliefs take center stage. According to Reformed theologian Philip Ryken, worldview is the "framework of beliefs and convictions" through which we interpret our lives, the universe, and reality. Ideally, this structure is *well-reasoned* and will deliver "a true and unified perspective on the meaning of human existence."[13] For Ryken, the quality of a worldview is partly determined by its development through reason. The Reformed philosopher Ronald Nash defines worldview as "a conceptual scheme, by which we consciously or unconsciously place or fit everything we believe and by which we interpret and judge reality."[14] By "conceptual scheme" Nash means the arrangement of ideas. Worldview is thus fundamentally a pattern of ultimate ideas. Randy Nelson similarly defines worldview as an interpretive "conceptual framework that allows us to make sense of reality" and stresses the mental contents of worldview.[15] Worldview, from this perspective, is essentially a belief system.

For many Evangelicals, the core elements of the Christian worldview answer questions pertaining to the existence and nature of God, the nature and purpose of human beings, the nature of morality, the human condition and the need for salvation, and truth and its knowability. The answers to these core belief questions lead to different, although sometimes overlapping, worldviews.[16] William Lane Craig and J. P. Moreland, two of the most influential contemporary

13. Philip Graham Ryken, *Christian Worldview: A Student's Guide*, Reclaiming the Christian Intellectual Tradition (Wheaton: Crossway, 2013), 20.
14. Ronald H. Nash, *Worldviews in Conflict: Choosing Christianity in a World of Ideas* (Grand Rapids: Zondervan, 1992), 16.
15. Randy W. Nelson, "What Is a Worldview?," in *Christian Contours: How a Biblical Worldview Shapes the Mind and Heart*, ed. Douglas S. Huffman (Grand Rapids: Kregel, 2011), 26.
16. Nelson, "What Is a Worldview?," 28–32.

Evangelical philosophers, continue the "mentalist" emphasis in their definition of worldview as "an ordered set of propositions that one believes, especially propositions about life's most important questions."[17] Albert Wolters's influential book *Creation Regained* defines worldview as "the comprehensive framework of one's basic beliefs about [ultimate] things."[18] The decisive element that shapes our worldview and guides our life, for these Evangelical thinkers, is cognitive beliefs, not emotions or interests.[19]

Others have proposed that beliefs play an important role in a worldview but do not fundamentally determine it. For Michael Goheen and Craig Bartholomew, worldview offers answers to ultimate questions about life, humanity, the world, evil, and salvation; they point us to the mental aspects of worldview. However, they don't intellectualize the concept. While worldview articulates basic beliefs, beliefs don't wholly determine a worldview.[20] Instead, these beliefs are "embedded in a shared grand story [and] are rooted in a faith commitment [and] give shape and direction to the whole of our individual and corporate lives."[21] Worldview is not *fundamentally* determined by beliefs. To have a worldview is to have fundamental beliefs, but beliefs arise from grand stories that are further rooted in faith commitments. Moreover, worldview beliefs are more often unarticulated; they are *pre*theoretical.[22] We are not often consciously thinking about them.

James Olthuis defines worldview as "a framework or set of fundamental *beliefs* through which we view the world and our calling and future in it."[23] At first glance, such a definition may seem mentalist, but on closer inspection, we see that it isn't. For Olthuis, worldview describes what the world is like (description) and what it should be like (prescription), but it is not primarily driven by mental beliefs. Rather, worldview is shaped by faith and life experience. Faith is not mental assent to certain doctrines, such as believing *that* Jesus rose from the dead; faith is believing *in* Jesus and entrusting the whole self to God. Of course, faith need not necessarily be Christian.[24] Everyone has faith in an ultimate reality, whether that ultimate reality is God, gods, or something

---

17. J. P. Moreland and William Lane Craig, *Philosophical Foundations for a Christian Worldview*, 2nd ed. (Downers Grove, IL: IVP Academic, 2017), 15.

18. Albert M. Wolters, *Creation Regained: Biblical Basis for a Reformational Worldview*, 2nd ed. (Grand Rapids: Eerdmans, 2005), 2.

19. Wolters, *Creation Regained*, 2–6.

20. Michael W. Goheen and Craig G. Bartholomew, *Living at the Crossroads: An Introduction to Christian Worldview* (Grand Rapids: Baker Academic, 2008), 24–25.

21. Goheen and Bartholomew, *Living at the Crossroads*, 23.

22. Goheen and Bartholomew, *Living at the Crossroads*, 25–26.

23. James H. Olthuis, "On Worldviews," *Christian Scholar's Review* 14, no. 2 (1985): 155 (italics added).

24. Olthuis, "On Worldviews," 157.

impersonal.[25] While mental beliefs are part of worldviews, they are neither decisive nor most important. Ultimate worldview questions are not finally answered by beliefs alone. Whatever those answers are, they reveal our faith commitments and our whole selves.

One of the leading figures in worldview studies is James Sire. Importantly, he acknowledges the evolution of his understanding of worldview. While he once defined worldview with propositional and conceptual descriptions, he now defines it as "a commitment, a fundamental orientation of the heart, that can be expressed as a story or in a set of presuppositions."[26] Believing and thinking occur through the heart. Unlike the popular understanding of the heart in contemporary US culture, the Bible's Hebraic understanding is that the heart is more than just the seat of emotion. The heart is also the place where wisdom, desire, will, spirituality, and intellect reside.[27]

Naugle has provided the most thorough study of worldview to date. He acknowledges that worldview in its most general and uncontroversial sense is the interpretation of reality. His more robust definition describes worldview semiotically (that is, through a system of signs): "Worldview is a semiotic system of narrative signs that has a significant influence on the fundamental human activities of reasoning, interpreting, and knowing."[28] Mental beliefs expressed in propositional statements—such as "God created the world good," "The world is corrupted by sin," and "The world can only be redeemed by Jesus"—can be elements of a worldview. But a worldview is much more. It reflects the central interpretive grid of human beings, which Naugle, drawing from Scripture, argues is rooted not in the mind and its beliefs but in the heart. The heart is the "innermost part of things. . . . [And] to know a person's heart is to know the actual person."[29] All parts of being human, such as thinking, acting, and feeling, arise from the heart.

Tied to the heart is our innate connection to signs. We use various forms of language to communicate, whether by sound, written word, or bodily movement. Moreover, besides God's speech, God is semiotically understood. The Father is known when we behold the Son, who is the Father's perfect image. And we know the Spirit through the sign of the Spirit *proceeding from* the Father and the Son.[30]

---

25. See Roy A. Clouser, *The Myth of Religious Neutrality: An Essay on the Hidden Role of Religious Belief in Theories* (Notre Dame, IN: University of Notre Dame Press, 2005).

26. James W. Sire, *Naming the Elephant: Worldview as a Concept*, 2nd ed. (Downers Grove, IL: IVP Academic, 2015), 141.

27. Sire, *Naming the Elephant*, 143.

28. Naugle, *Worldview*, 253. The field of semiotics looks at how signs communicate things spoken, through language, and even how unspoken signs or symbols are communicated.

29. Naugle, *Worldview*, 268.

30. Naugle, *Worldview*, 292–93.

The primary mode of human communicative and meaning-making activity is story. Think about the best speakers you've heard. Did they tell compelling stories? Why do movies and shows immerse us in their worlds? Because they tell good stories. Why is it that commercials don't merely lay out the facts of their products but convey them in images and stories? Because images and stories capture our hearts. It's no wonder that the most frequent mode of evangelism is sharing personal testimonies. Indeed, we can locate our worldview by identifying the stories we have internalized. Many Christians often find that their worldviews have been shaped broadly by the story of a good creation that became marred by sin, which explains the evils in the world. The solution to evil comes through redemption in Jesus Christ. This is the basic Christian story.

How is the renewal perspective any different from the basic Christian story? Every tradition adds its own variations and specific details to the story. In the case of Pentecostalism, adherents align their own stories to the Acts 2 narrative of Pentecost, where the Spirit was poured out on all flesh and the church was birthed, commissioned, and empowered to share the gospel to the ends of the earth. This is a biblical story, so it's available to any Christian tradition, but Pentecostals tend to emphasize it more than other traditions do. Pentecostals allow the story of Pentecost to color their lenses, thereby linking any life experiences to and grounding them in the universal outpouring of the Spirit. For our purposes, we define **renewal worldview** as a fundamental orientation of the narrated body that implicitly and often subconsciously imagines and understands reality. We all have a worldview. We inherit our worldview through narrative signs, emotions, beliefs, and actions, not just through propositional beliefs about ultimate questions that are often indistinguishable from Theology 101. In fact, most of our propositional beliefs are grounded in our bodily involvement in the world. Through narrative signs, emotions, beliefs, and actions, we further develop, modify, and express our worldview, an indwelt process that is often subconscious. For Pentecostals, the narrative signs, emotions, beliefs, and actions are rooted in the Pentecostal story we hear, tell, and live out. In this way, our definition of worldview is very much in line with that of Sire, Naugle, and Olthuis.

Thinking Holistically about Worldviews

As Naugle has argued, a general feature of worldview is that it is an interpretive grid of reality that directs our lives. Not a single aspect of our lives is untouched by our worldview. Worldview is systemic in this way. However, *systemic* is not necessarily *systematic*. Worldview can have inconsistency within itself. For example, one could be motivated by the stories of Jesus and thus believe that one ought to help the poor. But within that same worldview, shaped also by the US work ethic and capitalistic history, one could believe that God only helps those who help themselves, thus possibly creating an unhealthy generalized view of the poor.

Worldview is like a pair of permanent glasses that we wear. Better yet, it is like our outward appearances. Our skin color, sex, and gender play an incredibly powerful role in scripting and habituating our reality. Our worldview lens always already interprets reality for us. This doesn't mean that we are mere passive passengers of our understanding. We also actively participate in the development and changing of our worldview. However, a graver concern arises any time interpretation is mentioned. If worldviews interpret our understanding, then are we mired in the problem of relativism, which claims any worldview is true? Can we truly understand reality if we are left only to interpretations?

While there *are* relativistic worldviews, this isn't the case for Christian worldviews. By acknowledging from the outset that the Creator God exists, Christian worldviews are committed to the view that truth must, at minimum, correspond to God and God's creation. Objective states of affairs do exist independent of our interpretations. However, given that we only know through our worldviews, *our* knowledge is always subjective. Are we then back to square one? Are we left only to our interpretations of God's reality? The Christian philosopher Alvin Plantinga can help us with these questions.

According to Plantinga, warrant is a certain quality or quantity that, if we have enough of it, turns mere belief into knowledge. It is even unnecessary at times to provide evidence or arguments to have enough warrant for knowledge. Very broadly speaking, if the equipment we need for knowing (what Plantinga calls our cognitive faculties), such as our sensory system and brain, is working properly at the time of our believing and is successfully designed to produce true beliefs, then our beliefs can have enough warrant to qualify as knowledge. For example, Plantinga argues that God heals our cognitive faculties that were damaged by sin so that we can know God even if we don't arrive at that knowledge through some elaborate argument or extraordinary evidence. Therefore, our interpretive worldview beliefs *can* qualify as knowledge. This view is, of course, dependent on a particular Christian worldview.

Because a worldview is like permanent glasses, we often become accustomed to and unaware of its presence. This does not mean that we can't or shouldn't think about our worldviews. We ought to think about them so that we can examine them for their rightness and direct them appropriately, especially through narrative and embodied means. Yet our tendency is to operate in our interpretations without thinking about them and to consciously reflect on our worldviews only in punctuated moments. Even those of us who teach about worldviews don't often reflect on our own; rather, we simply operate in them, especially when we are outside our classrooms and offices. Always thinking about one's own worldview is impractical—doing so would stunt our life experiences and make us terrible company! Attempting to reflect on our worldviews all the time would be like a guitarist thinking about every finger movement or a runner thinking about every step. If we don't allow our bodily knowledge to take over, then we could easily stumble over our finger placements or lag behind in split-second movements that could mean the difference between winning and losing.

Because worldview is pretheoretical, we must be vigilant in guarding against foreign intrusions. This is a difficult task because our worldviews are often shaped pretheoretically. Much of our outlook on life occurs through life experiences, emotive judgments, and the stories in which we find ourselves. Yes, we must be vigilant against extraneous ideas, but the heart is susceptible to emotive and bodily-active appeals if we have not trained our emotions and dispositional actions (what we could call our virtues). This is why worldview descriptions that lionize belief are too simplistic. They blind us to the sneaky power of stories, emotions, and actions.

Yet we can't merely think in defensive terms. Such a posture already locates us in an "us versus them" story. The directing of our worldviews must include immersing ourselves in beauty, goodness, and truth, which are ultimately realized in God, who alone is *absolutely* beautiful, good, and true. But we cannot accomplish this immersion in solitude, as if developing an "orthodox" worldview necessitates the life of a desert hermit who lives on top of a pillar (we wouldn't mention it unless it really happened!).[31] Worldview formation occurs socially because we are social animals, and our stories are social stories. Each of us received a name that arose out of our unique social unit with its own (hi) story and expectations (or lack thereof). As we immerse ourselves in the social history and continuing story of our faith, we become—in our hearts and, indeed, in our whole beings—more and more attuned to God and what God is accomplishing and revealing in the world. Our pursuit of beauty, goodness, and truth solidifies our attraction toward these transcendentals and directs our lives while keeping our hearts guarded against antithetical worldviews.

Renewal Contributions to Worldview Studies

As we said above, a renewal perspective will not revolutionize worldview studies. There is no distinctive renewal approach to worldview that is unique to

---

31. It might interest some of you to read about the life of Simeon the Stylite. See Robert Doran and Susan Ashbrook Harvey, eds., *The Lives of Simeon Stylites*, trans. Robert Doran (Collegeville, MN: Liturgical Press, 1992).

Pentecostalism. A renewal worldview is holistic and will be similar to the definitions and descriptions provided by Bartholomew, Goheen, Olthuis, Sire, and Naugle. Renewal traditions strongly emphasize the emotional, participatory, and experiential elements of their spirituality. A renewal perspective, therefore, emphasizes the importance of not only beliefs but also emotions and actions in worldview formation, and it highlights how emotions and actions shape beliefs just as much as beliefs shape them. In this way, it rejects Ryken's view that beliefs necessarily precede emotions.[32] Beliefs are often embedded in emotions and actions, and emotions and actions can direct our beliefs. This last point is an important contribution made by Reformed charismatic philosopher James K. A. Smith.

According to Smith, the tendency to place believing or thinking at the center of worldview reveals a commitment to the theory that humans are fundamentally thinking or believing beings. The "person-as-thinker" model is found in the early modern philosophy of René Descartes, whose search for an absolutely certain foundation of knowledge led to "the thinking mind."[33] Perhaps you have heard the saying, "I think, therefore, I am," made famous by Descartes. Since even the existence of a good God and his own body could be doubted, Descartes believed that he needed to find something he could not doubt. Yet in order to doubt his own thinking, he needed to exist. Therefore, for Descartes, the thinking mind, not the body, was the fundamental feature of humanity.[34] Since everyone can wield reason, reason transcends the biases that arise from our individual and cultural contexts that are necessitated by our bodily locations.

Smith appreciates his Reformed tradition for diminishing this once-dominant view of humans as thinking things by turning to the preeminence of belief over thinking. All thinking arises from worldviews that are made up of fundamental beliefs that define our commitments and trusts. However, Smith is concerned that this "person-as-believer" model still disparages our God-given bodies. What are we without our bodies? Our life experiences—the highs and lows of our emotional lives, the joys of fellowship (including the obligatory after-church potluck!), the thrill of sporting events, the intimate touches of our loved ones—cannot occur without our bodies. These experiences make us who we are. They determine our understanding of the world and our place in it.

In place of these two previous models, Smith offers the "person-as-lover" model. As embodied creatures, we are primarily driven by our hearts and

32. Ryken, *Christian Worldview*, 28.
33. James K. A. Smith, *Desiring the Kingdom: Worship, Worldview, and Cultural Formation* (Grand Rapids: Baker Academic, 2009), 42–43.
34. René Descartes, *"Discourse on Method" and "Meditations on First Philosophy,"* trans. Donald A. Cress, 4th ed. (Indianapolis: Hackett, 1998), 65.

hands, which means that the fundamental elements of our worldviews are
not ideas but desires and actions.[35] Think about your own pursuit of meaning
and purpose. Are you driven merely by some idea or theory? Not likely. We are
driven by our desires. Sometimes we don't even know what we desire until we
partake in the particular activity. While beliefs can direct our emotions and
actions, our emotions and actions often direct our beliefs. Their relationship
is not a one-way street. Worldview is not fundamentally mental but emotive
and kinesthetic, and Smith arrives at this model by starting not with the mind
but with the body.

Since Pentecostalism is not primarily a doctrinal movement, it's best to
understand its heartbeat as the emotional, experiential encounter with the
Holy Spirit that grabs hold of our bodies, souls, and minds. In constructing
the elements of a Pentecostal worldview, Smith thus turns to Pentecostal worship, which is an experiential, embodied affair. (People don't joke about Pentecostals swinging on chandeliers for no reason!) Upon examination, Smith
discovered five elements that Pentecostals all share. First, Pentecostals have
a radical openness to God, specifically to the surprising work of the Spirit.
Second, the world is "enchanted" with the presence of the Holy Spirit along
with angelic and demonic spirits. Third, the body is not separated from the
mind, as seen in Descartes. Bodily healing and even prosperity are important
to Pentecostals. Fourth, against the primacy of mental beliefs in Reformed
and Evangelical traditions, Pentecostal practices exhibit a knowledge that is
more emotive and narrative.[36] Emotions are not mere physiological feelings,
like pain from a stubbed toe. They are themselves a way of knowing the world
that is different from mere beliefs. In the Pentecostal refrain, "I know that I
know that I know," we exhibit a kind of trust in our knowledge that sometimes
cannot be verified by ideas. For example, we don't know with our minds that
we are speaking anything intelligible when we are speaking in tongues, but
we know in our hearts that we are communing with God as the Spirit groans
with sighs too deep for words. This emotive knowledge is not relegated solely
to the religious realm. For example, a grumpy person and a cheerful person
will interpret the world differently. To one, the world and people are nuisances.
To the other, everything is just unicorns and rainbows.[37]

Emotive knowledge often arises from stories. The stories we hear and the
stories we live out detail our conflicts, meanings, and purposes. While beliefs

35. Smith, *Desiring the Kingdom*, 47–48.

36. James K. A. Smith, *Thinking in Tongues: Pentecostal Contributions to Christian Philosophy* (Grand
Rapids: Eerdmans, 2010), 12.

37. We jest, but this outlandish example clearly illustrates the power our emotions have over
our worldview.

are also part of stories, the embedded and eliciting emotions of our stories color our beliefs in a variety of ways. For Smith, this emotive, narrative knowledge is more fundamental than beliefs. For example, something gets lost when a story is broken down into mere details and facts. The idea of the story may get transmitted, but the emotive "pull" of the story disappears. Worldview thus cannot be fundamentally about beliefs because beliefs are shaped by our underlying emotions and the stories we embody.

Fifth, to return to Smith's list of worldview elements shared by all Pentecostals, he observes that they saw the outpouring of the Holy Spirit in contemporary times as the sign of Jesus's imminent return and the beginning of the end times, which oriented them toward justice and mission. But how does an end-times narrative motivate Pentecostals toward justice? Isn't social justice a politically liberal idea? Not so when we study renewal history. While charismatics have been traditionally socially conscious, classical Pentecostals have also exhibited great concern for justice and equality. For example, the initial years of the Azusa Street Revival, which began in 1906, which blurred the lines between color, gender, and socioeconomic levels.[38] This countercultural witness to a deeply racist, sexist, and classist Western world was made possible because people saw the Holy Spirit enrapture people of all colors, genders, and socioeconomic levels for kingdom work. Then and now, God is no respecter of persons. Social justice, for early Pentecostals, was not a politically partisan idea.[39] It was underwritten by the work of the Holy Spirit.

Smith's five Pentecostal worldview elements only make sense when the body is taken seriously. A renewal perspective on the transcendentals of beauty, goodness, and truth must arise from our embodiment even as it integrates beliefs. Michael Palmer, a Pentecostal philosopher, takes embodiment seriously and argues that worldview is a set of fundamental beliefs *and* practices. Importantly, he does not identify fundamental beliefs with propositions alone. Fundamental beliefs consist of propositional beliefs, significant narratives, and important norms, such as ethical and aesthetic standards, and they arise and become meaningful within the social context of experience and practice, especially as these active elements evoke an emotional response.[40]

As testified by these renewal scholars, worldview is not merely mental. Mental beliefs arise from, are integrated with, and shape emotions and practices.

---

38. Smith, *Thinking in Tongues*, 44–45.

39. We are not arguing that contemporary social justice movements are identical to the divine call for justice in Scripture. Nevertheless, biblical justice is greatly concerned with justice in the social realm.

40. Michael D. Palmer, "Elements of a Christian Worldview," in *Elements of a Christian Worldview*, ed. Michael D. Palmer (Springfield, MO: Logion, 1998), 24–30.

Again, this holistic impulse is due to the embodied spirituality of renewal Christianity. Doctrinal confessions that determine one's orthodox standings within the Christian faith (or denomination) are not most important; rather, it is one's encounter with God in Christ through the Holy Spirit that impacts one's emotions, actions, and beliefs.

Our approach to worldview in this book is thus **triperspectival**.[41] This seemingly complicated word points toward a straightforward reality: the integration of three perspectives (hence the "tri" prefix). Thus our renewal worldview is triperspectival because it integrates the emotional (soul), the active (body), and the mental (mind). Knowing beauty, goodness, and truth requires more than having beliefs about them. Our fundamental bodily orientation dictates that our knowledge of beauty, goodness, and truth requires an emotive aspect; we must not only know the good but love the good. And our practical lives direct our loves just as they are directed by our loves. To have a worldview in a robust sense is to participate in beauty, goodness, and truth. Our book thus recommends thinking lucidly about the transcendentals and also participating in them. For if God is absolutely beautiful, good, and true, then to know and participate in the transcendentals is to image, know, and love God in our lives. Shouldn't that be our desired goal?

To live holistically in the Spirit requires *knowing* that the Spirit guides us toward beauty, goodness, and truth. It also requires *living out* and *desiring* beauty, goodness, and truth as we seek to truly know them. If we don't embody beauty, goodness, and truth, they'll persist as ideal abstractions, betraying our renewal spirituality. If our claim that Pentecostalism is experiential and holistic is true, then any philosophical account of a renewal worldview *must* grapple with the intellectual attributes of life in the Spirit and pay close attention to the experiences that fund the renewal imagination. Now that we've discussed the intent of this book, below is an overview of how its contents flow.

Overview of the Book

This book is broken up into three parts, each named, respectively, after the transcendentals of beauty, goodness, and truth. Although the three transcendentals are usually ordered as truth, goodness, and beauty, giving priority to knowledge and what defines reality, we will approach these topics in reverse order.[42] Reversing the order stems from our argument *against* a mere mentalist approach of worldview and *for* a triperspectival approach that integrates the

---

41. Triperspectivalism was first introduced by the Reformed theologian John Frame, but we recognize its universal appeal in different traditions.

42. This is the approach of theologian Hans Urs von Balthasar, discussed in chap. 3.

emotional (soul), the active (body), and the mental (mind). Participating in beauty, goodness, and truth entails integration where the three intertwine in our human experience. Our experiences and reflections do not form a simple linear motion from aesthetics to ethics to epistemology. Nevertheless, because renewal spirituality tends to give precedence to experiential encounter, we believe the most natural starting point for a renewal worldview, if it is to reflect a renewal ethos, is beauty. Beauty exists in the realm of aesthetics as it considers perceptions and emotional responses. From experience we'll move to action, where we introduce goodness as it relates to ethical reasoning. From there we'll formulate our beliefs in pursuit of truth.

Because this book *introduces* the concept of a renewal worldview, we'll spend time doing some important historical and comparative legwork. This will help give us a better scope of the narrative threads that precede our contemporary renewal traditions. Each of the book's three parts comprises four chapters that pose the issues at hand and span all the way from ancient history to contemporary issues. The first chapter of each part considers the particular concept from a practical standpoint within our contemporary setting, while the final chapter of each part brings together the theoretical work of the preceding chapters.

Part 1, "Renewing Beauty," kicks off with chapter 1, "Aesthetic Formation: How Perceptions Shape Us." In chapter 1 we discuss the importance of beauty for worldview studies, demonstrating how perceptions shape us spiritually. To make our case, we look at the work of John Berger and Maurice Merleau-Ponty concerning visuality and perception. Our perceptions affect our emotions, which is the first leg of our triperspectival approach to Christian worldview.

Chapter 2, "A Historical Survey of Beauty and Aesthetics," sets the historical parameters of Christian aesthetics by tracing its roots through the Old Testament accounts of Bezalel and Oholiab, and then through the classical philosophers of Greece. It looks at the aesthetic theories of Plato and Aristotle in order to demonstrate the Greek influence on concepts of beauty and aesthetics in early Christian thought. It then traces the evolution of aesthetics, highlighting in particular the late nineteenth- and twentieth-century aversion to beauty and how this affected theological aesthetics and the church. This chapter looks briefly at the modern development of beauty, highlighting the work of Immanuel Kant, but then shows how the atrocities of the World Wars rendered beauty an escapist ideal. This historical piece is important because it demonstrates the antipathy of both the modern church and the art world toward each other, which helped the secular mind imagine a world devoid of God. It also shows that there is a resurgence of theological aesthetics in Christian discourse and why this is important for understanding global Christianity.

Chapter 3, "Contemporary Christian Aesthetics: Begbie, Balthasar, and Hart," traces some significant Christian aesthetics that arose out of the twentieth and twenty-first centuries. It contrasts Protestant and Catholic traditions through the creational aesthetics of Jeremy Begbie and the eschatological aesthetics of Hans Urs von Balthasar, respectively. It also offers a third position, via the work of Eastern Orthodox theologian David Bentley Hart, as another point of contrast.

The last chapter of part 1 is the constructive chapter. Chapter 4, "A Renewal Perspective on Beauty, Aesthetics, and Embodied Spirituality," shows what the Acts 2 narrative and the lived renewal experience can teach us about a renewal aesthetics. Since Pentecostalism is an experiential expression of Christianity, part of understanding a renewal worldview entails understanding how Pentecostals experience the world and interpret their experiences—especially since experiences can be understood aesthetically. This chapter demonstrates both the historical lineage of a renewal perspective and its contrast with other major traditions discussed in chapter 3.

Part 2, "Renewing Goodness," follows the same blueprint as part 1, with four chapters on goodness that engage practical contemporary issues and span from ancient history to today. Chapter 5, "Civic Engagement: How to Be Salt and Light in the World," demonstrates practically how a renewal ethic can guide cultural and political engagement. It gives practical advice on how to make ethical decisions in Christian love and gives guidance on political engagement that looks at both policy and character. Our worldview affects our actions toward others, which is the second leg of our triperspectival approach to Christian worldview.

Chapter 6, "A Historical Survey of Goodness and Ethics," sets the historical parameters of Christian ethics by tracing its roots through the classical philosophers of Greece and the kingdom of God motif in Hebraic ethics. The virtue tradition is highlighted with the Greek philosophers Plato and Aristotle. Hebraic ethics revolves around justice and the kingdom of God and shows the close relationship between Jesus's ethics and Isaiah. We also demonstrate that Hebraic ethics is not one dimensional but triperspectival, as it draws from various ethical perspectives. We then make a great jump to the modern period to present and contrast Immanuel Kant's deontological ethics and John Stuart Mill's utilitarian ethics. The wide historical gap we make between the two is intentional in order to introduce the representatives of the ethical theories that are vital to understanding the (tri)perspectives of renewal (and Hebraic) ethics within the page limitations.

In chapter 7, "Contemporary Christian Ethics: Niebuhr, MacIntyre, and Hauerwas," we compare and contrast the work of three significant Christian ethicists from the late twentieth and twenty-first centuries. We consider the

Christian realist ethics of Reformed theologian Reinhold Niebuhr and the virtue ethics of Catholic Alasdair MacIntyre. We also consider a third position of Christian pacifism in narrative ethics as championed by Methodist Stanley Hauerwas.

Finally, chapter 8, "A Renewal Perspective on Goodness, Ethics, and Civic Engagement," is the constructive chapter of part 2. This chapter locates the narratives of renewal ethics in the good news of the kingdom of God that culminates for the church in the Pentecost narrative of Acts 2. Pentecost and the outpouring of the Spirit equip the church for living out the ethical mission of the kingdom of God. Participating in this mission of God, however, should occur not through rote obedience but through the formation of our virtues, our sanctified change into Christ's image. We thus propose the importance of pursuing virtues through the lens of loving God and loving people, especially by enacting the Beatitudes and the fruit of the Spirit. We then provide an explanation of triperspectival ethics and how we can look at certain biblical ethical issues through a triperspectival lens. We end the chapter by exploring political engagements in our contemporary times. While justice often takes center stage in the political arena, we argue that reconciliation is the goal of renewal ethics.

Following suit, part 3, "Renewing Truth," offers four chapters that focus on truth, looking at renewal epistemology and what constitutes belief. In chapter 9, "Cultural Apologetics: How to Speak Truth to Culture," we demonstrate practically what it means to speak truth, in love, in a misinformation age. Continuing the holistic theme of the book, the work of this chapter is to direct apologetics away from a rationalist approach and to consider the role the body plays in knowing. It draws on insights from behavioral economics to demonstrate how we are more often driven by cognitive biases and heuristics than by our reflections. Against traditional apologetics, which assumes that we are primarily thinking beings, we propose that Paul Gould's cultural apologetics better connects with the longings of our hearts by targeting culture's imagination and presenting Christianity as not only true but satisfying.

In chapter 10, "A Historical Survey of Truth and Knowledge," we show how Scripture has dealt with matters of truth and the knowledge of reality in order to biblically ground the subsequent discourse. This chapter sets the historical parameters of Christian epistemology by tracing its roots through Greek philosophy and the New Testament writings of Paul and John. It explores pre-Socratic views on ultimate reality and their quest for philosophical knowledge. It then looks at the rationalism and empiricism of Parmenides and Heraclitus, before diving into Plato's and Aristotle's understandings of form and matter. We give special attention to John's philosophical use of "Word" in John 1 and to the Greek reference concerning the metaphysics of God in Acts 17:28. We then trace the evolution of epistemology and the origins of the two great schools of rationalism and empiricism that arose in the seventeenth century. We consider the rationalism of René Descartes and Gottfried Wilhelm Leibniz, the empiricism of John Locke and David Hume, and the chastened rationalism of Immanuel Kant.

Chapter 11, "Contemporary Christian Epistemologies: Plantinga, Zagzebski, and Lindbeck," traces some significant Christian epistemologies that arose out of the late twentieth and twenty-first centuries. We contrast the Catholic virtue epistemology of Linda Zagzebski with the Protestant, externalist epistemology of Alvin Plantinga. As a third option, we explore the postliberal epistemology of George Lindbeck, giving particular attention to his participatory correspondence theory of truth.

Finally, in chapter 12, "A Renewal Perspective on Truth, Epistemology, and Holistic Knowledge," we show what the Acts 2 narrative and the lived Pentecostal experience can teach us about a renewal epistemology. We mine Steven Land's concept of Pentecostal spirituality for its triperspectival view of truth, and we elucidate James K. A. Smith's concept of narrative, affective knowledge to provide a Pentecostal epistemology that recognizes the importance of embodied spirituality and rightly ordered knowledge, practice, and affections.

We wrap up with an epilogue that highlights and rearticulates the pneumatological approach we've taken along the way. We also suggest that renewal worldviews can and will take on many different forms throughout our global reality.

This book attempts to offer a broad, adaptable approach to renewal worldview that can help Christians live renewed in a pluralistic age. It is our hope that you will find this approach illuminating, along with its philosophical, theological, and practical insights.

Now, let us embark together on this journey of renewal!

Study Questions

1. How does our lived experience of the Spirit affect our theological insight about God and the world?

2. How are beliefs embedded in emotions and actions? How can emotions and actions direct our beliefs?

3. Why can't we define a renewal worldview solely by its beliefs or ideas?

PART 1

Renewing Beauty

+ 1 +

Aesthetic Formation

How Perceptions Shape Us

Key Words

Affect: *Being moved emotionally, which causes a change in someone or something.*

Enchanted naturalism: *The belief that God is present and involved in all facets of life, and miracles occur as a grace of God's presence, not as a suspension of what is natural.*

Expectations: *Beliefs about what is to occur.*

Invisibility: *That which surrounds and affects the visible.*

Perception: *The reception and interpretation of sensory information.*

Significant form: *The combination of colors and lines that relate to each other in such a way that an aesthetic emotion ensues.*

Visibility: *Something's ability to be seen.*

What moves you? Can you recall a time when you experienced something that forever changed the way you view the world? Perhaps you read a heartrending book, or watched an especially poignant film, or were completely enraptured by a painting. Each of these instances likely allowed you to see or experience something from a perspective beyond your own. Maybe you empathized with a story's protagonist who faced a crucible. Maybe a barrier broke where you were able to clearly see a unique perspective of the world. In each case something about the *way the experience was presented* to you captivated

3

your attention. Our perceptions of our experiences shape our worldview. **Perception** is the reception and interpretation of sensory information—it constitutes our awareness of things through our senses. Not only do our perceptions shape us, but the aesthetic attributes of our experiences have the ability to cut through our sober, rationally established assessments of the world. The term **affect** refers to being moved emotionally, which causes a change in someone or something. And it is our *affections* that profoundly shape our views and desires, which help develop our worldviews.

Even the physical spaces we inhabit structure our views of the world. Our memories of events have a look and feel to them. Our sense of the world is affected by our repeated movement within and outside the walls and corridors of our locales. This sense of place imprints on us, and we can't separate these impressions from our understandings of and feelings toward life and its events. Similarly, cities also imprint on us. A city that is well or poorly designed can affect the whole morale and political climate of a community. People traverse the same streets over and over every day. Do the city's surroundings elicit communal solidarity or drab isolation? Those feelings can manifest as a social climate of hope or of despair, and the social climate we live in also affects our worldviews. Painting the walls of drab buildings may seem like a small gesture, but it can actually be an important step on the way toward a hopeful community.

What does all this mean for a renewal worldview? It means the aesthetic realm is not an afterthought in worldview formation. Whether or not we like to admit it, we are constantly shaped by our perceptions—which is why we believe that the appropriate starting point for assessing worldview formation is at the base level of experience. If we focus on how experiences are perceived in a renewal worldview, then we can better understand what drives a Pentecostal's actions and thinking. As discussed in the introduction, many worldview studies focus on the mentalist aspects of worldview, positing that what someone *thinks* about the world shapes his or her actions and perceptions. We believe that worldview formation is far more integrated at every level, but if there has to be a starting point, it would be the experience itself, not the intellectual reflection on the experience. So in our renewal worldview, we'll start at the beginning, exploring the aesthetic realms of experience and perceptions.

To start this chapter, we will look at what Scripture has to say about experience and perceptions. This will show us that even the Bible recognizes that experiences move us to action. Then we will look at how perceptions work and what *seeing* actually entails. We argue that a person's worldview is drawn primarily from his or her social imaginary, and a person's social imaginary is primarily funded by his or her experiences. Having this understanding helps us take a step back to really appreciate the significance of our experiences.

Thus, this chapter commences the first leg of our triperspectival approach to Christian worldview.

Whatever Is Pure, Pleasing, and Commendable

As a final exhortation to the church in Philippi, Paul describes what sorts of things the Philippians should ascribe value to: "Finally, beloved, whatever is true, whatever is honorable, whatever is just, whatever is pure, whatever is pleasing, whatever is commendable, if there is any excellence and if there is anything worthy of praise, think about these things" (Phil. 4:8). What Paul calls "worthy of praise" are the things we should value. They fall into three realms: epistemology (what is true), ethics (what is honorable, just, and pure), and aesthetics (what is pleasing, commendable, and excellent). By breaking down what Paul is saying here, we can see that the matters we address in this book (beauty, goodness, and truth) are also the matters we should value as being worthy. And as we mentioned in the introduction, we hold to a triperspectival approach to Christian worldview that integrates the emotional (soul), the active (body), and the mental (mind). Since we have chosen to start at the point of experience, we'll first engage that which is pleasing, commendable, and excellent (aesthetics) before discussing what is honorable, just, and pure (ethics) and finally moving to what is true (epistemology). Indeed, one could even argue that Jesus took a similar approach.

Moved by the Suffering of Others

On many occasions in the Gospels, Jesus saw or experienced something, was moved, and then reacted to what he experienced. The Greek verb *splanch-nizomai*, which means "to be moved with compassion," is used throughout the Gospels to describe Jesus's reaction toward people. It's related to the word *splanchnon*, which refers to the inner parts of a person, like the heart, lungs, liver, and kidneys, and denotes the "seat of the affections." When Jesus encountered someone or something and felt deeply moved, these were the words that were used. For instance, Jesus was moved by the weariness of the crowds who were "harassed and helpless" (Matt. 9:36). In many cases, Jesus reacted to his affections with miraculous acts. For example, Jesus miraculously fed a crowd of five thousand after feeling compassion toward them (Matt. 14:14; Mark 6:34). He did the same after being moved with compassion toward a crowd of four thousand (Matt. 15:32; Mark 8:2). He raised a boy to life after being moved by the tears of the boy's widowed mother (Luke 7:13). He healed two blind men on the roadside after being moved by their request for healing (Matt. 20:34). He healed a leper after being moved by his request for healing (Mark 1:41), and he healed a possessed boy after being moved by a request from his father (Mark 9:22). In each case Jesus saw something (like the weary crowds) or listened to the pleas of the people, was moved, and then reacted out of, not in spite of, his affections. Experience and rightly guided emotions ordered Jesus's actions.

Jesus also used the same words in some of his parables to describe positive emotional reactions that led to restorative actions. The parable of the good Samaritan (Luke 10:25–37) saw a Samaritan—a social adversary to the Jews—being moved to compassion (v. 33) by a Jew who was brutally beaten and left for dead. The Samaritan's affections caused him to break social barriers and act generously and lovingly toward the Jew. Similarly, the parable of the lost son (Luke 15:11–32) saw the father run undignified toward his returning son. The father was filled with compassion at the mere sight of his son (v. 20). The point here is that Jesus demonstrates actions as taking place after his affections were stirred. While Jesus could certainly act out of logical deduction—do something that makes the most rational sense—here his actions are prompted by emotion. That's not to say we should *only* act out of emotion and never think things through! But it does show us the powerful place experience and affect hold, both in how we see the world and in the decisions we make.[1] We'd like to take this line of thought one step further and claim that even the *way* things appear to our senses powerfully affects us and helps shape our views of the world. This involves the aesthetic dimension of what we experience.

Moved by Aesthetically Striking Experiences

How are we moved by aesthetic things? While this section intends to further provide a scriptural basis for aesthetic formation, to gain better clarity on what is meant by "aesthetic formation" we must take a brief detour into the field of aesthetics. Philosopher Clive Bell developed an "aesthetic hypothesis" to define a theory of aesthetics that takes into account the role of human emotions. Bell begins by dogmatically stating that the beginning of any aesthetic system must be the personal experience of a particular emotion, and any object that evokes such an emotion is a work of art.[2] Since all art evokes a particular emotion, there

---

1. A common counterargument to this point is that our hearts are deceptive, and we cannot trust our emotions to help us make decisions, which is often based on Jer. 17:9. This argument is used frequently against the Pentecostal emphasis on experience and emotion. While this expresses that we should use caution before trusting our emotions and intuitions, it would be wrong to reactively disregard them altogether. We believe the triperspectival approach we are advocating for creates checks and balances between reason, action, and emotion. This approach thus protects us against any of these elements taking complete precedence over worldview formation.

2. Clive Bell, "The Aesthetic Hypothesis," in *Aesthetics*, ed. Susan Feagin and Patrick Maynard (Oxford: Oxford University Press, 1997), 15.

must be something about art that elicits an emotional response. This intrinsic quality that all art holds, for Bell, is its "significant form." **Significant form** is the combination of colors and lines that relate to each other in such a way that an aesthetic emotion ensues.[3] Bell believes that one is moved profoundly when viewing an artwork's significant form because it expresses the emotion of its creator. In other words, the very lines and colors of an artwork convey something to the viewer that the artist felt.[4] Artists, for Bell, can convey an "emotion felt for reality," which reveals itself through an artist's own masterful rendering of line and color.[5] In Bell's view of artist-as-conveyor-of-ultimate-reality, the artist becomes a prophet of the way things truly are. While what Bell is saying may put a little too much stock into the role of the artist, it does show that an object's form—how it presents itself to our senses—is crucial for evoking emotion from our experience of it. The more aesthetically striking something is, the more the experience of perceiving it sticks with us.

Let's now apply Bell's theory to two of the more extravagant aesthetic experiences recounted in Scripture. Peter, James, and John were struck by the glory of Christ at his transfiguration (Matt. 17:1–8; Mark 9:2–8; Luke 9:28–36). They were not struck by the ethics of what was happening, nor did they reason themselves into awe. They had the awesome aesthetic experience of seeing the heavens open up and Christ transfigured before their eyes. Similarly, it was not an intellectual breakthrough that struck Paul on the road to Damascus. Paul was knocked down because of the thunderous voice of God and the brilliance of light that flashed around him (Acts 9:1–19). In both cases we can understand these experiences as conveying significant form, with God as the artist who conveys something about ultimate reality—to Peter, James, and John at the transfiguration and to Paul on the road to Damascus. But Scripture does not only demonstrate dramatic instances of glory as those that resonate deeply. It also depicts subtle experiences as expressively beautiful and formative.

Moved by Subtle Sensory Experiences

Perhaps the noblest act of worship in the Bible was one that came not extravagantly but quietly. It nevertheless came about as an evocative sensory experience. John's account of Jesus's anointing at Bethany saw Jesus and the disciples gathered at Lazarus's house for a dinner to honor Jesus (John 12:1–8). Lazarus's sisters, Mary and Martha, were present, and as a sign of honor Mary took out a pint of expensive perfume and poured it out on Jesus's feet, wiping his feet

3. Bell, "Aesthetic Hypothesis," 15.
4. Bell, "Aesthetic Hypothesis," 15.
5. Bell, "Aesthetic Hypothesis," 159.

with her hair. Judas was angered at the apparent wastefulness of the act (that perfume was worth a full year's wages), claiming that it could have been sold and the money used to help the poor. But Jesus replied, "Leave her alone. She bought it so that she might keep it for the day of my burial. You always have the poor with you, but you do not always have me" (vv. 7–8). We know that Mary's act of love speaks to the fact that Jesus would be crucified later that week. The perfume was bought to anoint Jesus at his burial, but Mary anointed him early, presumably in anticipation of what was to come. This honoring of Jesus while he was alive gives credence to the sentiment, "What we say at funerals should be said while they're still here." Mary was blessing Jesus while he was present in her midst. Jesus's response should not be viewed as a denigration of the needs of the poor but as an affirmation of Mary's act of choosing Jesus as her priority.

The aesthetic component of this experience that was dramatically affective involved scent and the human sense of smell. This means that what was arguably the Bible's greatest act of worship relied not on music or art or preaching but on the olfactory sense. The significance of scent is that it lingers and stays on objects, sometimes for days, permeating surrounding spaces. The sweetness or stench of a scent creates a totally different atmosphere for locations that would otherwise be commonplace. If the scent of the perfume lingered on Jesus, then he was reminded of Mary's act of love wherever he went. Any room he stepped into quickly took on a fragrance that evoked Mary's love for him. This is especially significant considering what was to occur in the coming days, when Jesus would experience the Last Supper, the prayer at Gethsemane, a trial, beatings, and finally his own crucifixion. While there's no way of knowing if the scent indeed stayed with him all week, it's interesting to wonder if Jesus could still smell the aroma of Mary's perfume while he was beaten, his body broken. Perhaps when Jesus hung on the cross and gasped for air, the scent of Mary's love was just enough to remind him why he was there. Being a disciple means not only receiving the blessing of the cross but also blessing Christ on the cross.

As can be seen, the aesthetic components of experience are essential for shaping our perceptions of those experiences. The world we see, hear, touch, taste, and smell shapes our understanding of self and everything we go through. We're not beings-separate-from-experiences, but we're beings-in-the-world[6] who affect and are affected by the world. Our experiences shape us, and through those same experiences we shape our surroundings. While the biblical witness has shown us how important the aesthetic components of experience are for

6. This concept, first introduced by philosopher Martin Heidegger, refers to one's existential understanding of self in relation to others. See Martin Heidegger, *Being and Time*, trans. John Macquarrie and Edward Robinson (New York: Harper & Row, 1962), 33.

determining actions, next we will look at what it means to be a person who relates to his or her surroundings through experience and how this shapes worldview. We'll consider how perceptions situate us in the world and how aesthetic appreciation helps us gain a richer quality of life.

Understanding Experience Philosophically

Our perceptions are not just one-sided. When we become aware of something, we are not the only party involved. Becoming conscious of something else necessarily entails the "something else" that we've become conscious of. Consider our sense of sight, for example: *seeing* the world entails looking at something *as it relates to* us.[7] Philosopher Maurice Merleau-Ponty defines vision as the "precession of what is upon what one sees and makes seen, of what one sees and makes seen upon what is."[8] In other words, vision has to do with making visible the world we are confronted by, while *we* become visible to the world. We use our sense of sight to see both objects before us and the spaces we occupy. So through sight we come to know ourselves and the world we inhabit. It should be noted that although we are pinpointing the sense of sight here, one can certainly come to an understanding of self and the world without sight. All the senses are used in our perceptions, and we sense and feel our way through the world holistically. Someone who lacks the sense of sight can absolutely still come to know their own agency as a perceiver and come to know the world they inhabit. So while Merleau-Ponty, our main dialogue partner in this section, focuses on sight, the ideas presented can be applied, directly and through analogy, to perception in general.

Part of seeing is our awareness of the fact that we can be seen—that we are fully part of the visible world.[9] As Merleau-Ponty states, "My body simultaneously sees and is seen. That which looks at all things can also look at itself and recognize, in what it sees, the 'other side' of its power of looking. It sees itself seeing; it touches itself touching; it is visible and sensitive for itself."[10] Our senses, therefore, not only supply our brains with data from our experiences but also enable our sense of community by making us aware of our relatedness to others. For Merleau-Ponty, therefore, vision entails an "undividedness of the sensing and the sensed."[11]

7. John Berger, *Ways of Seeing* (London: Penguin Books, 1972), 7.

8. Maurice Merleau-Ponty, "Eye and Mind," in *The Merleau-Ponty Aesthetics Reader: Philosophy and Painting*, ed. Galen Johnson (Evanston, IL: Northwestern University Press, 1993), 147.

9. Berger, *Ways of Seeing*, 9.

10. Merleau-Ponty, "Eye and Mind," 124.

11. Merleau-Ponty, "Eye and Mind," 125.

The place of "undividedness" is the body. **Visibility** refers to something's ability to be seen. If something is visible, it can be known through the sense of sight. Merleau-Ponty argues that in order for something to be visible, it must have a corporeal, or bodily, analogue. Ideality—the state in which something becomes an ideal—cannot be separated from the physicality of the thing that's perceived. Mauro Carbone, interpreting Merleau-Ponty, states that "ideality is constituted by those images as their excess, and it is precisely *through* their appearance that it manifests itself."[12] Thus the ideas we form about things come from our experiences of the things' concrete objectness, or "flesh," as Carbone states it.

Another important aspect of visibility is *in*visibility. **Invisibility** is that which surrounds and affects the visible. The invisible outlines the visible and creates the contours of what we can perceive.[13] While the invisible itself is not visible, it exists relative to what is visible.[14] This means that what we see brushes up against what we cannot see, and while we cannot see it, we know it by its relation to what we can see. Someone who is a visionary is able to bring all that is visible to light and points to that which stands beyond what we can see. Visionaries cast light on that which transcends our everyday experiences.

For Merleau-Ponty, artists are visionaries in that they are able to make visible that to which people have become blind.[15] Visionary artists are able to present to our senses what sits at the boundary of the visible and the invisible. Art isn't merely a copy or reproduction of something else; it is a reconstitution of perceptual elements (forms, textures, values, etc.). And as a reconstitution, art becomes its own object with its own "flesh" that is made visible. Art makes its own meaning as well, and in so doing it tells us something about the world and our experience of it. This is similar to Bell's point that artists are prophets of the way things truly are. If artists have the ability to illuminate what is visible and help us gain a sense of what is invisible, then perhaps they do have the ability to demonstrate a deeper sense of reality to us. Perhaps this is part of the reason art affects us so deeply. If art truly does reveal what is visible and makes known what is invisible, then our worldview can be profoundly shaped as we experience the world *through* art.

Another reason art affects us so deeply is because it makes things that are familiar to us appear unfamiliar and new. Literary theorist Victor Shklovsky

12. Mauro Carbone, *The Flesh of Images: Merleau-Ponty Between Painting and Cinema*, trans. Marta Nijhuis (Albany, NY: SUNY Press, 2015), 9.

13. Galen Johnson, "Ontology and Painting," in Johnson, *Merleau-Ponty Aesthetics Reader*, 37.

14. Maurice Merleau-Ponty, *The Visible and the Invisible*, ed. Claude Lefort, trans. Alphonso Lingis (Evanston, IL: Northwestern University Press, 1968), 257.

15. Maurice Merleau-Ponty, "Cézanne's Doubt," in Johnson, *Merleau-Ponty Aesthetics Reader*, 69.

states that we experience the artfulness of an object by making objects unfamiliar.[16] We tend to make the things we experience in the world compact and habitual. We go through our lives creating shortcuts and routes that we repeat over and over again. While this makes going about our business more efficient, it also causes us to lose the wonder of seeing or experiencing something for the first time. We lose our sense of awe as we gaze at the beautiful face we've just encountered. Artists try to erase shortcuts and habituation in order to purposefully make things difficult. As Shklovsky writes, "Art removes objects from the automatism of perception."[17] To make his point, Shklovsky cites writer Leo Tolstoy, who had the ability to describe something as if he were seeing it for the first time.[18] Tolstoy was a master at making the familiar seem strange. By talking about things as if they were new, he invited readers to recapture the wonder, excitement, and novelty of first experiences.

Consider a phrase that you might hear uttered repeatedly in a drawing class: "Draw what you see, not what you know." What this phrase points to is the fact that our brains make shortcuts for us. If we were told to draw a tree, we would likely draw the cartoonish thing we've seen in coloring books and on TV shows. This is because the concept "tree" latched on to that reduced form in our minds. But if we don't allow concepts to adopt reduced forms and if we instead look at objects in front of us as if they are foreign, then we will begin to focus on what we're supposed to focus on in art: line, shape, form, gesture, and so forth. We see the formal correspondences of our visual stimuli, not whatever shortcut our minds have created. Another technique artists use when something is looking too familiar is to look at the drawing or painting in a mirror. Sometimes our brains will try to "fix" problems that they perceive, like straightening out crooked noses or making oddly shaped faces more proportional. The technique of inversing a portrait can help the artist see forms afresh. Changing how we see forms exposes their "problems," thereby allowing us to recapture an appropriate sense of realism. Another technique artists use to see things anew is to turn both the painting and the reference photos upside down. This simple but significant shift allows the artist to pay closer attention to the formal relations, not the shortcuts.

Drawing techniques such as these teach us something about slowing down and recognizing the aesthetic aspects of the experiences that shape us. Paying attention to *all* that is visible—even and especially the small things—helps us foster a richer and more intentional quality of life. In a similar way, as we'll

16. Victor Shklovsky, "Art as Technique," in *Modern Criticism and Theory: A Reader*, ed. Antonio Barrenechea (London: Longman, 1988), 20.

17. Shklovsky, "Art as Technique," 21.

18. Shklovsky, "Art as Technique," 23.

see through the remainder of this chapter, a renewal worldview approaches the world in wonder and newness.

Parameters of the Pentecostal Imagination

Openness and expectation each play an important role in approaching the world in wonder. In his book *Thinking in Tongues*, James K. A. Smith contends that the Pentecostal worldview is marked by an openness to God's action in the world, both natural and supernatural.[19] Pentecostals often use interventionist language to talk about God's action in the world. They see God working in the supernatural, defying or even suspending the laws of nature.[20] Smith, however, states that there is some distance between what is espoused explicitly and what is believed implicitly by Pentecostals when they refer to the "supernatural." While Pentecostals often use interventionist language, they implicitly hold to a noninterventionist supernaturalism in which the supernatural does not act outside of the natural order because the natural order itself is open. If the natural order is closed and ordered, and totally empirically comprehensible, then miracles and the supernatural can only come about by defying nature. But if the natural order is open, then divine interventions are possible occurrences that take place in an "enchanted naturalism."[21] In an **enchanted naturalism**, God is present and involved in all facets of life, and miracles occur as a grace of God's presence, not as a suspension of what is natural. As Smith writes, "A miracle is a manifestation of the Spirit's presence that is 'out of the ordinary,' but even the ordinary is a manifestation of the Spirit's presence."[22] Miracles may be surprising to us because they are outside of our expectations, but if God is already present in the natural, then miraculous experiences are not *super*natural. God moves within the laws of a created order that is open. Pentecostals see the Spirit's presence as a regular, natural occurrence in everyday life, not as a suspension of the natural order. The physical and the spiritual realms are two aspects of the same reality. Although adopting an enchanted naturalism might seem like we're harking back to a medieval worldview where reality was understood through an interventionist lens, Pentecostals have a theological understanding of reality that's noninterventionist.

19. James K. A. Smith, *Thinking in Tongues: Pentecostal Contributions to Christian Philosophy* (Grand Rapids: Eerdmans, 2010), 33–41.

20. James K. A. Smith and Amos Yong, eds., *Science and the Spirit: A Pentecostal Engagement with the Sciences* (Bloomington: Indiana University Press, 2010), 36.

21. Smith, *Thinking in Tongues*, 98.

22. James K. A. Smith, "Is There Room for Surprise in the Natural World? Naturalism, the Supernatural, and Pentecostal Spirituality," in Smith and Yong, *Science and the Spirit*, 47.

Secularity and the Social Imaginary

In his book *A Secular Age,* philosopher Charles Taylor helpfully distinguishes between the medieval worldview and today's secular age. His distinction can help us understand how the renewal understanding of enchantment occurs *within* a naturalist frame and not as an intervention. Taylor's study seeks to uncover how, in the West, the conditions of belief changed toward secularization.[23] Five hundred years ago, it was unthinkable to hold a nonreligious worldview, but today secularism is a totally viable option. Secularity, for Taylor, was once understood as merely a contrast to the sacred. If you worked as a priest, you had a sacred vocation, but if you worked as a blacksmith, you had a secular vocation. Then throughout modernity the idea of secularity began to refer to any nonreligious identity. This sense of secularity marked the decline of the sacred and the viability of carrying a secular identity.[24] Taylor argues, however, that we currently live in a third sense of secularity where living a secular life is a viable option among many other options. While the second sense of secularity supposed our society would continue to secularize,[25] the third sense of secularity says the world is still very religious although pluralistically diverse. Today in the West there are a number of prevalent religious beliefs (Christianity, Islam, Judaism, Buddhism, etc.), along with many New Age, pseudoreligious worldviews that are not declining but growing. The world isn't secularizing but diversifying.

The third sense of secularity that we live in today marks a shift in our Western "social imaginary," which Taylor defines as "the ways people imagine their social existence, how they fit together with others, how things go on between them and their fellows, the expectations that are normally met, and the deeper normative notions and images that underlie these expectations."[26] Whereas the medieval social imaginary was deeply entrenched in a theocentric worldview, our present secular age is radically pluralistic and holds many theistic and nontheistic worldviews together. The medieval worldview saw natural phenomena like earthquakes and floods as acts of God. All of society was known in a context where God and the church reigned and where the world was seen as "enchanted." An enchanted world in the Middle Ages was a "world of spirits, demons, and moral forces which our ancestors lived in."[27] Today most of Western society holds a social imaginary that's disenchanted and rationalized,

---

23. Charles Taylor, *A Secular Age* (Cambridge, MA: Harvard University Press, 2007), 28.
24. Taylor, *Secular Age,* 15.
25. James K. A. Smith, *How (Not) to Be Secular: Reading Charles Taylor* (Grand Rapids: Eerdmans, 2014), 21.
26. Charles Taylor, *Modern Social Imaginaries* (Durham, NC: Duke University Press, 2004), 23.
27. Taylor, *Secular Age,* 25–26.

what Taylor calls the "immanent frame." As the opposite of transcendence, immanence refers to that which is within something. The immanent frame thus refers to the Western social imaginary, which is solely constituted by a natural, rather than a supernatural, order.[28] It does not register in one's realm of possibility that reality could be "haunted" by something beyond the material world. If we adopt an immanent frame, that means we're locating our sense of reality in the world around us, whereas a transcendent frame locates our sense of reality beyond what's around us. The immanent frame is this-worldly, whereas the transcendent frame is otherworldly.

An Enchanted Naturalism in an Immanent Frame

If it is true that today we see ourselves as existing in an immanent frame, then Smith's assertion that Pentecostals actually hold to a form of naturalism makes sense. Since Pentecostalism as a global movement developed in the early twentieth century, it has always been in close proximity to modern and late modern ideology and should *not*, therefore, be understood in premodern terms. Pentecostalism has not reverted back to the interventionist, transcendent frame of the Middle Ages. Rather, Pentecostals critique modern materialism by affirming a spiritual reality that coextends with the physical. Pentecostals, in other words, believe that the naturalist worldview of modernity must be amended to account for the spiritual reality that the Enlightenment shunned. The physical is not below the spiritual; rather, both the physical and the spiritual make up a holistic reality. This critique is not a wholesale rejection of modernity, however. It merely suggests the renewal proclivity toward adopting, critiquing, and then modifying modern naturalism to better suit a renewal worldview—one that is open to the Spirit *in* the created order. Thus, Smith's notion of "enchanted naturalism" should be understood as a holistic late modern worldview. Affirming both the physical and the spiritual, Pentecostals are open to spiritual encounters and able to see the physical affecting the spiritual and vice versa. If the physical and the spiritual are both part of the same reality, then why shouldn't physical manifestations correspond with spiritual circumstances? And conversely, why should anyone dismiss the spiritual ramifications of physical actions? The theme of spiritual holism will be picked up further in chapter 4 of this book, but for now we can see that a renewal worldview affirms both the spiritual and the physical and sees them both as part of a unified reality.

If we understand the renewal worldview as operating under an enchanted naturalism, then an adherent's most appropriate response to the world is a

28. Taylor, *Secular Age*, 542.

sense of newness and wonder. Since every experience has both physical and spiritual ramifications, we should understand how experiences affect us bodily, emotionally, and spiritually. And, as we've noted above, since the aesthetic components of experience shape our perceptions of those experiences, we must learn to slow down and fully appreciate our sensory intake before interpreting it. This slowing down establishes an aesthetic approach to living. If Shklovsky is right about art having the ability to make old things and experiences seem new again, then maybe living in an artistic, or aesthetic, frame of mind can help us approach the world in newness and wonder. By "aesthetic frame of mind," we are not advocating for living in a carnal or self-gratifying way.[29] An aesthetic frame of mind is not only about aesthetic *pleasures*; it entails the full appreciation of our experiences at the sensory level. Living aesthetically, in this sense, requires a kind of humility—we allow the world to enchant us. When we slow down and really learn to "see," we take things away from their normal connections. We make them novel and strange. When things become foreign to themselves, we can once again see them in a new light, and we become filled with wonder by their newness.

Leaning on the work of Taylor and Smith, we see that a person's worldview is drawn from his or her social imaginary, which is funded by his or her experiences. And as mentioned above, our experiences occur through our senses. Smith draws the connection between sensory intake and worldview, writing that "our worldview is more a matter of the imagination than the intellect, and the imagination runs off the fuel of images that are channeled by the senses."[30] While our sensory intake will be interpreted through an interpretive lens, we must slow down and come to appreciate our experiences aesthetically to get a rich sense of what it means to exist as a being-in-the-world. One significant aspect of the renewal worldview is its ability to imagine the world otherwise.[31] Here a Pentecostal's aesthetic approach to experience takes on theological significance. The eschatological vision of the kingdom of God—of a redeemed reality breaking in today—marks the interpretive lens from which our experiences are interpreted.

29. This is what Kierkegaard argues against in *Stages on Life's Way*. He states that a person passes through three stages of existence. The first and most shallow is "the aesthetic," which constitutes sensory experience and the pleasures. The second stage is "the ethical," where a person rises above the pleasures of the aesthetic and begins to follow the rules of society. Here we come to know ourselves in terms of the promises and commitments we've made with each other. Finally, the third stage is "the religious," which is, for Kierkegaard, the highest stage of existence. This is where the person gives him- or herself over to a higher power, like God, and leaps, by faith, into the unknown in pursuit of God. See Søren Kierkegaard, *Stages of Life's Way: Studies by Various Persons*, trans. and ed. Howard Hong and Edna Hong (Princeton: Princeton University Press, 1988).

30. James K. A. Smith, *Desiring the Kingdom: Worship, Worldview, and Cultural Formation* (Grand Rapids: Baker Academic, 2009), 57.

31. Smith, *Thinking in Tongues*, 84.

Our experiences help to shape these interpretive lenses, just as they are known through the same lenses. What we are arguing for is the phenomenological[32] significance of experience as it shapes our hermeneutic.[33] In other words, we are highlighting the way experience shapes our interpretive lenses.

Experience and Expectation

Finally, to close out this chapter we'd like to briefly discuss the role of expectation in a renewal worldview. Expectations are beliefs that shape the way we perceive our experiences. If you recall from above, our triperspectival view of worldview posits that beauty, goodness, and truth all influence and inform each other. **Expectations** are epistemic in that they are beliefs about what is to occur. Anticipation is the emotion we feel that's associated with expectation. So, by definition, the concept of expectation belongs in the category of epistemology, whereas anticipation belongs with aesthetics. Expectation, however, comes about through the imagination and is thus also formed by our experiences, which fund our imaginations. For instance, if we've experienced something with newness and wonder, we might come to expect a similar experience when similar circumstances arise. One peculiar aspect of a renewal worldview is that it entails a constant expectation of newness that comes from experiencing the Spirit. The renewal expectation, therefore, is to encounter God. Pentecostals should be open to what that encounter entails. When a believer is filled with the Spirit, the Spirit refreshes the believer with newness and spontaneity. Just as John 3:8 states, "The wind blows where it chooses, and you hear the sound of it, but you do not know where it comes from or where it goes. So it is with everyone who is born of the Spirit." Radical openness to the work of the Spirit and the expectation of encountering God are part and parcel of a renewal worldview.[34]

This sense of expectation can easily be demonstrated with worship. If a worshiper enters a worship service fully expecting to experience the Spirit, that person will very likely interpret something from the songs, the sermon, the Scripture reading, or the communal interactions as a divine encounter. Since the worshiper expects to feel the Spirit, his or her senses, both physical and spiritual, are tuned in to these encounters. Now imagine someone who enters the service with an expectation to *not* experience God. Perhaps they came to

32. Phenomenology is the philosophical study of direct experience.
33. Hermeneutics is the philosophical study of interpretation.
34. We are not arguing that the old and constant are somehow less valuable than the new. The Spirit works through all things. As the example of worship in the following paragraph indicates, experiencing a new encounter with the Spirit often occurs through traditioned worship.

church reluctantly and look at every element of worship through a lens of skepticism. The preached words about God's provision might sound like emotional manipulation, the number of times a line is repeated in the bridge of a worship song may come across as annoying, and the friendly communal gestures from other worshipers may be read as fake or inauthentic. From this example we can see that a person's expectations, which arise from the person's unique interpretive lens, can lead him or her to interpret such experiences either as positive encounters with God or as inauthentic forms of emotional manipulation. But in both cases, expectation drove the interpretation of the experience.

You might have noticed a cycle beginning to form: we experience something, we reflect on our experience, we interpret our experience, the meaning of this experience shapes our expectations, and then the cycle begins again with an experience. This cycle has come to be known as a hermeneutical circle, where understanding a part of something determines the whole, and then the whole determines the part. Our experiences are the parts, and our interpretive lens (renewal worldview) is the whole. Beginning with the aesthetic components of experience (the parts) ultimately leads us to understand the renewal worldview (the whole).

Conclusion

Our hope is that, through this chapter, we've convinced you of the importance of experience, perception, and aesthetics for shaping a person's worldview. We began by looking at what the Bible has to say about perceptions and emotional responses to situations. Then we discussed how experiences can be understood philosophically, before examining the parameters of the renewal imagination, which is essential for understanding a renewal worldview. Now that we've discussed experience and aesthetic formation, we can begin to look at the experience of beauty and how that's understood in a renewal worldview. The next three chapters will take us on a journey through history and around other Christian traditions as we explore how beauty and aesthetics have been discussed through the ages and around the world.

Study Questions

1. What are some of the benefits of starting with experience when determining a renewal worldview?

2. According to Shklovsky, how can art help us experience something anew?

3. Why are openness and expectation important for a renewal worldview?

+ 2 +

A Historical Survey
of Beauty and Aesthetics

Key Words

Aesthetics: *The philosophical study of value as it pertains to matters of sensed perception.*

Beauty: *The quality in an object that, upon its perception, gives a person pleasure and radiates the way an object should be.*

Claritas: *An object's ability to shine forth the inner luminosity of a thing. Derives from Thomistic thought.*

Disinterestedness: *Perceiving something for its own sake and not to receive something from it. Derives from Kantian thought.*

Experience: *The conscious perception of the surrounding world.*

Poetics: *The act of making or producing something, bringing forth something that did not exist beforehand. Derives from classical Greek thought.*

How exactly does *beauty* shape our worldview? From the outset it seems categorically wrong to assume that a mere aesthetic feeling can tell us anything about how we orient ourselves in this world. But as we argued in the introduction of this book, a renewal worldview does not merely look at rational beliefs and adopt a mentalist approach to worldview. Instead, Pentecostals take a holistic approach to worldview, linking the story of Pentecost to their lived experience, even before they reflect on those experiences intellectually. If by

experience we mean the conscious perception of the surrounding world, then we must also account for the aesthetic components that accompany perception. We experience things through our five senses of touch, taste, smell, sight, and hearing, and when we reflect on those sensed perceptions, we're doing aesthetics! The word "aesthetics" comes from the Greek word *aisthētikos*, which means "perceptible by the senses." So **aesthetics** is the philosophical study of value as it pertains to matters of sensed perception. This includes issues concerning taste, aesthetic judgment, beauty, and the nature and evaluation of art. When we call something beautiful, we've made a value judgment of our experience of it. We reflect on the object's physical characteristics, see those characteristics working together, and then surmise that the object is beautiful. So understanding beauty is significant for understanding our experiences because the things we deem beautiful have already been judged favorably by our senses.

If *truth* corresponds with what is epistemologically right, and if *goodness* corresponds with what is morally right, then *beauty* corresponds with what is aesthetically right. So while **beauty** is typically defined as the qualities in an object that give a person pleasure upon its perception, it also radiates something honest and ineffable about the object—a sense that it is the way it should be. There's a teleological component to beauty, so when we think something is beautiful, we think it is reflecting accurately the way it's supposed to be. Considering this, we can think of at least three reasons why understanding beauty and aesthetics is important for understanding worldview: (1) Beauty is what we really care about! It's what drives our leisure time and what we pay money for. Beauty reflects that which gives us pleasure by the mere perception of it and gives us the sense that it is exactly how it should be perceived. (2) Creative output is important for human flourishing. Civilizations in times of peace make things. They make poetry, paintings, sculptures, songs, and dances as they reflect on what is most important to them as a society. During times of war and strife, people are so caught up in the work of simply surviving that they tend not to have time either to reflect on beauty or to make beautiful things. Creative output is a sign of a healthy society that's ready for deep reflection, inventive problem solving, and the celebration of life. (3) Finally, beauty inspires our passions and gives us aspirations for human flourishing. It is both what we pursue and what makes our pursuits worthwhile.

This chapter continues our exploration of beauty, aesthetics, and the arts. It briefly surveys how beauty has been understood biblically and historically, thus creating a context from which we can assess the church's relationship with matters of beauty and the arts in subsequent chapters. This chapter is by no means exhaustive. In fact, the opposite is true! It is concise and selective but also, we hope, ample enough to give us some common language for dialogue.

Hebrew Concepts of Beauty

The Hebrew Scriptures, at first blush, seem to put the pursuit of beauty in the back seat relative to the pursuit of truth and right living. For instance, Proverbs 31:30 states, "Charm is deceitful, and beauty is vain, but a woman who fears the LORD is to be praised." The aesthetic gratifications of charm and beauty are seen as epistemologically dangerous (deceitful) and morally self-serving (vain). Appropriately, therefore, what happens inside is favored over what happens outwardly. This sentiment is even repeated in the New Testament as 1 Peter 3:3–4 states, "Do not adorn yourselves outwardly by braiding your hair and by wearing gold ornaments or fine clothing; rather, let your adornment be the inner self with the lasting beauty of a gentle and quiet spirit, which is very precious in God's sight." But a scriptural account of beauty is not merely dualistic, pitting physical beauty against truth and moral integrity. The relationship between beauty, truth, and goodness is more complex than this simple polarization. In fact, many Old Testament heroes were praised for their physical beauty. Along with women such as Sarah, Rebecca, Rachel, and Esther, men such as Joseph, David, and Absalom were also lauded for their physical appearances. The beauty between lovers is recounted throughout Song of Solomon. It's not beauty per se, or even the pursuit of beauty, that is deemed deceitful and immoral. Rather, it is the idolization of beauty that is to be avoided. Beauty's power so enraptures us that it can become central to our lives. Saying that one should not live *solely* for the vanity of beauty is very different from saying one should not pursue beauty at all.

While the Old Testament does at times talk about the beauty of God (Pss. 27:4; 50:1–2; Isa. 33:17), it also ties beauty to God's creative acts (Pss. 19:1; 50:2; 104:1–35). The things God creates are good, beautiful, and wonderfully made. Moreover, they have an eschatological purpose, according to Qoheleth, the writer of Ecclesiastes: "He has made everything beautiful in its time; also he has put eternity into man's mind, yet so that he cannot find out what God has done from the beginning to the end" (Eccles. 3:11 RSV).[1] God makes things beautiful from the start but also draws things toward a *telos* of beauty. A tree sprout is already physically beautiful, but another aspect of its beauty is the fact that it will grow to be a stout and glorious tree. The sprout's beauty is already *and* not yet—it's beautiful in both its design and its potential. As these examples show, the Old Testament associates beauty with God and with God's creative work. But it also reveals a God who calls and empowers people to make beautiful things.

---

1. While the NRSV translates the Hebrew word יָפֶה (*yapheh*) as "suitable," the RSV translates it as "beautiful," which aligns more closely with the intended meaning within the context of this verse. Thus we use the RSV for this particular passage.

The first people in the Bible who were filled with the Spirit to perform a special task were the artists Bezalel and Oholiab. In Exodus 35:30–36:1, Moses tells the people that Bezalel and Oholiab were specially anointed to design and adorn the tabernacle, which housed the ark of the covenant. The passage states,

> Then Moses said to the Israelites: See, the LORD has called by name Bezalel son of Uri son of Hur, of the tribe of Judah; he has filled him with divine spirit, with skill, intelligence, and knowledge in every kind of craft, to devise artistic designs, to work in gold, silver, and bronze, in cutting stones for setting, and in carving wood, in every kind of craft. And he has inspired him to teach, both him and Oholiab son of Ahisamach, of the tribe of Dan. He has filled them with skill to do every kind of work done by an artisan or by a designer or by an embroiderer in blue, purple, and crimson yarns, and in fine linen, or by a weaver—by any sort of artisan or skilled designer.
>
> Bezalel and Oholiab and every skillful one to whom the LORD has given skill and understanding to know how to do any work in the construction of the sanctuary shall work in accordance with all that the LORD has commanded.

This passage gives us a great sense of how the Old Testament views beauty, aesthetics, and the arts. First, Bezalel was chosen, called, and filled with the Spirit to adorn the tabernacle, carving, engraving, and mounting gems and precious stones into the walls and facades of the tabernacle. The Spirit's filling gave him wisdom to best discern what to do and elevated his abilities and expertise. Wisdom was granted so that he could better perform artistically. The judgments Bezalel would make were aesthetic, not moral. We can infer, therefore, that God not only allows artistic efforts of beauty and craftwork but that God also desires and even inspires such endeavors! Bezalel and Oholiab were specially anointed to carry out these tasks, and they were called to teach their expertise to others (35:34). If beauty comes from God, and if God desires and inspires us to make beautiful things, then we can't reasonably assert an anti-aesthetic dualism from Scripture. Yet some Christians see the arts as dangerous for our spiritual development. Some of the disdain toward the arts comes from Christians misreading texts like Proverbs 31:30, and some goes back to the classical Greek influence on early Christianity. It is to this latter issue we now turn.

Greek Poetics

Christians today are often caught between two opposing attitudes toward the arts. On the one hand, as we noted above, some view the arts as dangerous vehicles of corruption. Examples are plentiful: the Reformation-era icono-clasm that led to the removal and destruction of artworks that once adorned churches, the banishing of dance in most Fundamentalist and Holiness circles, the pre–Jesus Movement designation of rock and roll as "the devil's music," the boycotting of films with anything higher than a PG rating, and so forth. But on the other hand, many Christians view the arts in a positive light as vehicles of moral and spiritual formation. Here Christians seek to use the arts in the context of worship through all types of music, visual art, dance, film, stage acting, and so on and have sought to engage the arts publicly from Christian perspectives.[2]

We can see these opposing attitudes begin to form early on in Western history, even in Plato and Aristotle. Before discussing their philosophies, however, let's define a term that's pertinent to us here: "poetics." In our common vernacular, poetics simply means "the art of writing poetry." But in philosophy, the term has a much broader meaning. **Poetics** derives from the Greek word *poiēsis*, which refers to "production" and means a "behavior aimed at an external end."[3] It's the activity of bringing forth something that did not exist beforehand. So when the Greeks approach topics of art, creativity, aesthetics, and perception, they articulate a *poetics*. This distinction is important for us to articulate because both Plato and Aristotle held to the objectivity of beauty and saw art as an imitation, but their poetics differed when it came to the *effects* of art. One viewed the act of making positively and the other negatively, and, as we will see later, this influenced divergent theological views on beauty and the arts that still affect our worldviews today.

Both Plato and Aristotle held to an imitation theory of art, although their views differed on the ontological perceptions of forms (as will be discussed in chap. 10). Plato held to a dualistic understanding of the arts, promoting the superiority of spiritual life, soul, and intellect over the material world.[4] He saw the material senses as mere copies of the ontological[5] reality of Forms.[6] Art, for Plato, is either something that can participate in the ideal truth, beauty, and

2. For a larger treatment on artistic engagements from a Pentecostal/charismatic perspective, see Steven Félix-Jäger, *Pentecostal Aesthetics: Theological Reflections in a Pentecostal Philosophy of Art and Aesthetics* (Leiden: Brill Academic, 2015); and Steven Félix-Jäger, *Spirit of the Arts: Towards a Pneumatological Aesthetics of Renewal* (New York: Palgrave Macmillan, 2017).

3. Roger Crisp, "*poiēsis* (Greek, 'production')," in *Cambridge Dictionary of Philosophy*, 3rd ed., edited by Robert Audi (Cambridge: Cambridge University Press, 2015), 838.

4. Gesa Elsbeth Thiessen, ed., *Theological Aesthetics* (Grand Rapids: Eerdmans, 2005), 11.

5. The philosophical study of ontology concerns the nature of being and asks questions about existence and reality.

6. Plato, *The Republic*, trans. Francis MacDonald Cornford (New York: Oxford University Press, 1941), 509.

harmony of Forms or something that can misconstrue these ideals, triggering one to be captivated by mere materiality. This second possibility is what Plato feared, causing him to hold a negative view of the arts. For Plato, art thrice removes a person from reality since it's a mere copy of a second-rate copy (the material thing being represented) of the Forms.[7] Accordingly, Plato advocated banishing the representative arts from his "ideal society" in *The Republic*.[8] So Plato's imitation theory of art saw art as copying nature and, in so doing, causing people to drift further away from reality.

Aristotle also held to an imitation theory of art, but unlike Plato, he viewed representation in a positive light.[9] Aristotle understood forms to be immanent, not transcendent. Aristotle's main critique of Plato regards the problem of *chōrismos*, or separation. He saw Plato as separating Forms, which are supposed to be the ultimate causes of things, from the things they are supposed to be the causes of. If the Forms are transcendent, how can they be the cause of the "whatness" or essence of a thing? Aristotle writes, "It would seem impossible that the substance and that of which it is the substance should exist apart; how therefore, could the Ideas, being the substances of things, exist apart? In the *Phaedo* the case is stated in this way—that the Forms are causes both of being and of becoming; yet when the Forms exist, still the things that share in them do not come into being, unless there is something to originate movement."[10]

So while Plato viewed art negatively, seeing it as a representation thrice removed, Aristotle viewed art as able to bring one closer to reality because the essence of the thing is embodied immanently *within* it.[11] Moreover, Aristotle thought the arts were actually helpful for human development because they allowed a person to express and even release emotions in a healthy way. He called this release, purification, or purgation of emotions *catharsis*. Art could, for instance, allow a person to cathartically purge the feelings of sorrow, terror, or pity in the controlled space of a performance as opposed to the uncontrolled space of regular human interaction. Art could also have a positive social effect

7. Jeremy Begbie, *Resounding Truth: Christian Wisdom in the World of Music* (Grand Rapids: Baker Academic, 2007), 81.

8. Plato, *Republic*, 511.

9. Gordon Graham, *Philosophy of the Arts: An Introduction to Aesthetics*, 3rd ed. (New York: Routledge, 2005), 104.

10. Aristotle, *Metaphysics*, trans. W. D. Ross, in *Basic Works of Aristotle*, ed. Richard McKeon (New York: Random House, 1941), 991.

11. Aristotle, *Poetics*, trans. Ingram Bywater, in McKeon, *Basic Works of Aristotle*, 1451. Aristotle here is referring to poetry rather than visual art, but the idea that art brings one closer to the ideal is present. Aristotle particularly claims that poetry is more important because it points toward universals rather than particulars. Universals point toward the essence of a thing, while the particular (in the case of history) only states what happened in one instance.

through imitation. Instead of showing the way things *are*, art can show the public the way things *could* or *should* be. Aristotle's poetics, therefore, sought to re-create nature and thus correct its faults. Unlike Plato's sense of art as imitation, Aristotle's view was of art as a positive force that, through catharsis, could reestablish appropriate relations to the world.[12]

As we'll see in part 3 of this book, classical Greece influenced many of our Western concepts of truth and knowledge. Likewise, our Western theories of beauty and aesthetics are heavily influenced by the Greeks, especially by the thought of Plato and Aristotle. Their divergent poetics later influenced two of the most prominent Christian thinkers of church history—Augustine and Thomas Aquinas, respectively—especially as it concerns the topic of beauty.

Greek Influence on Christian Concepts of Beauty and Aesthetics

Although there were significant Christian writings on beauty and aesthetics (though scattered and not formally systematized) by earlier Christian thinkers such as Justin Martyr, Irenaeus, and Origen, to name a few,[13] the North African theologian, philosopher, and church bishop Augustine of Hippo was so influential that he'll serve as our representative of Western patristic thought and its view of art and beauty. For Augustine, both truth and beauty come from God, and the perception of beauty consists of appreciating symmetry and the right proportions of members.[14] Conversely, beauty's opposite is chaos, which brings about dysfunction and destruction. Several biblical allusions lend themselves to this idea. For instance, in Genesis 1:1, God created all things *ex nihilo* (out of nothing): "In the beginning God created the heavens and the earth" (RSV). Then in verses 2–3, God's creative acts are not *ex nihilo* but rather bring order to the existing chaos: "The earth was without form and void, and darkness was upon the face of the deep; and the Spirit of God was moving over the face of the waters. And God said, 'Let there be light'; and there was light" (RSV).[15] The

12. While we would like to endorse a more positive outlook on the arts than that of Aristotle's predecessor, Augusto Boal points out that Aristotle's poetics has its own problems. It creates a vehicle for oppression as those in power can use the arts to reinforce, even habituate, the values that put them in power in the first place. Instead, Boal suggests we pursue a poetics that starts from the ground up—that emanates out from the people. Boal's poetics does away with passivity and with the idle spectator, and it sees every person as an actor. See Augusto Boal, *Theater of the Oppressed*, trans. Charles and Maria-Odilia Leal McBride (New York: Theatre Communications Group, 1985).

13. Excerpts of Justin Martyr's *Dialogue with Trypho*, Irenaeus's *Against Heresies*, and Origen's *De principiis* can all be found in Thiessen, *Theological Aesthetics*. Here each author holds an early premodern aesthetic view.

14. Thiessen, *Theological Aesthetics*, 12.

15. In Augustine's exegetical treatment of Gen. 1, in which he discusses the idea that God created *ex nihilo*, the dualism between beauty in creation and chaos in formlessness can be clearly

idea that God's beauty is found in order and symmetry prevailed throughout the aesthetics of the Middle Ages.

Augustine's Concept of Beauty and Aesthetics

Following Plato, Augustine's aesthetics was also dualistic. Art, for Augustine, can either lead us toward ultimate beauty in God *or* distract us away from God, leading us to an attachment to this world. This deviation from God happens because of art's sensory and material nature. Accordingly, Augustine formulated a hierarchy of good things in this world that ought to be seen in right perspective. At the peak of this hierarchy is God, above whom nothing can be perceived, and nothing (like art) can take attention away from this intended order without resulting in idolatry.[16] Unlike Plato, Augustine does not view art in a wholly negative light. Art is only bad when it is elevated above God in Augustine's hierarchy of good things. Art must therefore be handled with care because it *could* be viewed positively as a source for experiencing God's beauty with one's senses.

Augustine also asserts that our hearts must be cleansed to attain a vision of God and thus to see and comprehend God's beauty and truth. Augustine writes, "But, when the soul has properly adjusted and disposed itself, and has rendered itself harmonious and beautiful, then will it venture to see God, the very source of all truth and the very Father of Truth."[17] This idea of consecration before witnessing the beauty of God is a theme that carried on through the Middle Ages. It should also be noted that the derivative forms of Platonic thought acutely influenced Augustine, as Platonic language seemed helpful for expressing theological issues such as eternal life and heaven.

Aquinas's Concept of Beauty and Aesthetics

The most prevalent scholar of the late Middle Ages was Thomas Aquinas. Aquinas was the major philosophical and theological influence of this era, just as Augustine was for the patristic period. Aquinas lived in Italy in the thirteenth century and constructed his theological and philosophical works in the midst of political and philosophical conflicts. When conflicts began to arise between Aristotelian philosophers and Augustinian theologians, Aquinas embraced the Aristotelian side. The political arena in Italy also influenced Aqui-

---

seen. Augustine, *The Confessions of Augustine*, trans. E. B. Pusey (New York: Barnes & Noble Books, 2003), 300–303.

16. William Dyrness, *Visual Faith: Art, Theology, and Worship in Dialogue* (Grand Rapids: Baker Academic, 2001), 33.

17. Augustine, *The Divine Providence and the Problem of Evil*, in *Writings of Saint Augustine*, trans. Robert Russell (New York: CIMA, 1948), 1:328.

nas as "long-standing antagonisms between the See of Rome and the churches of the East—aggravated by a then two-hundred year old schism—significantly influenced the way that Aquinas would deploy his intellectual energies."[18] In the midst of this, however, Aquinas did not create a poetics for its own sake, since his focus was on God and not the arts. But he did absorb the traditional doctrines into his own system (*Summa Theologica*), which gives us insight into beauty and medieval aesthetics.[19]

Whereas Plato and Aristotle held to the imitation theory of art, Aquinas did not defend art except in the ways it bolstered Christian life. In his *Summa Theologica*, Aquinas interacted with several subjects, including metaphysics, theism, psychology, natural philosophy, and morality, in order to discuss the whole of Christian theology. Aquinas expanded on Augustine to claim that beauty did not simply come from God but that it was a *transcendental attribute* of God.[20] As Cynthia Freeland observes, for Aquinas, "human artworks should emulate and aspire to God's marvelous properties."[21] Like Augustine, Aquinas views art as having the potential to edify toward God, but unlike Augustine, Aquinas grounds beauty concretely as an attribute of God. Aquinas enthusiastically embraced Aristotelian thought and sought to synthesize Christian thought with Aristotle instead of Plato.[22] Aristotle's focus on the immanence of the form allowed the material aspects of a thing to be celebrated.[23]

Another distinct difference between Aristotle and Plato is that Aristotle claims there is a power called the "active intellect," which turns a person's sense data into ideas and thus makes the initial data knowable to the human being.[24] Aquinas contends that every mind has its own active intellect; thus

18. Romanus Cessario, "Thomas Aquinas: A Doctor for the Ages," *First Things*, March 1999, https://www.firstthings.com/article/1999/03/thomas-aquinas-a-doctor-for-the-ages.

19. Umberto Eco, *Art and Beauty in the Middle Ages*, trans. Hugh Bredin (New Haven: Yale University Press, 1986), 26.

20. Thomas Gilby, "Method of the Summa," in *Summa Theologica*, vol. 1, *Christian Theology*, by Thomas Aquinas, trans. and ed. Timothy McDermott (London: Blackfriars, 1964), 47.

21. Cynthia Freeland, *But Is It Art?* (Oxford: Oxford University Press, 2001), 38.

22. Healy, *Thomas Aquinas*, 8. Umberto Eco writes, "Aquinas demonstrated that it was possible to devise a metaphysics of beauty which was not Platonist. His aesthetics moved closer to a kind of humanism. There were other thirteenth-century examples of hylomorphic aesthetics, but none achieved the naturalistic vigour of Aquinas." Eco, *Art and Beauty in the Middle Ages*, 84.

23. "Hylomorphic Composition" was not a phrase that Aristotle used, but it was attributed to him later in order to refer to the twofold composition, material and formal, of everything that exists in the natural world. Ed Miller and Jon Jensen, *Questions That Matter*, 6th ed. (New York: McGraw-Hill, 2009), 74.

24. Aristotle and Aquinas embrace an epistemological empiricist approach to philosophy rather than the deductive rationalism that guided Plato and later Descartes—that is, sense data plays a critical role in knowledge over against the rationalist view that considers sense data as unnecessary for foundational knowledge.

every person is able to reason and make his or her own judgments.[25] Instead of art, Aquinas pointed to the priority of beauty; as an attribute of God, beauty can be experienced to a certain degree by human senses. Although one can delve deeper into these particular nuances, what can be stated about Christian medieval aesthetics is that beauty is intrinsically tied to the transcendent God. Medieval aesthetics also sought to understand beauty through particular aesthetic principles.

Fundamental Principles of Medieval Aesthetics

Freeland claims that medieval theory functioned according to three fundamental principles: proportion, light, and allegory.[26] These are the predominant principles that dictated artmaking in the medieval age, but one can see elements of this earlier, in the Roman era, and later, in the Reformation. Proportion was crucial in medieval aesthetics, and this principle can be traced back to Augustine's notion of divine beauty, which is found in order and symmetry, and even earlier to Plato and Aristotle, who claimed that the structures of art relate somehow to the Forms of the things represented. Aquinas finds beauty in forms of proportion: "We call a thing beautiful when it pleases the eye of the beholder. This is why beauty is a matter of right proportion, for the senses delight in rightly proportioned things as similar to themselves, the sense-faculty being a sort of proportion itself like all other knowing faculties. Now since knowing proceeds by imaging, and images have to do with form, beauty properly involves the notion of form."[27]

As an example, the emphasis on proportion can be seen in the construction of cathedrals. In fact, the formation of the cathedrals, particularly the guidelines about proportion, was dictated by the instruction of Augustinian scholars from the School of Chartres.[28] Cathedrals were built to emulate God's creation of the orderly cosmos. Nonfunctional elements and geometrical formations were used in the design of many aspects of the cathedral (portals, arches, windows, etc.). Geometric perfection and order were the goals of the process. The cathedral itself was designed to emulate a cross, with cross-arms that are proportional to the arms of a human figure, as is visible from an aerial view.[29]

25. Healy, *Thomas Aquinas*, 9.

26. Freeland, *But Is It Art?*, 38.

27. Thomas Aquinas, *Summa Theologica*, vol. 2, *Existence and Nature of God*, trans. and ed. Timothy McDermott (London: Blackfriars, 1964), 73.

28. Freeland, *But Is It Art?*, 38. Chartres was a thriving city in medieval France around 1200 CE. Freeland elaborates on the School of Chartres and its importance as a center for worship and education (36–42).

29. Freeland, *But Is It Art?*, 39.

Light and allegory were also central themes in Thomistic aesthetics. Plato understood light to be the ideal good,[30] but Aquinas saw light as signifying an inner perception of God. He called this ability to shine forth the inner luminosity of a thing *claritas*.[31] Accordingly, cathedrals were designed to accentuate light. The tall buildings fortified by vaulted ceilings and flying buttresses allowed for stained glass windows to adorn the walls. Today we think of gothic cathedrals as dark and scary, but this is ironic. In those days when there was no electricity, these cathedrals were the most illuminated buildings in the world! The windows allowed streams of light to pour in and fill the white stone walls with beautiful patches of colored light. This light symbolized the illumination that comes from the heavenly Father, and the height of the cathedrals represented heaven.[32] These symbols acted as allegories for a transcendent reality that was present in the space. Freeland writes, "For medieval philosophers like Aquinas, allegory was a logical way to understand how God is present in the world. Each thing in the world could be a sign from God."[33] Allegory was a core principle, along with proportion and light, in a Christian medieval poetics.[34]

Modern Aversion to Beauty

While pre-Enlightenment movements like the Renaissance,[35] and styles such as baroque and rococo, offered artistic innovations and some of the greatest works of art the world has ever seen, the art of the Western world was still largely representational, functioning within a Greek-inspired poetics. The next biggest shift in Western philosophical understandings of beauty and aesthetics came during the Enlightenment, when concepts of beauty and aesthetic judgment shifted from a theological starting point to an anthropocentric one. Kant's

30. See Plato's analogy of the sun in *Republic*, 507.
31. Aquinas, *Summa Theologica*, 2:73.
32. Freeland, *But Is It Art?*, 41.
33. Freeland, *But Is It Art?*, 41.
34. We have been emphasizing Western as opposed to Eastern art and artmaking. Eastern art and iconography, however, played a major, influential, and at times controversial role in Western art, particularly in the late Middle Ages and during the Reformation. As we are only discussing the premodern landscape of Western art, the Eastern influence on art will only be addressed concerning its effects on Western art. Treating the subject here would likely be an injustice to Eastern art as the intricate nature of iconography would be rendered too briefly.
35. The Renaissance, and particularly the movement within the Renaissance known as the Reformation, can conceivably be spoken about in both premodern and modern terms. Although one might argue that the Renaissance and Reformation fit better ideologically and historically with the late medieval era, they dictate the turning from the premodern to the modern era. An exact starting date for any era is unfeasible because of the fluid nature of cultural progression.

aesthetics, outlined in his *Critique of Judgment,* clearly portrays the modern turn from the divine toward the human.

Kant believed that we do not have to rely on God to understand the role of art or to determine if something is beautiful.[36] Aquinas said that the principles of integrity, proportion, and *claritas* in objects had the ability to elicit a response of beauty in the perceiver, and he saw these demarcations as a sort of general revelation of the transcendental of beauty, which was properly located in God. Kant, on the other hand, believed that beauty only comes from human discernment, and he eschewed any sort of objective rootedness. Kant recognized two types of judgment that are used to discern things: *determinate judgment,* which is subject to law, and *indeterminate judgment,* which is free-flowing. Aesthetic judgment is this free-flowing judgment that is disinterested (not influenced by outside considerations) and nonconceptual. For Kant, one can utilize reason through creative judgment. Aesthetic pleasure is not the visceral experience itself; it's the reflection on the visceral experience. There is no physical or material correlative of what is perceived and judged aesthetically. Value judgments, such as when we consider something to be beautiful or sublime, are evident not because the objects portray beauty or sublimity but because this is how the viewer sensually responds to the object upon perceiving it.[37] The thing itself doesn't have the aesthetic pleasure; the pleasure is a second-order thing. In this sense, Kant doesn't look at the "beautiful" stone but finds beauty in the stoniness of the stone. This is a big move away from an objectivist understanding of beauty and an even bigger move away from Aquinas and the medieval theologians who saw beauty as a transcendental, objective quality located in God. In Kant's view, beauty exists not objectively as a transcendental but subjectively in the realm of perception and aesthetic reflection.

Yet for Kant there is a sense of universality in beauty. When we look at something and believe it is beautiful, we look at it with the sense that everyone *ought* to agree with us in thinking that it's beautiful. We assume that it is, or should be, universally perceived as beautiful. The "ought" in aesthetic judgment, however, is conditional and not categorical. As Kant writes, "The ought in aesthetical judgment is therefore pronounced in accordance with all the data which are required for judging and yet is only conditioned. We ask for the agreement of everyone else, because we have for it a ground that is common to all; and we could count on this agreement, provided we were always sure that the case was correctly subsumed under that ground as rule of assent."[38] We

36. Immanuel Kant, *Critique of Judgment,* trans. J. H. Bernard (Overland Park, KS: Digireads.com, 2010), 113.
37. Kant, *Critique of Judgment,* 54.
38. Kant, *Critique of Judgment,* 55.

may in fact believe that others ought to view the same object as beautiful too, but we're then inclined to ask others if they agree. In other words, even in our pronouncement that something is beautiful, we understand that others might not see it that way—and that's okay because we recognize that our perception of beauty lies subjectively in the eye of the beholder. There is freedom in our disinterestedness; hence, aesthetic judgment is free.

The idea of disinterestedness, noted above, is another important concept developed by Kant. **Disinterestedness** essentially means that a person perceives something for its own sake and not to receive something from it. A disinterested viewer is not an *un*interested viewer but a viewer who sees in art a "purposeful-ness without purpose."[39] Art does not need to educate or be used as a means to some other end. It does not need to carry any sort of utility. Rather, to the disinterested viewer, art is the end in itself. This concept led Enlightenment thinkers and modern art connoisseurs to appreciate "art for art's sake." Before the Renaissance, much art in the West was made in service to the church, and even during the Reformation one would not have appreciated art for aesthetic contemplation alone.[40] This idea, coupled with the human-centered, subjective understanding of beauty, would radically change how art and aesthetics were viewed and understood in the West. These shifts also allowed for the modern person to, in a way, shun beauty. If beauty is no longer objectively tied to God, then we can do away with it. But why would someone want to do away with beauty?

The great novelist Leo Tolstoy distinguished between the objective and the subjective notions of beauty in his essay "What Is Art?" Beauty, he claims, can be seen as the objective perfection found in God, or it can be subjectively de-fined as that which is pleasing without the aim of advantage. The first of these definitions is, as Tolstoy states, fantastical, rooted in nothing.[41] It is, in any case, a metaphysical claim, which is neither provable nor observable. Therefore, Tolstoy opts for the second, "intelligible" definition, which derives from ob-servation.[42] Many aesthetic theories claim that the observance or transmittance of beauty is foundational for aesthetics. Tolstoy, however, sees these theories as wrong and claims that people will only find the true meaning of art when they let go of the idea that the aim of art is beauty or pleasure.[43]

39. Graham, *Philosophy of the Arts*, 18.
40. William Dyrness, *Reformed Theology and Visual Culture: The Protestant Imagination from Calvin to Edwards* (Cambridge: Cambridge University Press, 2004), 11.
41. Leo Tolstoy, "What Is Art?," in *Aesthetics*, ed. Susan Feagin and Patrick Maynard (Oxford: Oxford University Press, 1997), 166–67.
42. Tolstoy, "What Is Art?," 167.
43. Tolstoy, "What Is Art?," 168.

Tolstoy uses the tautological statement "Enjoyment is good because it is enjoyment" to dismiss the definition of art as something that transmits enjoyment via beauty. Instead, he believes art is the transmittance of feelings from artist to viewer by an artifact.[44] As Tolstoy writes, "To evoke in oneself a feeling one has once experienced, and having evoked it in oneself, then, by means of movements, lines, colors, sounds, or forms expressed in words, so to transmit that feeling that others may experience the same feeling—this is the activity of art."[45] In this way, art is a human activity that constitutes the transmittance of feelings from person to person.[46] Viewing art merely as the transmittance of feeling has allowed the modern viewer to devalue the significance of beauty in art.

While Kant's decisive move to relocate the source of beauty from God to the subjective perceptions of the viewer paved the way for artists and theorists to move away from the topic of beauty, the decline of beauty was not merely due to a rationalistic shift in thinking. Instead, beauty's decline was largely due to major societal changes that took place in the West during the modern era. The early twentieth century was beleaguered by some of the worst atrocities history has ever seen. After the Spanish-American War of 1898, the early parts of the next century were followed by World War I (1914–18), the Armenian genocide in Turkey (1914–15), the Great Depression (1929–39), the Spanish Civil War (1936–39), Hitler's Holocaust (1933–45), and World War II (1939–45). During these hardships, the idea that life was good and beautiful came into question. When people faced the ugly realities of war and devastation, beauty began to look like kitschy escapism.[47] When everything in society is hard, beauty does not look like a redemptive ideal or attribute, but like a mask that covers up the real ugliness of life.

Kathleen Marie Higgins sees beauty as a feeling that helps us gain a renewed love of life.[48] But what if this love is lost and all we see is misery? If beauty enhances the natural order of things, what if nature is ugly? Part of the modern decline of beauty is, for Higgins, the mind's newfound ability to see beauty mixed with the ugliness of life. When we look at the world through a lens of cynicism, unsullied beauty appears to be from a time that's far removed. So instead of striving for beauty, we oppose it, finding it unconnected to our reality.[49]

44. Tolstoy, "What Is Art?," 169.
45. Tolstoy, "What Is Art?," 170.
46. Tolstoy, "What Is Art?," 171.
47. Kathleen Marie Higgins, "Whatever Happened to Beauty? A Response to Danto," *The Journal of Aesthetics and Art Criticism* 54, no. 3 (Summer 1996): 282.
48. Higgins, "Whatever Happened to Beauty?," 282.
49. Higgins, "Whatever Happened to Beauty?," 283.

Arthur Danto, however, sees beauty making a resurgence in our present age. While beauty may never again be seen as *normative* for our creative output, it can still play a pivotal role for many creative and artistic expressions. If an artwork's content is best expressed through beauty, then it should be beautiful! But that's not to say the artwork *must* be beautiful to be considered good.[50] Beauty is required of the artwork if and only if beauty is integral to the artwork's meaning.[51] Art does not need to be beautiful to be excellent. Rather, artistic excellence dictates what the work of art is supposed to be or do.[52] For Danto, beauty is an aesthetic characteristic of our myriad experiences, not a divine attribute or transcendent ideal. Yet even as it has become more difficult to talk about beauty as a transcendental, we are at least able to see the resurgence of beauty as it makes its way back into our conversations.

Conclusion

Through this (very) brief and selected survey, we can begin to see the difficulties that surround the concepts of beauty and aesthetics when we think about them in terms of theology and worldview. If one of our foundational faith claims is that beauty is objectively rooted in God, then it would be wrong to simply dismiss beauty as kitschy escapism. Yet by holding on to these concepts of beauty, we can appear culturally out of touch, as if we're oblivious to what's going on in the real world. Perhaps the fix is to approach beauty by its eschatological function rather than by its essence.[53] This change of approach allows us to welcome beauty back into our theological vocabulary in a way that fully engages what is happening in the world around us. An eschatological beauty is one that in trying times elicits hope, not escapism.

A renewal worldview envisions the Spirit's aesthetic role in this way: beauty is the aesthetic component of the eschatological Spirit's inbreaking. Beauty, therefore, corresponds with those moments when we catch a glimpse of God's vision for reality. To be clear, this idea is not exclusively Pentecostal. Many other Christian traditions adhere to a concept of the kingdom of God as "already and not yet," while some even see beauty as an eschatological inbreaking of what is to come.[54] Yet understanding this concept through the narrative framework

50. Arthur Danto, *The Abuse of Beauty: Aesthetics and the Concept of Art* (Chicago: Open Court, 2003), 37, 58.

51. Danto, *Abuse of Beauty*, 9, 13, 97.

52. Danto, *Abuse of Beauty*, 107.

53. This does have biblical precedence, after all (see Eccles. 3:11).

54. See W. David O. Taylor, *Glimpses of the New Creation: Worship and the Formative Power of the Arts* (Grand Rapids: Eerdmans, 2019); and Kin Yip Louie, *The Beauty of the Triune God: The Theological Aesthetics of Jonathan Edwards* (Eugene: Pickwick, 2013).

of Pentecost allows it to speak in theological terms consistent with Pentecostal thought and practice. Thus, a renewal theological aesthetics would seek to understand how beauty's eschatological power reflects the Spirit of Pentecost. This is the sort of theological aesthetics that coheres with a renewal worldview, and it is what we will attempt to construct in chapter 4.

Since beauty corresponds with what is right aesthetically, the most beautiful moments will be those when God's full vision, for us and for the world, is realized. Let's not forget the aesthetic experience of sight when we read 1 Corinthians 13:12: "For now we see in a mirror, dimly, but then we will see face to face. Now I know only in part; then I will know fully, even as I have been fully known." The fullness, completion, and rightness of that moment can only be described as beautiful. Can *beauty* be our apologetic? We will consider these concluding reflections in greater depth and detail in the subsequent chapters of part 1.

Study Questions

1. How can Christians talk about the beauty of God in our present era?

2. How do our concepts of beauty affect our worldviews?

3. Should we see beauty as a subjective feeling that's located "in the eye of the beholder" or as an objective property that objects hold?

✛ 3 ✛

Contemporary Christian Aesthetics

Begbie, Balthasar, and Hart

Key Words

Axiology: *The philosophical study of the nature of value and of what kinds of things are valuable.*

Five Solas: *The key theological convictions of the Reformers, which include* sola Scriptura *(Scripture alone),* sola fide *(faith alone),* sola gratia *(grace alone),* solus Christus *(Christ alone), and* soli Deo gloria *(glory to God alone).*

Perichoresis: *A theological term that refers to the divine relationality between the persons of the triune God.*

Ruach: *The Hebrew word for spirit, breath, or wind.*

Sublime: *The aesthetic quality of greatness that inspires awe.*

Theological aesthetics: *The interdisciplinary study of theology and philosophical aesthetics.*

What gives things worth? We tend to value an object based on its uniqueness and demand. For instance, if something is rare and a lot of people want it, we consider it valuable. The scarcer the object is, the more value we ascribe to it. But there are abstract things we value that are not directly quantifiable, like happiness or love or beauty. So when we concern ourselves with what is valuable, we may have to take a step back and think philosophically about value. Sometimes we have to go deeper than merely stating that a thing

35

does or does not have value. We must ask why things do or do not have value, and how these values come about in societies, communities, or traditions. The philosophical field of **axiology** is concerned with the nature of value and with what kinds of things are valuable. The two basic forms of axiology are ethics, which looks at moral values, and aesthetics, which looks at values concerning sensed perceptions. Ethics asks questions like, What is right and wrong? And how can we make moral judgments? Aesthetics, on the other hand, asks questions like, What is beauty? And what makes art successful? While all of part 1 of this book is concerned with matters of aesthetics, this chapter in particular will look at how some significant theological traditions have understood God and the Christian faith in light of aesthetical reflection.

Having only formed in the early 1900s, Pentecostalism is still rather young as a theological tradition. This means older Christian traditions have had more time to flesh out theological ideas systematically. Many of these traditions have such firm foundations in their systematics that they have been able to move beyond the customary doctrines and approach interdisciplinary subjects theologically. Since Pentecostalism is still the new kid on the *theological* block, it will, as a point of comparison, serve us well to see how other Christian traditions have dealt theologically with matters of aesthetics. Thus, we will proceed first by overviewing the field of theological aesthetics, and then by looking at the work of Jeremy Begbie as representative of a Protestant theological aesthetics, Hans Urs von Balthasar as representative of a Roman Catholic position, and David Bentley Hart as representative of an Eastern Orthodox position. This will give us a better context for framing our own renewal aesthetics in the next chapter.

An Overview of Christian Theological Aesthetics

As was discussed in the previous chapter, before the Enlightenment, matters of aesthetics were seen as theological matters because Christians reflected on beauty as an attribute of the divine. After the Enlightenment, however, philosophers began to look at matters of perception, taste, beauty, and the arts apart from theology, so aesthetics became its own separate field of philosophical inquiry. Thereafter, two separate but related fields formed: aesthetics and theological aesthetics. If aesthetics proper is the philosophical study of value as it pertains to sensed perception, then **theological aesthetics** is a branch of aesthetics proper that can be defined as the interdisciplinary study of theology and philosophical aesthetics. While theology studies religious matters—namely, the nature of God in relation to humanity—aesthetics is the axiological field that studies sensed perceptions. Thus, theological aesthetics concerns itself with religious matters as they are perceived through sensed experience. It takes seriously the religious experience of the Christian life, reflecting on theo-aesthetic concepts such as beauty, imagination, inspiration, ritual, sacrament, creation, discernment, revelation, and so on.

In terms of theological method, theologians typically take one of two approaches when engaging theological aesthetics: either they address concepts like the ones mentioned above systematically through a theo-aesthetic lens, or they explore the theological implications of aesthetic sociocultural practices from particular worshiping communities. Theologian Alejandro García-Rivera takes the former approach in his book *The Community of the Beautiful,* where he argues that the Christian community is the recipient of God's self-disclosure, experiencing the beauty of God through communal engagements and God's revelatory signs.[1] Given this basis, García-Rivera spends the rest of the book teasing out the theological and philosophical implications that belong to such a statement. This means he is creating a theological system that is rooted in the theo-aesthetic foothold stated above. Conversely, Ashon Crawley takes the latter approach in his book *Blackpentecostal Breath.*[2] Crawley observes the liturgical and oratorical worship practices of Pentecostal traditions that are composed primarily of African Americans. Based on these, he creates an interdisciplinary study that looks at the theological implications arising from an examination of the historical, political, cultural, and economic conditions that affect African Americans. Because these conditions shape Black Pentecostal worshiping communities, we can look at the aesthetics of their worship practices and gain insight into their faith tradition. García-Rivera's is an inside-out approach that takes a theological idea and systematically teases out implications, whereas Crawley's is an outside-in approach that begins with the aesthetic expression (the worship act or ritual) and then traces the sociocultural and theological roots that evince the expression. Both approaches are important for theological aesthetics and show how the aesthetic realm is important for our understanding of a Christian worldview. Both approaches can guide the way we interpret aesthetic experiences theologically, but one starts with the theo-aesthetic idea and the other starts with the experience itself.

The theologians we engage below use the first approach as they let a particular theo-aesthetic idea drive their systems. In the next chapter we will put forth a renewal aesthetics that also takes the first approach. For the rest of this chapter, however, we will survey three contrasting theological aesthetics from prevalent theologians who stand as exemplars of their tradition's aesthetical

1. Alejandro García-Rivera, *The Community of the Beautiful: A Theological Aesthetics* (Collegeville, MN: Liturgical Press, 1999), 82.

2. Ashon Crawley, *Blackpentecostal Breath: The Aesthetics of Possibility* (New York: Fordham University Press, 2017).

thinking. While no theological tradition is monolithic, and other individuals have put forth books that are worthy of consideration, the three chosen theologians are each highly influential figures within their respective traditions of Reformed Protestantism, Roman Catholicism, and Eastern Orthodoxy. Through their work, we can gain a clearer view of how the three traditions contrast as we move toward constructing a renewal perspective.

Begbie as Representative of Protestantism

How might a Protestant theologian form his or her theological aesthetics? Some of the key theological convictions of the Reformers are summed up in five Latin phrases known as the **Five Solas:** *sola Scriptura* (Scripture alone), *sola fide* (faith alone), *sola gratia* (grace alone), *solus Christus* (Christ alone), and *soli Deo gloria* (glory to God alone). These slogans comprise the main convictions of Protestant theology, which claims that the salvific, justifying grace of God comes by faith in Jesus Christ alone. Scripture is the source of written divine revelation that teaches and guides people in matters of salvation and the Christian faith. A Protestant theological aesthetics holds these convictions in high regard and, unlike the aesthetics of the Catholics or Orthodox, pays less attention to church traditions as a formative force for theological aesthetics. The main source funding the Protestant theological project is Scripture. We should notice, too, that the Spirit is not mentioned in the Five Solas. This shows a major point of contrast between Protestantism and Pentecostalism, even as Pentecostalism is typically seen as a faction of Protestantism. We will discuss this further in the next chapter.

Given all this, we can expect a Protestant theological aesthetics to be principally based on Scripture and centered on Christ (Christocentric), and to be especially focused on matters of salvation. And if the theological reflection is primarily rooted in Scripture, then it makes sense for a theological aesthetics to start where the Bible starts: the story of creation. Many aesthetics that begin with creation see human creativity as analogous to God's creative acts. People are made in the image of the Creator God, so they reflect and honor God through creativity.[3] Since only God's initial creation is "out of nothing" (*ex nihilo*), every person's creativity flows from the substance of God's initial creation. This line of thinking is what I (Steven) have elsewhere called a "creational aesthetics."[4]

3. See Hilary Brand and Adrienne Chaplin, *Art & Soul: Signposts for Christians in the Arts,* 2nd ed. (Downers Grove, IL: InterVarsity, 2001); L. Clifton Edwards, "Artful Creation and Aesthetic Rationality: Toward a Creational Theology of Revelatory Beauty," *Theology Today* 69, no. 1 (2012): 56–72; and Abraham Kuyper, *Wisdom and Wonder: Common Grace in Science and Art* (Grand Rapids: Christian's Library, 2011).

4. Steven Félix-Jäger, "Creational Aesthetics and the Challenge of Conceptual Art," *Religion and the Arts* 20 (2016): 663–73.

A creational aesthetics sees God's creation as fundamentally good, humans as imitating creators, and creativity as spiritually mediated.[5] The key is to see how a person's creative acts help reveal the glory of God in a post-lapsarian (i.e., after the fall) world.

While Anglican theologian Jeremy Begbie (b. 1957) also begins his aesthetics with the trinitarian God's creation *ex nihilo*, his sense of creation is not viewed solely as a model for creativity but also as intricately tied to matters of the fall and redemption. For Begbie, creation is an act of grace that opens God up to the possibility of God's suffering. Because of God's trinitarian relationality, even without creation God is already relational. Relationality can be seen through the perfect loving community of God, which comprises God's very nature. Since creation is separate from God, it opened the possibility of deviating from God. Out of God's love, God also created a covenant with creation, which allowed the world the ability to move and be free as its own entity.[6] This covenant made way for the possibility of rejecting God. Thus, the possibility of God's suffering was opened up through creation and made most evident in the life of Christ from the incarnation through the cross.

Christ plays a crucial role in Begbie's aesthetics. For one, Begbie sees creation as coming into being through spontaneous, unpredictable acts, and since Jesus is the Word (John 1), he is the supreme orderer of the cosmos.[7] It's through the Word of God (Christ) that creation was ordered. The light was separated from the dark, and the waters from the waters, and the skies from the dry land, all through the Word of God when God *said*, "Let there be . . ." (Gen. 1). After the fall, it is once again Christ, as the Word of God, who reorders things and sets them right! Begbie writes, "The one who has put all things under his feet is none other than the one who has borne the full weight of the world's evil as man."[8] It is through Christ's death and resurrection that the world can be redeemed and order can once again be brought to the disorder wrought by sin.

But Christ is also the *telos*, or ultimate aim, of humanity as he embodies the fullness of a redeemed created reality. Here Begbie uses the metaphor "Christ as mediator of the cosmos," showing that Christ, the one who is present as the originator of all things, is also involved throughout world history. Christ is our connection to the transcendent God. He is our path for salvation and our link to new life. These notions of orderer and reorderer help us grasp the pertinent role Christ takes in creation and in our creativity. Just as Christ is

---

5. Félix-Jäger, "Creational Aesthetics," 666.

6. Jeremy Begbie, *Voicing Creation's Praise: Towards a Theology of the Arts* (London: T&T Clark, 2000), 171.

7. Begbie, *Voicing Creation's Praise*, 175.

8. Begbie, *Voicing Creation's Praise*, 176.

mediator of the cosmos, so are Christians "priests of creation" as we share in God's creative purposes.[9] Everything God has done since the fall has been to draw creation back to Godself through Christ, and it is our duty as humanity to respect, develop, and steward God's creation. Our task as image-bearers is to help reconcile creation to God, and it is in this way that we too become mediators like Jesus.

Putting all this together, Begbie's theological aesthetics begins in our present context of fallen creation, where the Creator God acts through Christ, inviting creation to be redeemed and remade into a new creation. Human creativity thus has significant theological implications. When *our* creations reinforce the ministry of reconciliation God has called us to, we have agency in God's work on earth, partnering with the Creator God who draws creation back to Godself.

Begbie exemplifies a Protestant theological aesthetics because his theology checks off many of the key Protestant theological convictions. Significantly, his aesthetics is scriptural, beginning with the Genesis account of creation and synthesizing the whole biblical narrative of salvation. Furthermore, Begbie's theology focuses on the supremacy of Christ for matters of faith and salvation and understands creative acts through that framework. Begbie's approach is helpful for us as we attempt to craft a renewal aesthetics in the next chapter because it demonstrates what it means to enter into God's work of creation and redemption and what creative roles we can play as stewards. However, our renewal aesthetics will differ in that it will be decidedly pneumatocentric (focused on the Spirit), whereas Begbie's aesthetics only makes brief mention of the Spirit when he talks about the Trinity. Doesn't the Spirit play a significant role in creation?

A trinitarian reading of Genesis 1 tells us that the *Ruach* of God "swept over the face of the waters" (v. 2). **Ruach** is the Hebrew word for spirit, breath, or wind, so trinitarian Christians read Genesis 1:2 as saying that "the Spirit of God" was hovering over the chaotic waters. So, while the Word of God was a major agent in ordering creation, the Spirit of God was active too. In fact, the second-century church bishop Irenaeus said that God worked through both the Word and the Spirit to create: "For always present with him are the Word and Wisdom, the Son and Spirit, by whom and in whom he made all things freely and of his own will, to whom he also speaks, when he says, 'Let us make man after our image and likeness.'"[10] We can also say that the Spirit plays a crucial role in redemption and salvation since it was the Spirit of God that raised Christ

---

9. Begbie, *Voicing Creation's Praise*, 177.

10. Irenaeus, *Against Heresies* 4.20.1, quoted in Andrew Raddee-Gallwitz, ed., *The Cambridge Edition of Early Christian Writing*, vol. 1, *God* (Cambridge: Cambridge University Press, 2017), 34.

from the dead (Rom. 8:11) and that dwells in the hearts of believers (1 Cor. 3:16). It's the Spirit of God that empowers the church today (Eph. 2:21–22) and grants us to once again eat from the tree of life (Rev. 2:7). While Begbie is helpful to an extent, a renewal aesthetics will be seen through a pneumatological lens. Such an approach will speak more directly to the commitments and sensitivities of renewal spirituality.

Balthasar as Representative of Catholicism

Catholics have rich traditions of theological aesthetics to draw from. Although pre-Reformation theologians are accessible to both Catholics and Protestants, Protestants tend to be most conversant with Reformation theologians like Martin Luther and John Calvin and some of the Protestant theological giants that followed, such as John Wesley and Jonathan Edwards. Catholic theologians, on the other hand, tend to draw from a longer historical lineage looking all the way back to the work of Thomas Aquinas, Boethius, and Augustine to supplement their theological aesthetics. This is certainly the case for Swiss theologian Hans Urs von Balthasar (1905–88), who, like Boethius, explores the transcendentals of truth, beauty, and goodness in his magnum opus—a multivolume trilogy of works known as *The Glory of the Lord* (*Herrlichkeit*), *Theo-Drama* (*Theodramatik*), and *Theo-Logic* (*Theologik*). Most theologians and philosophers who focus on the transcendentals start with truth and progress to goodness and then beauty. Balthasar, however, made aesthetics his starting point in *The Glory of the Lord* and, in so doing, crafted one of the most robust and influential theological aesthetics ever. As is evident, Balthasar inspired us to take a similar approach in this volume.

Systematicians often take classic events of the Christian faith and build entire theologies around them, teasing out all the insights and implications that arise from the events. For instance, a theologian might look at the resurrection of Christ as that major turning point in salvation history that not only proves true everything that was said about Jesus but also gives hope to believers and reasons for persisting in the faith.[11] In this manner, Balthasar's entire systematic theology begins with aesthetic considerations of the glory of the Lord revealed in the life of Christ. As a method, Balthasar looks at the aesthetic dimension of glory as seen through the "eyes of faith."[12] The eyes of faith are the spiritual

11. This is the starting point for Wolfhart Pannenberg, who saw the resurrection of Christ as historically revelatory and key for knowing the identity of Christ. See Wolfhart Pannenberg, *Jesus— God and Man*, trans. Lewis Wilkins and Duane Priebe, 2nd ed. (Philadelphia: Westminster, 1977).

12. Hans Urs von Balthasar, *The Glory of the Lord: A Theological Aesthetics*, vol. 1, *Seeing the Form*, trans. Erasmo Leiva-Merikakis (San Francisco: Ignatius, 1982), 44–45.

senses that we use to encounter Christ as he shows himself. It is faith that's the
theological act of perception. Our bodily senses become saturated with faith
when we believe with the eyes of faith, and it is here, through the grace of faith,
that we experience God in and through the world. We see Christ radiating forth.
Here's how Balthasar states it: "There is a moment when the interior light of the
'eyes of faith' becomes one with the exterior light that shines from Christ, and
this occurs because man's thirst, as he strives and seeks after God, is quenched
as he finds repose in the revealed form of the Son."[13] For Balthasar the glory of
God is revealed to us in Christ and recounted in Scripture.

Beauty has a form which is perfectly revealed in Christ through the incarnation. If beauty is a transcendental and belongs in God, then we see the form of
beauty when God enters creation through the incarnation. We know the form
of beauty because we see it incarnated in Christ. Thus, Christ becomes the
standard from which all other forms can be measured.[14] Christ is, therefore,
the center of the Christian faith. Concerning Balthasar's method, Aiden Nichols writes, "Balthasar sets himself the task of trying to perceive the objective
form of revelation, in creation and in Jesus Christ, in all its splendid, harmonious and symphonic fullness."[15] Since the revelation of God is experienced,
we must be able to recognize the aesthetic components of our experiences,
so what Balthasar is really after is to see how the world *perceives* the revelation
of God's grace.

If the transcendent Creator God were to become part of creation, we would
be able to see and experience God *as* part of the material world. Our knowledge
of God would be more complete than that of a theophany (a visible manifestation of God) because God would *be* one of us! This is the significance of the
incarnation—the transcendent God entered creation in order to save it. Jesus
is thus the *full revelation of God*, not just a divine manifestation. Jesus is God in
the flesh. Since Jesus is the fullness of God's revelation, then the glory of God
emanates from Christ. Jesus is the object of true beauty, and as we gaze upon
him, our ability to truly see God is illuminated. So Christ (the object of faith)
draws us (the subject of faith) to the form of beauty, which is rooted in God and
revealed in Christ. This is also why Catholicism could be considered a religion
of beauty—it is God's beauty that's made tangible through the incarnation, not
the **sublime** (the aesthetic quality of greatness that inspires awe). God's self-
revelation in Christ is one that is intimately present *as* humanity—enfleshed,
beautiful. Yet the purpose of Christ is to lead us into the *logos* and to the Father.

13. Balthasar, *Glory of the Lord*, 190
14. Balthasar, *Glory of the Lord*, 451.
15. Aiden Nichols, *A Key to Balthasar: Hans Urs von Balthasar on Beauty, Goodness, and Truth*
(Grand Rapids: Baker Academic, 2011), 13.

Our perception of God's beauty is our awareness of God's self-emptying, divine love. This perception is made evident in Christ through the incarnation. To this point Balthasar states, "Christian contemplation can marvel, in the self-emptying of divine love, at the exceeding wisdom, truth and beauty inherent there. But it is only in this self-emptying that they can be contemplated, for it is the source whence the glory contemplated by the angels and the saints radiates into eternal life."[16] Our ability to contemplate the beauty of God is made possible by the incarnation, and God's self-emptying love is most evident on the cross. Here God's glory shines forth more brilliantly than ever because it is juxtaposed with his humiliation.[17]

To understand this point, let's consider one of the main principles of art and design: contrast. Contrast is the arrangement of opposite elements and effects and is used to differentiate and highlight objects. For instance, if you're painting and you want to make a color really pop, then one thing you could do is contrast it with a complementary color. Colors that are across from each other on the color wheel are called direct complements (i.e., blue and orange, red and green, yellow and purple). Direct complements affect each other in two major ways: first, mixing in a color's direct complement can make the original color appear duller—for example, by adding a bit of blue to orange. Adding a complement deadens a color's brilliance. Second, a color will appear brighter if its complement is placed near or around it. So if you're painting and you want something orange to pop, then surround it with objects that are deep blue. Artists also contrast textures, values, shapes, and other elements to create visual separation and order. In the same way, Christ's glory radiates more when he's on the cross because the purity and beauty of God is contrasted with the debasement of the cross.

Although God's beauty is evident in things that are deemed beautiful, beauty is more than a mere aesthetic property for Balthasar. It is "radiance from the depths of Being."[18] Beauty's correspondence with God's transcendental of beauty means it can only be truly known through the eyes of faith. As Nichols writes, "Beauty thus speaks of the meaning of that which transcends and yet inheres in all existents."[19] God's glory radiates from Christ, the revelation of God, and can be experienced by us as grace. So Balthasar's christological aesthetics focuses on our experience of God's self-emptying love.

16. Hans Urs von Balthasar, *Explorations in Theology I: The Word Made Flesh*, trans. A. V. Littledale and Alexander Dru (San Francisco: Ignatius, 1989), 113.
17. Balthasar, *Explorations in Theology*, 114.
18. Balthasar, *Glory of the Lord*, 389.
19. Nichols, *Key to Balthasar*, 42.

Beginning at the end, Balthasar's aesthetics focuses on that which breaks into our present—the glory of the Lord. One does not need to rely on the church or the authority of tradition to accept the truths of faith. Rather, the eyes of faith reveal Christ's beauty, giving perceptible evidence toward the Christian faith's truth and goodness. Like Begbie, Balthasar starts from a christological vantage point, which can lead to a neglect of the Spirit's role in a theological aesthetics. However, a pneumatological reading of Balthasar might help a re-newal aesthetics nuance the concept of beauty—if the beauty of the Lord is definitively known in Christ, then the Spirit, inspiring our social imaginaries, allows us to envision Christ's glory in our lives today. The Spirit allows us to be fully cognizant of, and participate in, the beauty of the Lord collectively today, even as the incarnation and the cross entered history millennia ago. A pneumatological imagination can speak to Balthasar's ideas, recognizing the beauty of God breaking into our present state, and by witnessing our own beautification as we move in pursuit of the beautiful Christ.

Hart as Representative of Eastern Orthodoxy

Of all the Christian traditions out there, Eastern Orthodoxy has arguably the richest aesthetic tradition of *image*. Like Catholicism, Eastern Orthodoxy holds to ancient liturgical and theological traditions. But while Catholicism traces its roots back to the western Roman Empire, Eastern Orthodoxy traces its roots to the eastern Roman Empire. The Orthodox draw heavily from Eastern, Greek-speaking theologians such as Maximus the Confessor (ca. 580–663 CE), Pseudo-Dionysius the Aeropagite (ca. fifth or sixth century CE), and John of Damascus (ca. 675–749 CE), and from medieval Byzantine theology. Eastern Orthodox theologians have developed a sophisticated theology of icons, which is essential for their theological aesthetics.

An icon can be considered a form of liturgical art from the Eastern Ortho-dox tradition. Its function, however, is not merely representational but also deeply religious.[20] While icons are typically paintings of Christ, the saints, heavenly hosts, or theological concepts, they can best be understood as rep-resentations of heavenly realities. In worship, icons help believers focus on divine things, acting as windows into a heavenly realm. So when one looks at the eyes of Jesus in an icon, he or she is actually looking *through* the icon to the spiritual reality it depicts. The worshiper sees the real eyes of Christ.

20. Leonid Ouspenksy, "The Meaning and Language of Icons," in *The Meaning of Icons*, by Leonid Ouspensky and Vladimir Lossky, trans. G. E. H. Palmer and E. Kadloubovsky (New York: St. Vladi-mir's Seminary Press, 1999), 31.

Icons apart from their spiritual vision, however, are merely wooden boards. The Holy Spirit empowers the transfiguration of matter, which gives the icon revelatory power. In fact, for Orthodox Christians, icons are revelatory in the same way the Scriptures and the cross are revelatory.[21] Icons are made out of material but are prayerfully made so they depict the "deified protoype" of a subject's likeness. They are images "not of corruptible flesh, but of flesh transfigured, radiant with Divine light. It is Beauty and Glory, represented by material means and visible in the icon to physical eyes."[22] Icons signify things beyond themselves, revealing transfigured reality. Therefore, icons are not art per se but presence.

Icons can also be considered theology in image form. Throughout the early Middle Ages, they served to educate illiterate Christians about the faith. They depict theologically dense symbols in their portraiture, expressing doctrines like the incarnation or the nature of Christ's divinity. Their symbols represent theologically significant characteristics of Jesus or the saints, like compassion or wisdom. By reflecting on the presence of God, icons inform theology just as they depict theological concepts.

Icons do not merely depict beauty in an aesthetic sense, but they materially depict the transcendental of beauty. As theologian Leonid Ouspensky writes, "The beauty of an icon is the beauty of the acquired likeness to God and so its value lies not in its being beautiful in itself, but in the fact that it depicts Beauty."[23] Iconic beauty, therefore, seems to reject the Kantian notion that beauty is in the eye of the beholder (as discussed in chap. 2). The beauty of an icon is its participation in and revealing of divine Beauty. This sense of beauty is not concerned with a viewer's aesthetic judgment of the piece. Orthodox theologian Paul Evdokimov sees beauty as belonging to and pointing back to God. Beauty is the shining forth of God's grace to creation, he says, and the icon "is a target, the point which centers the whole household on the brilliant shining forth of the beyond. It is never simply a decoration."[24] The icon is that which centers us to see God's Beauty.

Considering all of this, let's now look at how contemporary Eastern Orthodox theologian David Bentley Hart crafts his theological aesthetics. Hart's theological aesthetics takes a cue from Gregory of Nyssa, but it also enters into dialogue with Balthasar, the Catholic theologian discussed above. In *The Beauty of the Infinite*, Hart sets out to create a theology that's equipped with

21. Ouspenksy, "Meaning and Language of Icons," 30.
22. Ouspenksy, "Meaning and Language of Icons," 36.
23. Ouspenksy, "Meaning and Language of Icons," 35.
24. Paul Evdokimov, *The Art of the Icon: A Theology of Beauty*, trans. Steven Bigham (Pasadena, CA: Oakwood, 1990), 76.

its own rhetoric and internal logic.[25] Following Balthasar, Hart starts with beauty (as opposed to starting with truth or goodness) but draws heavily on Gregory's notion of perichoresis. **Perichoresis** is a theological term that refers to the divine relationality between the persons of the triune God. It states that God is communal by nature because the persons of the Trinity co-inhere and interpenetrate in relationship even before creation. In other words, God is relational in Godself through the co-inherence of the Father, Son, and Spirit. The term "perichoresis" was first found in Gregory but then later developed by Maximus. Hart states that Christian rhetoric should be drawn first from the point that God is infinite. Since God is infinite, differences can find their harmony in God through God's perichoretical co-indwelling relationality.[26] God is infinite beauty because God is triune in a divine harmonic relationality. So for Hart, beauty isn't just a characteristic of a static God but the outworking of God's triune nature.

Like Balthasar, Hart also sees God's beauty as taking definitive form in Christ.[27] God's beauty is infinite but is tangibly known in Christ through the incarnation. Creation is "the radiance of divine glory," and it can be seen as an icon of the triune God.[28] Since God's triune relationality is infinite beauty, it radiates as an *excessus*[29] that's evident in creation and finds its ultimate form in Christ. While Balthasar's aesthetics is predominately teleological, focusing on Christ's glory, Hart's aesthetics is largely trinitarian, focusing on divine relationality. By situating God's beauty in God's relational co-indwelling, Hart shows us how God relationally radiates beauty, which draws us back to relationship with God through Christ. Typically, Orthodox theologies are profoundly pneumatological, so Hart differs from the norm a bit. Though Hart doesn't ignore the Spirit, he also doesn't make the Spirit his main theological point of departure.

Hart's relational, trinitarian aesthetics can be helpful for a renewal aesthetics because a pneumatological imagination properly understood *is* a trinitarian imagination. A renewal aesthetics might begin with the present reality of the Holy Spirit in the life of believers, but the Spirit always points back to Christ,

25. David Bentley Hart, *The Beauty of the Infinite: The Aesthetics of Christian Truth* (Grand Rapids: Eerdmans, 2004), 3. Hart begins his project responding to the postmodern critique of metanarratives. Drawing from Milbank, Hart agrees that metanarratives should not be the sole arbiters of power, but he does not believe we can simply remove all rhetoric of ultimacy. While the postmodern critique shows rhetoric triumphing over the dialectic, Christianity can still make contributions to knowledge as it too has its own rhetoric with internal logic.

26. Hart, *Beauty of the Infinite*, 183.

27. Hart, *Beauty of the Infinite*, 441.

28. Hart, *Beauty of the Infinite*, 240.

29. Hart specifically uses the Latin term *excessus*, which means "departure" or "a going out."

who reveals the Father. So a renewal aesthetics would start with a present experience of beauty revealed by the Spirit, who is active in the present.

Conclusion

Many theological aesthetics have been written from a diverse array of Christian traditions, but this brief survey gives us a good starting point that will be important in articulating a renewal aesthetics in the next chapter. As we noted at the beginning of the chapter, no tradition is monolithic, and while this comparison only considered one prevalent theologian to exemplify each tradition's aesthetic thinking, the theologians we engaged have proven to be influential in and beyond their traditions. Comparing and contrasting three well-developed, influential theological aesthetics from a Protestant, a Catholic, and an Orthodox vantage point helps us see what a renewal aesthetics shares with each of these traditions and how it might differ.

One commonality found in each of these is that they all seek to understand beauty theologically as a quality or characteristic of God. They excavate aesthetic issues pertaining to beauty (particularly the beauty of Christ), the incarnation, the cross, images, and sacraments. Since most of what was discussed was dealt with through christological and ecclesial lenses, none of these traditions articulate their aesthetics from the vantage point of the universal outpouring of the Spirit. This, we argue in the next chapter, is what makes a renewal aesthetics unique. If we approach a theological aesthetics from a pneumatological vantage point, a number of questions may arise: Does the Spirit have a role in creation? How does the Spirit demonstrate and connect us to God's beauty? Does the Spirit help people experience the transcendent beauty of God? Does the Holy Spirit also inspire artists? Does the Spirit play an eschatological role in the creation of art? These are the sorts of questions that we will address as we detail a pneumatological aesthetics that is distinctively Pentecostal, which will then become the base for a renewed Christian worldview.

Study Questions

1. How can a robust theological aesthetics give us a sense of what we value in life?

2. Compare and contrast the role of beauty in the three theological aesthetics described above.

3. What are the strengths and deficiencies of each of the three theological aesthetics?

+ 4 +

A Renewal Perspective
on Beauty, Aesthetics,
and Embodied Spirituality

Key Words

Christian imagination: *The lens that shapes the way a Christian interprets life events and experiences.*

Embodiment: *The manifestation or expression of something in a tangible form.*

Pneumatological imagination: *The lens that shapes the way Pentecostals interpret life events and experiences, which is particularly inspired by the Pentecostal experience of the Spirit.*

Renewal aesthetics: *The interdisciplinary study of the theological doctrine of the Spirit and philosophical aesthetics.*

Spiritual holism: *A sense of spirituality that recognizes the significance of body and emotion in spiritual health.*

Have you ever had a shared experience with someone, and you each came away from it with wildly different interpretations of what actually happened? Sometimes we might remember the facts of our experiences differently, but more often what differs is how we *interpret* the facts of our shared experiences. A quick recovery from an illness can be seen as a reason to praise God's heart for restoration, or as a reason to applaud modern medicine, or as a reason to marvel at the human immune system. It's not the facts of the experience but the frameworks in which we interpret the experience that lead us to different conclusions. Pentecostals believe, of course, that the Spirit can enter into any framework, breaking down the walls that guard our hearts. Nevertheless, in order to understand a renewal worldview, it is important to grasp *how* Pentecostals interpret their experiences.

When we talk about a renewal worldview, we are talking about the way Pentecostals experience and interpret the world. Because Pentecostalism is a very experiential expression of the Christian faith, and because experiences can be understood aesthetically, part of understanding a renewal worldview entails how Pentecostals *see* the world theologically and aesthetically. As discussed in chapter 1, seeing the world entails looking at something as it relates to us.[1] Our seeing involves both our perceptions and our interpretation of those perceptions as they are filtered through our frameworks of interpretation. Therefore, the question we should ask is, Do Pentecostals have a unique framework for interpreting and understanding experiences and perceptions? We believe the answer to that question is yes, and in this chapter we seek to explore what a Pentecostal theo-aesthetic framework looks like and how it shapes a renewal worldview.

We will first define a renewal theo-aesthetic framework by adopting Amos Yong's concept of the pneumatological imagination. Through this framework we will look at how theo-aesthetic matters such as inspiration and beauty can be understood generally. Then we will discuss Pentecostalism's embodied spirituality and how it affects the way Pentecostals view the world aesthetically and use the arts as embodied, liturgical practices. These topics will nuance the renewal aesthetics we adopt for our renewal worldview.

Beauty and the Pneumatological Imagination

A **Christian imagination** is the lens that shapes the way a Christian interprets life events and experiences. The term "imagination" does *not* refer to fantasies or whatever Christians make up. Rather, a Christian imagination negotiates the interpreted biblical witness relative to a person's everyday experience of the world. We will take this broad concept of Christian imagination and define it more particularly to envision a renewal perspective. Theologian Amos Yong's concept of the **pneumatological imagination,** one of his most novel ideas, suggests that Pentecostals see themselves as beings-in-the-world through a lens that shapes their interpretation of life events and experiences. This lens is particularly inspired by the Pentecostal experience

1. John Berger, *Ways of Seeing* (London: Penguin Books, 1972), 7.

of the Spirit.[2] The pneumatological imagination helps Pentecostals perceive the Spirit's work and presence in all things. Yong claims that the Pentecostal experience of the Spirit shapes every aspect of a Pentecostal's inhabited self-understanding. It is "a way of seeing God, self, and world that is inspired by the Pentecostal-charismatic experience of the Spirit."[3] One could say a Pentecostal's imagination is baptized by the Spirit.

A **renewal aesthetics** is the interdisciplinary study of the theological doctrine of the Spirit and philosophical aesthetics. For our particular renewal aesthetics, we will adopt Yong's concept of pneumatological imagination and focus on how the Spirit affects the aesthetic components of our experiences. Since all our experiences come about through our five senses, we can focus on the sensory and aesthetic properties of our experiences even before we think through and frame our experiences into social, linguistic, or cultural constructs. To discuss the aesthetic component of experiences, we will draw on the work of twentieth-century philosopher and psychologist John Dewey. Dewey sees experience as coming from the interaction of the experiencer and the object or situation being experienced.[4] Experience is, therefore, not merely a psychological concept that happens within a person but a transaction that involves the conditions surrounding the experience.

Dewey writes, "There are sources outside an individual which give rise to experience. It is constantly fed from these springs."[5] Objects and events are known as such by the reflection that occurs after the experience to which they are connected. Earlier we defined perception as the reception and interpretation of sensory information (chap. 1), and we defined experience as the conscious perception of the surrounding world (chap. 2). These definitions must be understood together since experiences constitute our perceptions of the world. Dewey helps us see the aesthetic dimension of experience, since experience is perceived, appreciated, and reflected upon.

An aesthetic experience, therefore, entails the reactions we have toward objects or events upon perceiving them. It is our sense of awe as we stand on top of a mountain and gawk at the vast landscapes surrounding us, our sense of beauty as we gaze into the eyes of someone we love, or our sense of disgust when we pass by the rotting carcass of a dead animal on the side of the road. Aesthetic responses can be good, bad, or something in between—they

---

2. See Amos Yong, "The Pneumatological Imagination: The Logic of Pentecostal Theology," in *The Routledge Handbook of Pentecostal Theology*, ed. Wolfgang Vondey (London: Routledge, 2020), 152–62.

3. Amos Yong, *Discerning the Spirit(s): A Pentecostal-Charismatic Contribution to Christian Theology of Religions* (Sheffield: Sheffield Academic Press, 2000), 102.

4. John Dewey, *Experience and Nature* (Chicago: Open Court, 1925), 18.

5. John Dewey, *Experience and Education* (New York: Touchstone, 1997), 39–40.

are gut-level responses to the unity or disjunction of an object or experience. Aesthetic responses arise out of our fascinations, as our senses get enraptured by something unalloyed. The pneumatological imagination situates our aesthetic experiences. It organizes even our gut-level responses within a renewal theo-aesthetic framework. A renewal aesthetics is the way we understand our sensed perceptions through a pneumatological imagination.

Now that we have a grasp of the aesthetic dimension of experience, we can look at the particular experience of beauty. Like every other experience, a Pentecostal's aesthetic response to beauty should be understood through the lens of a pneumatological imagination. Since aesthetic responses are felt in a context where the Spirit is ever-present and working, beautiful moments for Pentecostals are those that display the Spirit's unifying and redeeming work when the Spirit breaks into the present. Balthasar, as noted in the previous chapter, sees God's glory radiating as a kenotic (self-emptying) gesture. In a similar way, Pentecostals see Pentecost as that pivotal kenotic moment where the Spirit is poured out on all flesh (Acts 2). It is the event of Pentecost that enables the pneumatological imagination to view all things as being saturated by the Spirit of Pentecost. Pentecost, however, was not the Pentecostal story's end but its beginning. The universal outpouring of the Spirit birthed and empowered the church with the Spirit to carry on Christ's ministry of expanding the kingdom of God. The kingdom of God was inaugurated by Christ, but we'll only see it in its fullness once Christ returns and sets all things right. So experiencing the Spirit today is experiencing God breaking into our present circumstances. It is us perceiving a foretaste of what is to come. The pneumatological imagination's aesthetic response to this foretaste is a response of beauty.

For Balthasar, Hart, and Begbie, beauty in its ultimacy is known in Christ. Christ is, after all, the visible image of the invisible God (Col. 1:15), and the transcendental of beauty is properly located in God. So Christ is the perfect image of God's beauty. While a renewal aesthetics would not refute these points, it would look to highlight the Spirit's role in one's perception of divine beauty. The Spirit is, after all, the Spirit of Christ who testifies on Christ's behalf (John 15:26). Since the universal outpouring of the Spirit is the start of the renewal story, the story's end, or *telos*, is the eschaton. So in a renewal aesthetics we can see the aesthetic pursuit of beauty as us participating in the *telos* of the universal outpouring. As we pursue the beauty of God, we are moved by the Spirit toward God's glory. Balthasar's theological aesthetics (discussed above in chap. 3), especially as it deals with teleology, helps us articulate our renewal aesthetics.

Theologian Patrick Sherry states that beauty bears an eschatological function because through it we catch a glimpse of the transfiguration of the cosmos.

Those beautiful moments that enrapture our theological imaginations do so because they exhibit God's intentions for the world. Likewise, the arts, as producers of aesthetic responses, can help give us a foretaste of what is to come. As Sherry writes, "The arts, in their highest achievements, glimpse eternal beauty, and anticipate and give a foretaste of the reality beyond, which is to come."[6] The response of beauty that's elicited from an artwork can offer us the hope of a new reality with new possibilities. Art functions prophetically when it becomes a vehicle for the Spirit to break through our social consciousnesses and relay a new sense of hope. It should be noted, however, that in a renewal aesthetics, it is not the art that gives us a new hope but the Spirit through the art. Pentecostals view God as the bringer of hope and believers themselves as "a temple of the Holy Spirit" (1 Cor. 6:19). God does not indwell artistic objects or divinize them as if they were the hearts of believers or even the ark of the covenant—the Spirit's agency is unique and not enfleshed in art. The Spirit, however, is ever present and at work in and through all things, which does mean that the Spirit works *through* objects. In other words, art can be a vehicle for the Spirit but not a home.

While Catholicism's nuanced sense of visual theology becomes a rich source for us to draw from, one major theological distinction between Catholic and Pentecostal thought as it pertains to aesthetics concerns the nature of God's presence on earth. For Catholics, the beauty of Christ shines forth and reaches out from the fractures and mysteries of everyday life.[7] This line of reasoning can lend itself toward panentheism, where God, as Christ, is in all things.[8] One can begin to view objects as divinized as the real presence of Christ shines forth in our everyday reality. The cosmic Christ, the anointed one, permeates the created order and is seen through the eyes of faith, making God present and knowable. Pentecostalism, on the other hand, promotes a theology of encounter that's pneumatological. It is in the communion of believers, when two or more are gathered (Matt. 18:20), that the presence of God is made manifest. God isn't summoned from on high in these communal gatherings—the Spirit is already present. Rather, the believers, in solidarity, turn their hearts toward the Spirit and open themselves up to whatever the Spirit wants to do. Objects

6. Patrick Sherry, *Spirit and Beauty: An Introduction to Theological Aesthetics*, 2nd ed. (London: SCM, 2002), 144.

7. Charismatic Catholics, who are considered part of the global renewal tradition, take a more pneumatological approach to life and spirituality, recognizing the transforming presence of the Spirit in worship and at work in the world. See John Boucher and Therese Boucher, *An Introduction to the Catholic Charismatic Renewal* (Cincinnati: Franciscan Media, 2017).

8. For more on this, see Richard Rohr, *The Universal Christ: How a Forgotten Reality Can Change Everything We See, Hope for, and Believe* (New York: Convergent, 2019); and Teilhard de Chardin, *The Divine Milieu* (New York: Harper & Row, 1960).

and rituals do not hold any mediatory power to unlock the Spirit's presence, but any experience where the Spirit is present *becomes* sacramental. The arts are not mediatory in themselves, but they become occasions for communal gathering and spiritual invocation. The concept of "holy ground" is, for Pentecostals, any place where the Lord is present. Balthasar believes the eyes of faith are pivotal in seeing Christ shine forth in the mundane, but for Pentecostals it is a faith of expectancy that readies a person for an encounter with the Spirit.

Closely tied to the Spirit's presence and the Christian imagination is the theological concept of inspiration. In Sherry's view inspiration forms a bridge between the doctrine of the Holy Spirit and aesthetics.[9] Theologians typically talk about inspiration in reference to the Bible. In particular, they discuss how the Holy Spirit inspired the words of Scripture (2 Tim. 3:16), making Scripture both authoritative and reliable. Sherry suggests, however, that we widen our theological concept of inspiration to include any of the Spirit's creative communication.[10] This widening of inspiration, Sherry argues, has a long tradition in Christian thought: "If we look back over the centuries, we find that earlier generations of Christians had a far wider understanding of inspiration than the contemporary theological one, which tends to be restricted to biblical inspiration, and the associated ideas of canonicity, inerrancy, and authority."[11] Inspiration should, accordingly, entail the ways in which God allows us to share in God's creativity.[12] This relocates the concept of inspiration from biblical inscription to the doctrine of creation. Approaching inspiration in this way opens us to seeing the Spirit inspiring every aspect of life. Wherever the Spirit's creative power is at work, so too is God's inspiration.

If divine inspiration arises out of a theological imagination, then the imagination could be understood as a storehouse for inspiration. Our religious experiences shape our theological imaginations, so when we're inspired, God speaks to us through our imaginations, using what we've already come to experientially know about God and the world. As we think about artistic inspiration from a theological standpoint, this view of the theological imagination suggests that God inspires artists in two ways: (1) by directly communicating something to an artist through a religious experience, and (2) by endowing the artist's imagination through religious experiences, which the artist could later draw from. The Spirit inspires the artist either directly or indirectly, but in both cases the Spirit is involved in artistic inspiration through the imagination.

9. Sherry, *Spirit and Beauty*, 100.
10. Sherry, *Spirit and Beauty*, 106.
11. Sherry, *Spirit and Beauty*, 107.
12. Sherry, *Spirit and Beauty*, 103.

Furthermore, the Spirit's inspiration is also at work in the reception of art. While the Spirit inspires artists in their artmaking, the Spirit also inspires on-lookers with a deep sense of understanding. Theologically, we can think of "understanding" art as discerning or interpreting the Spirit or the Spirit's work in art. If the Spirit is active and present all over the world, then we should look for the Spirit's inspiration in all things, especially the arts, since they are the highest form of human expression. But we must pay close attention, as we continue to move toward a renewal aesthetics, to how the Spirit inspires artis-tic expression and, on the flip side, how experiences are perceived through a pneumatological imagination.

An Embodied Spirituality

The next thing to consider in a renewal aesthetics is the embodied nature of an aesthetic experience. One important aspect of renewal spirituality is what we might call "spiritual holism." Holism is the inclusion of a whole system or being. So, for example, a holistic attitude toward humanity considers the health of all aspects of humanity, including the physical, emotional, and spiritual. **Spiritual holism**, therefore, recognizes the significance of body and emotion in one's spirituality. Because Pentecostal spirituality is characterized by holistic, Spirit-filled practices, the idea of embodiment plays an important role in our understanding of a renewal aesthetics. **Embodiment** is the manifestation or expression of something in a tangible form. It is the incarnation of a feeling or expression—dancing when one feels joy, crying when one feels sorrow, or reaching out when one feels vulnerable. As holistic spirituality is part and par-cel to Pentecostalism, a renewal aesthetics recognizes the aesthetic sensibilities of embodied Pentecostal practices.

Holism in the Scriptures

Biblically, the Acts 2 narrative speaks of embodiment as the Spirit is poured out on all *flesh* (Acts 2:17, quoting the prophet Joel). This may seem to be only a subtle nod to embodiment, but the idea that God's Spirit is poured out on flesh—on materiality—shows that we should not have a dualistic understanding of human constitution. Our spirits do not oppose our flesh. Rather, God's good creation is reflected in both spirit and flesh, just as the spiritual reality of Pente-cost holistically subsumes both spirit and flesh. This line of thinking suggests a significant departure from the anti-material, dualistic understanding of human constitution that has come to define much Christian thought. For instance, some Christians view Paul's words in Galatians as suggesting the supremacy of the human spirit over the flesh: "Live by the Spirit, I say, and do not gratify the desires of the flesh. For what the flesh desires is opposed to the Spirit, and what the Spirit desires is opposed to the flesh; for these are opposed to each other, to prevent you from doing what you want" (Gal. 5:16–17). This passage does not juxtapose the human spirit with the material body, however. Rather, it affirms *God's Spirit* over our fleshly nature. It is not depicting human flesh as something like an inferior prison to our spirit. In fact, this passage does not oppose materiality at all; it opposes the sinful desires that arise from being in a fleshly state.

Paul's use of the word "flesh" should be understood as the state of human existence for those living apart from God. The Greek word translated here as "flesh" is *sarx*, which connotes acting or making decisions according to the self. People who live by the flesh are living by their own power or accord, not by the power of the Spirit. Because flesh represents life under the old covenant before the reception of a new heart and new spirit (Ezek. 36:25–28), flesh in and of itself is too weak and frail to completely fulfill God's commands. Jesus, however, was able to fulfill all of God's commands despite human frailty and fleshly weakness, thereby paving the way for our redemption. There are two ages: the age of the flesh (the former way of life) and the age of the Spirit (the new life under Christ). This creates two communities or states of existence: a community in the Spirit that lives according to the Spirit and a community in the flesh that lives according to the flesh. Christians, Paul says, must be the community of the Spirit who belong to Christ.

Thus Paul does not deny human flesh or materiality but demonstrates what it means to live in the Spirit. In fact, a few verses later in Galatians 5, Paul tells us what a Christian life in the Spirit looks like: "By contrast, the fruit of the Spirit is love, joy, peace, patience, kindness, generosity, faithfulness, gentleness, and self-control. There is no law against such things" (vv. 22–23). Paul uses the agricultural image of fruit to show that a person who lives a life yielded to the Spirit will bear noticeable signs of a transformed life. Plants do not struggle to produce fruit; they produce fruit naturally, as a part of a healthy life. In the same way, when one is yielded to the Spirit, he or she naturally produces the fruit of the Spirit.

Taking this all together, we see that Paul is *not* perpetuating the Greek idea that the physical world is in itself sinful and opposed to the spiritual realm. Rather, Paul is still in line with the Hebraic tradition that promotes a holistic view of body-spirit unity in human constitution,[13] but he is arguing that one

---

13. James Nelson, *Embodiment: An Approach to Sexuality and Christian Theology* (Minneapolis: Augsburg, 1978), 46.

should be wholly given over to the Holy Spirit. This in turn brings us back to the idea of the Spirit being poured out on all flesh. The use of "flesh" in both Acts 2:17 and Galatians 5:16 comes from the same Greek word[14] and in both instances connotes acting of one's own accord, apart from God. But when the Spirit is poured out on all flesh, we are all grafted into the community of the Spirit and empowered to live by the Spirit rather than by the self. Since the universal outpouring motif frames the social identity of Pentecostals around the world, we can view life in the Spirit as a holistic life of worship wherein every part of the person honors and reflects the indwelling Spirit.

Worth noting is that the Acts 2 passage also implies global universality in its statement that the Spirit will be poured out on *all* flesh. Not only does it affirm our realities as physical beings, but it indicates that *anyone* can live a life in the Spirit through Christ. The radiance of the Spirit can be known in all places and by all people as Christ pours out the Spirit. Anyone can come to know the outpoured Spirit of God and thereby interpret his or her experiences through a pneumatological imagination. This passage, therefore, speaks toward our embodied *and* communal lives, so a renewal aesthetics would look at human experiences, appreciation, and worship through the lens of embodied spirituality.

Philosophical Understandings of Embodied Knowledge

In addition to the above case for embodiment on biblical grounds, we can also make a philosophical case for embodied, experiential knowledge. In fact, Enlightenment playwright, poet, and philosopher Friedrich Schiller argued for a holistic sense of knowledge and experience—one that is guided by the experience of beauty. In *Letters upon the Aesthetic Education of Man*, Schiller critiques the over-rationalized state of Enlightenment Europe, instead calling for a rationalism that reconciles reason with empirical, or "sensed," knowledge. Schiller perceives an overreliance on reason, over against a person's capacity for feeling, and wants to reintegrate feeling without neglecting rationalism. In this way humanity can be brought to a holistic state of being in communion with the elements of nature. While the gnostic Christians of antiquity denied the material realm, Schiller says the Enlightenment thinkers denied the sensual realm of emotion and passion. The symbiotic relationship between the sensual and the rational (the "senses and spiria")[15] can and should be regained.

---

14. While they are the same word, they have slightly different morphologies: Acts 2:17 uses the accusative feminine singular, whereas Gal. 5:16 uses the genitive feminine singular.

15. J. C. Friedrich von Schiller, *Letters upon the Aesthetic Education of Man* (Whitefish, MT: Kessinger, 2010), 11–16 (letter 6).

For Schiller, none other than the pursuit of beauty could enable the coopera-tion of the sensual and the rational.[16] Beauty and the arts live in the domain of play and function as equalizations between the two opposing forces and their detriments. The sensual instinct or "sense drive" (*Sinntrieb*, as articulated in the original German) is rooted in life as it is experienced through the senses, and the formal instinct or "form drive" (*Formtrieb*) is rooted in form—abstract configurations as experienced intellectually through reason. The play instinct or "play drive" (*Spieltrieb*) is rooted in the aesthetic qualities of experience (beauty) and exists as a both/and between sense and form—it is a "living form."[17] Beauty has the ability to free us from enslavement to either the sense drive or the form drive, and it gives us the freedom to choose between the two. This drive makes sense of our constitution as holistic beings. Not only do we think and feel, but we play! It is in this mode of free relationality that we discover beauty and are most fully alive.[18] One could say that renewal spirituality taps into the *Spieltrieb* as worshipers play, relate, and grow together. A renewal wor-ship service becomes a holistically generative space where relational equity emerges between oneself, God, and other worshipers. Worship could thus be seen as the relational form between persons through a *Spieltrieb* connection in an aesthetic state. Worshipers join in song as they celebrate the beauty of the Lord.

Embodied Knowledge and the Arts

Having established that holistic renewal spirituality involves the body and spirit and engages a full range of emotions, we can now consider how the arts are used to make evident these notions of holism. If we think of ourselves as perceiving bodies, then we can appreciate the significance of embodied action. Embodied action is not simply something we do but the manner in which we perceive and are perceived by the world.[19] We are "beings-in-the-world," who come to know our surroundings (the world) through experience. Our bodies

16. Schiller, *Letters*, 25–26 (letter 12).
17. Schiller, *Letters*, 31–34 (letter 15).
18. Some excellent studies link Pentecostal spirituality with the play drive. See Jean-Jacques Suurmond, *Word and Spirit at Play: Towards a Charismatic Theology* (Grand Rapids: Eerdmans, 1994); Nimi Wariboko, *The Pentecostal Principle: Ethical Methodology in New Spirit* (Grand Rapids: Eerdmans, 2012); and Wolfgang Vondey, *Beyond Pentecostalism: The Crisis of Global Christianity and the Renewal of the Theological Agenda* (Grand Rapids: Eerdmans, 2010).
19. For a deeper dive into embodiment and theology, see Steven Félix-Jäger, *Spirit of the Arts: Towards a Pneumatological Aesthetics of Renewal* (New York: Palgrave Macmillan, 2017); Elisabeth Moltmann-Wendel, *I Am My Body: A Theology of Embodiment* (New York: Continuum, 1995); and Ola Sigurdson, *Heavenly Bodies: Incarnation, the Gaze, and Embodiment in Christian Theology*, trans. Carl Olsen (Grand Rapids: Eerdmans, 2016).

are the locations from where we perceive. Movement, thus, gives us a sort of precognitive knowledge—what some philosophers and psychologists call "embodied knowledge." The body is already a knowing subject by gaining a sense of the world through perceptions, feelings, and intuitions. Our bodies move and have a sense of space and time even before we think about what's happening. It is only after our experiences that the mind forms ideas (more will be said about this in part 3 of this book). The embodied knowledge of experience is formative for worldviews because it constitutes our initial, precognitive understanding of the world. If we look at Christian worldview holistically, we must begin with our embodied experience of the world.

The body is a source of intrigue and taboo and is perhaps more familiar to us than most other perceivable objects because of our ability to evaluate our own bodies. The depiction of the human body thus communicates something about reality that is wholly relatable. There is a narration that goes along with the body that speaks to the heart and desires of a person, rather than merely his or her intellect. People can experience empathy when viewing a body because of the way the body in that particular moment or situation relates to the viewer's own experiences. As such, the implicit human narrative supplied by the imaged body functions as a powerful communicative tool.

Considering this, we believe the embodied liturgical actions of renewal worship help shape our sense of the world. Unique to Pentecostalism is the expressive manner in which its adherents worship. Indeed, it's hard to think of renewal spirituality without picturing vivid images of loud and emotive music coming from well-rehearsed worship teams, raised hands, swaying and dancing, shouts of affirmation, glossolalic prayers, prayerful intercessions, and the like. Pentecostals tend to incorporate music and embodied actions into every part of their worship services.[20] Music serves as a score of sorts, playing behind and underneath many aspects of the Pentecostal liturgy, including the sermon, ministry time, times of response, and even announcements. This creates a sense of flow in the worship service and ties every aspect together. In addition, Pentecostals often respond vocally to the sermons and are expressive in their singing. Without a doubt, the notion of embodiment is evident when Pentecostals gather to worship. And while much more can be said about the nature and practices of Pentecostal worship, our main point is that these actions in themselves are formative for a renewal worldview.

If the experience of bodily movement offers a precognitive sense of time and space, then we are already coming to know the inhabited world simply by

---

20. For more on this, see Steven Félix-Jäger, *Renewal Worship: A Theology of Pentecostal Doxology* (Downers Grove, IL: IVP Academic, 2022).

moving about in it. Embodied actions in worship are thus formative for anyone who participates, but renewal worship emphasizes these actions, which fosters an elevated sense of what these actions come to mean. For instance, the aesthetic experience of being emotionally moved by the resounding prosody between a melodic line and a lyric might be interpreted as an encounter with something transcendent, beyond the self. Then as the experience is interpreted through a pneumatological imagination, the transcendent encounter becomes known as a divine encounter with the Holy Spirit. David Morgan calls this the "sacred gaze"—when people see an object or event and attribute spiritual significance to it. He writes: "*Sacred gaze* is a term that designates the particular configuration of ideas, attitudes, and customs that informs a religious act of seeing as it occurs within a given cultural and historical setting. A sacred gaze is the manner in which a way of seeing invests an image, a viewer, or an act of viewing with spiritual significance."[21] In other words, it is a form of perception that attributes spiritual significance to experiences like the one discussed above.

Does breaking down the aesthetic experience like this expose it as *mere* experience devoid of any spiritual connection? Are our physical and mental responses to experiences spiritually neutral? We believe that because the very notion of spiritual holism entails the physical, mental, and emotional aspects of life, our spiritual encounters will have corresponding physical responses. In other words, spiritual holism means the physical affects the spiritual and the spiritual affects the physical. The embodied liturgical actions in themselves are mere movements, but in the context of worship we associate them closely with what's happening in and around us spiritually. The experiences we have are interpreted through our pneumatological imagination and, in turn, alter, expand, and even modify the imagination through which they are interpreted.[22]

The arts are significant in worldview formation because they represent the highest level of human sensory engagement.[23] The most aesthetically exquisite form of human bodily movement, for instance, is known as dance. Because dance starts at the point of movement, it has the ability as an art form to communicate a precognitive sense of the world through beautiful movement.[24] Both the dancer and the spectator conceptualize time and space in profound and

---

21. David Morgan, *The Sacred Gaze: Religious Visual Culture in Theory and Practice* (Berkeley: University of California Press, 2005), 3.

22. See chap. 3 of Félix-Jäger, *Renewal Worship*.

23. If you think back to our foray into historical aesthetics in chap. 2, this concept sits in stark contrast to Plato's negative view of art.

24. Marcia Mount Shoop, *Let the Bones Dance: Embodiment and the Body of Christ* (Louisville: Westminster John Knox, 2010), 12; and Maxine Sheets-Johnstone, *The Phenomenology of Dance* (Philadelphia: Temple University Press, 2015), 400.

reflective ways through dance. A level of intimacy between a person's body and his or her relation to time and space is forged through dance. And since the world we inhabit exists within the parameters of time and space, dance enables us to know the world intimately in a way that only deep reflection renders possible. The use of dance and dancelike bodily movement in Pentecostal worship provides intimate world-knowledge that informs the pneumatological imagination.

A similar case can be made for music. If dance kinesthetically engages space and time, music engages time auditorily through sound. We can think of music as the most aesthetically exquisite form of sound. Music elicits embodied and emotional responses. In fact, music and dance have historically been tied together, and it was only within the past five hundred years that music began to be appreciated disinterestedly.[25] Music's ability to affect a person's emotions and gestures has caused some to see it as potentially manipulative.[26] While it is certainly the case that music and the arts in general have been used to affect or even control social behaviors, this does not mean that music should therefore be avoided. Humans have bodies and emotions, so to worship God holistically is to worship God bodily, emotionally, *and* intellectually. To disregard the emotional or the bodily for fear of manipulation would be to restrict the potential for holistic worship. And just as dance can teach us about the world by reflecting on aestheticized movement, music does the same by adorning time with aestheticized sound. Our auditory experiences also shape our view of the world; the sounds we submerse ourselves in provide the soundtracks of our lives.

All the arts can and should be understood as significantly formative. Dance is aestheticized movement, and music is aestheticized sound, and in the same way visual art can be seen as aestheticized sight. Film could be seen as aestheticized sight and sound, and architecture could be seen as aestheticized sight and touch. Each art form is predicated on its sensory reception, so how we perceive objects relating internally (i.e., an object's artfulness in and of itself) and to other objects externally (i.e., an object's way of interacting with the world around it) affects what we perceive of the objects. Art is always made in a way that is perceivable. Art is not passed on telepathically from mind to mind, but rather the concept is transmitted and received somehow through our senses. The transmitting object is the artifact. For various reasons, artists care to communicate in a way that is creative and speaks on a deeper human

25. Daniel Levitin, *This Is Your Brain on Music: The Science of a Human Obsession* (New York: Plume, 2006), 257.

26. See Steven Brown and Ulrik Volgsten, eds., *Music and Manipulation: On the Social Uses and Social Control of Music* (New York: Berghahn Books, 2005).

register. Artists want to communicate in a way that is affective and not merely cerebral. Artists seem to know that it will take more than the expression of an idea to sway a person's desires. A striking visual, for instance, can conjure up manifold recollections for a viewer that move him or her emotionally and somatically. That visual has then communicated a message to the mind and heart of the viewer. Thus the concept and the embodied experience of the concept's signifier are inseparable. Art is communicative but in a way that is different, and more robust, than textual communication. Art is a text that is read by the heart.

The judgment of art follows its perception. Beauty, aesthetically speaking, refers to the rightness of a thing's composition according to a person's perception of it. As Kant has shown us, what we perceive is subjectively taken in. These perceptions are then viewed through our own interpretive lenses before we judge them. Visual art and film can help us transcend ourselves as we deeply empathize with the subjects of the artworks or films. They help us view other vantage points of being-in-the-world.[27] Architecture structures the space around us, so it orchestrates our movement within and outside communal settings.[28] Through it we learn kinesthetically and precognitively about spatiality. In each case, the sensed perception and the interpretation of the experience shape the way we view the world.

Art exists in a triadic relationship among the viewer, the object, and the community. The object only means what it does in the context of its community, and it can only be interpreted once it's perceived. If any of these parts is taken away, we've taken away the potential for art. We are not brains in a vat. Rather, we are thinking, perceiving, embodied people who make and value art in communities. S. Brent Plate argues that people from different cultures ascribe different meanings to things because their location and historical settings shape their interpretive lenses differently.[29] In other words, a person's religious and cultural beliefs change the way he or she views the world. Plate writes, "Religious myths and rituals alter the actual perception of the world."[30] So if we really want to get to know people and where they are coming from, we should study their "visuality." *Seeing* is a meaningful, world-constructing encounter.[31]

27. Robert Johnston, *Reel Spirituality: Theology and Film in Dialogue*, 2nd ed. (Grand Rapids: Baker Academic, 2006), 33–34.

28. Gaston Bachelard, *The Poetics of Space: The Classic Look at How We Experience Intimate Places* (Boston: Beacon, 1994), 4–7.

29. S. Brent Plate, ed., *Religion, Art, and Visual Culture: A Cross-Cultural Reader* (New York: Palgrave, 2002), 6.

30. Plate, *Religion, Art, and Visual Culture*, 22.

31. Plate, *Religion, Art, and Visual Culture*, 23.

The experiences we have through touch, taste, and smell are also formative. *Every* communal and liturgical action—the monthly church potlucks, the weekly hour spent at a prayer chapel, the daily devotional Scripture reading—forms us deeply. While the arts are evocative and touch us deeply, liturgical arts happen every week and are formative through habituation. Repeated actions can form habits for us, and, as philosopher James K. A. Smith argues, habits can form desires.[32]

In his book *Desiring the Kingdom*, Smith deals with the question "what makes humans human?" The modern trend, since the time of René Descartes, has been to say that thinking is what makes humans human. The fact that thinking is seemingly inescapable—Descartes could not *not* think—made Descartes presume that this very notion is the undeniable fact of human existence. Hence, Descartes made his famous statement "I think, therefore I am." But, like Schiller, Smith sees this overreliance on reason and thinking as neglecting the body, heart, and emotions, as well as relationships and the Spirit. If these things, like thinking, are also essential for our human existence, then they must be definitive. We should, therefore, be defined not as merely thinking beings but also as desiring beings that exist bodily, emotionally, and intellectually in this world.[33] What we love is what drives our actions. As Smith states, "What we desire or love ultimately is a (largely implicit) vision of what we hope for, what we think the good life looks like. This vision of the good life shapes all kinds of actions and decisions and habits that we undertake, often without our thinking about it."[34] Humans must be understood as holistic beings because we are more than our minds. The idea that "if we think like Christians, then we'll act like Christians" is flawed when improperly understood. (If it were a true statement, then we should question sermon-centric services.) Romans 12:2 does tell us that we should not be conformed to the patterns of the world but be transformed by the renewing of our minds—which, again, is not intended to pit the body against the mind. Renewing our minds entails being *fully* caught up in the presence and mission of God. Having a renewed mind means we are being transformed wholly, from the inside out. While the mind is seen here as corresponding to the core of our being, it isn't the only aspect of our being. Smith argues that true behavioral change happens when our desires change.

While loving or desiring, rather than thinking, makes us human, *what* we love and desire tells us what kinds of people we are. What are the things that

---

32. James K. A. Smith, *Desiring the Kingdom: Worship, Worldview, and Cultural Formation* (Grand Rapids: Baker Academic, 2009), 25–26.

33. Smith, *Desiring the Kingdom*, 24.

34. Smith, *Desiring the Kingdom*, 27.

consume your thoughts and desires? If those things drive your free actions, then those are the things that define what kind of person you are. If you live a party lifestyle that seeks to gratify the flesh, then your desires are only skin-deep and you follow a shallow, moral hedonism. If you live a life of devotion that serves others for the betterment of the kingdom of God, then you're driven by a desire to grow closer to God. But let's say you had a life-changing experience with God and now want your desires to shift from self-serving hedonism to kingdom-oriented living. How can you shift your desires? Simply believing in what's right is not enough. Scripture makes this point when James says, "You believe that God is one; you do well. Even the demons believe—and shudder" (James 2:19). When you're a disciple of Christ, your actions will reflect the kingdom of God. Being a disciple of Christ entails more than mere belief; it entails a life of obedience.

Smith says we can shape our desires by changing our actions. Because we are holistic beings, emotive and sensory actions form us. Just as an athlete enhances skills by developing muscle memory through repetition, we are formed spiritually through repeated liturgical actions. Christian practices such as fasting, prayer, Scripture reading, and communal worship help us draw close to Christ, which shapes our spiritual formation. Liturgies are, for Smith, the kinds of practices that most shape how we view ourselves. Either we can take part in a "secular liturgy"[35] of self-serving hedonism by repeatedly acting out secular practices or we can adopt a liturgy that brings us closer to Christ by repeatedly acting out those kingdom-oriented practices highlighted above. As mentioned, much more will be said about this in part 3 of this book, but for now we'd like to focus on how Smith has rearticulated spiritual formation through embodied practices. This gives us a strong footing for understanding how emotional, evocative, and sensory things help form us, and it shows the significance of the embodied actions in spiritual formation. This embodied, aesthetic formation penetrates the community when we perceive our own relatedness to everything that surrounds and shapes us. Since Pentecostal communities shape the narrative parameters of understanding, the visceral, experientialist actions that take place in worship are fundamental for Pentecostal formation. The aesthetic dimension of experience is thus an apt starting point for understanding a renewal worldview.

Smith agrees that one's worldview is constructed through the funding of the imagination.[36] Stories, myths, and pictures are the sorts of things that fund imaginations and create social imaginaries. The pneumatological imagination

---

35. Smith, *Desiring the Kingdom*, 39.
36. Smith, *Desiring the Kingdom*, 57.

is, as stated above, how Pentecostals imagine the world even before thinking about it. So for Smith, an important aspect of renewal spirituality is its ability to imagine the world otherwise. The Spirit is able to convert our imaginations from the "logics of power, scarcity, and consumption that constitute 'rationality' in our world"[37] to a pneumatological imagination of hope for a coming kingdom that has already begun. When we tie this "imagining otherwise" together with our renewal aesthetics, we can see the aesthetic response of beauty elicited from embodied renewal practices as offering us the hope of a new reality with new possibilities.

Conclusion

If the idea that Pentecostals rely primarily on intuition when following the Spirit's leading is true, then the weight a renewal aesthetics carries for a renewal worldview becomes palpable. An openness toward the aesthetic dimension is built into renewal spirituality,[38] so understanding a Pentecostal's aesthetic formation helps us grasp how Pentecostals see the world and why embodied practices are so important for renewal spirituality. In this chapter we adopted Yong's concept of the pneumatological imagination to circumscribe a Pentecostal theo-aesthetic framework, which allowed us to understand experience and interpretation. This framework also helped us recognize how the aesthetic response of beauty and the theological idea of inspiration are understood in a renewal aesthetics. Finally, we looked at embodied knowledge and how embodied practices help spiritually form Pentecostals.

As we close this chapter and part 1 of this book, we want to briefly reiterate how a renewal aesthetics affects and enhances a renewed Christian worldview. When we see the world through the eyes of faith, we see God's heart behind all things. We get a sense of God's plan and will for us, and we also take notice of what God is doing in the lives of others. If, through the eyes of faith, we can get a sense of the Spirit's role in our reception of divine beauty, the way we see all things will be dramatically affected. If beauty is seen as the Spirit eschatologically breaking into our present, then the glory of the Lord and of God's redeemed creation will remain at the forefront of our minds as we go about our lives. In other words, a good renewal aesthetics can sanctify our perceptions so that we always have a solid understanding of God's vision for the world.

37. James K. A. Smith, *Thinking in Tongues: Pentecostal Contributions to Christian Philosophy* (Grand Rapids: Eerdmans, 2010), 84.
38. Smith, *Thinking in Tongues*, 81.

Study Questions

1. How do you define the aesthetic response of beauty? What do you find most beautiful and why?

2. Why is an understanding of embodied knowledge important for a renewal worldview?

3. What sorts of embodied practices can positively aid your spiritual formation and why?

PART 2

+ Renewing Goodness +

+ 5 +

Civic Engagement

How to Be Salt and Light in the World

Key Words

Benevolence: *A disposition to do good that is characteristically kind and selfless.*

Eschaton: *The post-historic era where God reigns.*

Ethics: *The reflective activity of discerning moral content.*

Goodness: *The foundational basis for right actions that emerge from and influence our experiences and beliefs.*

Kingdom of God: *A spiritual reality, inaugurated by Christ, where God reigns as king.*

Kingdom of the world: *A reality that is antithetical to God, morally opposing God's will for a fully reconciled reality.*

Quietism: *A pejorative term that describes a form of Christian spirituality that sees passivity and the subdual of human effort as key to allowing divine action to take course.*

How should Pentecostals vote? This question may seem out of the blue for a book on Christian worldview, but it's more relevant to our topic than some might think. After discussing beauty, aesthetics, and embodied spirituality in part 1, we now move to a discussion of goodness. We are moving from experience to action. **Goodness** is the foundational basis for right actions that emerge from and influence our experiences and beliefs.[1] Human action is governed

---

1. Throughout part 2, any reference to "the good" refers to goodness as an objective reality.

individually through ethics and socially through politics, so a full exploration of goodness must consider how Christians should act through moral formation and what our social responsibility is toward others. We must look at *both* moral formation and civic engagement.

The reason political matters are important to discuss in a renewal worldview is because we are often told that to be a Christian we *must* hold to particular political views. This line of thinking tells us that politics helps define our Christian worldview. We would like to emphatically disagree with this view. Since a renewal faith is holistic, the Spirit guides *every* aspect of life. Our faith guides our actions both individually and socially, and no external political force should ever guide our faith. This must be acknowledged outright if we are to disentangle our Christian worldview from our national identities.

Since **ethics** constitutes the reflective activity of discerning moral content, our reflection on goodness focuses on both how we reason morally and how a renewal ethics guides our cultural and political engagement. This chapter discusses how to make ethical decisions in Christian love, looking at both character and policy. We will look at what the Bible says about moral action before we apply those ideas to civic action and political engagement. The subsequent chapters of part 2 will look at the history of Christian moral thinking and compare other views of Christian ethics and political engagement, before finally positing a constructive renewal perspective on goodness. This chapter sets the stage for part 2 by identifying the center of a renewal ethics as the Spirit of love.

Love as the Foundation of Renewal Ethics

Indispensable to the Christian faith is our commitment to love and to live a life guided by love. In fact, Jesus commands this of us: "This is my commandment, that you love one another as I have loved you" (John 15:12). On one occasion the Pharisees try to trap Jesus by asking him what the greatest commandment is. Jesus replies, "'You shall love the Lord your God with all your heart, and with all your soul, and with all your mind.' This is the greatest and first commandment. And a second is like it: 'You shall love your neighbor as yourself.' On these two commandments hang all the law and the prophets" (Matt. 22:37–40). In those days the entire Hebrew Bible was known as "the law and the prophets," so Jesus is essentially saying that all Scripture hinges on the commandments to love.[2] These two commandments belong together because they entail the same

---

2. Michael Floyd, "The Production of Prophetic Books in the Early Second Temple Period," in *Prophets, Prophecy, and Prophetic Texts in Second Temple Judaism*, ed. Michael Floyd and Robert Haak (London: T&T Clark, 2006), 276.

action: love. The difference is that the first commandment refers to the vertical relation of loving God, whereas the second refers to the horizontal relation of loving others. Many pastors and scholars have noticed that these vertical and horizontal directions of love form a cross.[3] Fittingly, the cross can be seen as the quintessential sign of God's love. Christ hangs upright, aiming toward God in the ultimate act of *loving obedience* to the Father as he "humbled himself and became obedient to the point of death—even death on a cross" (Phil. 2:8). But his outstretched arms on the cross also indicate Christ's *loving embrace* of us. It is through Christ's sacrificial act of love that we are once again brought back into the family of God.

We will look at how a renewal ethics approaches love a little later in this section, but for now it's important to note that love must root *any* Christian ethics, no matter the tradition. The Bible makes it abundantly clear that every moral action must be rooted in the love of God. John 13:35 states, "By this everyone will know that you are my disciples, if you have love for one another." But love does not just come from anywhere, nor does it indicate mere good feelings toward others. *Christian* love is love that is rooted in God, who *is* love. As 1 John 4:7–8 states, "Beloved, let us love one another, because love is from God; everyone who loves is born of God and knows God. Whoever does not love does not know God, for God is love." John then relates this type of love to the cross in verse 9: "God's love was revealed among us in this way: God sent his only Son into the world so that we might live through him." This is a love that is sacrificial—a love that is divine.

The popular tautological maxim "Love is love" implies that any love between persons is of the same kind, so no expression of love should be disfavored. While this is a nice sentiment, the term "love" in English is ambiguous and thus must be delineated further. By "love" do we mean feelings of affection? Do we mean feelings of obligation toward something or someone? Do we mean feelings of attraction or desire? The concept of love might be broad enough to encapsulate all of these connotations, but Christian love, in particular, is *agapic* (sacrificial) and oriented toward helping others and caring for them. Paul famously demonstrates the characteristics of Christian love in 1 Corinthians 13:4–7: "Love is patient; love is kind; love is not envious or boastful or arrogant or rude. It does not insist on its own way; it is not irritable or resentful; it does not rejoice in wrongdoing, but rejoices in the truth. It bears all things, believes all things, hopes all things, endures all things." This sort of

3. See Albert Tate, *How We Love Matters: A Call to Practice Relentless Racial Reconciliation* (New York: Faith Works, 2022), 15; Jim McNeely, *Grace in Community: Real Life Grace from the Book of 1 John* (Seattle: Vox Dei, 2014), 142; and Robert Dean, *For the Life of the World: Jesus Christ and the Church in the Theologies of Dietrich Bonhoeffer and Stanley Hauerwas* (Eugene, OR: Pickwick, 2016), 30.

love is commonly referred to as **benevolence**, which means a disposition to do good that is characteristically kind and selfless. So we can say that Christian love is (or at least should be) characteristically benevolent. Through these passages we can conclude that any Christian ethics must be rooted in divine love. This sense of Christian love is sacrificial and characteristically patient, kind, humble, steadfast, and hopeful. These passages together form the foundation for a Christian ethics.

While the Old Testament describes God as abounding in love (Neh. 9:17; Ps. 86:5), demonstrating unfailing love (Pss. 31:16; 94:18; 143:8; Isa. 54:10), and demonstrating compassion (Ps. 103:8–13; Lam. 3:22), it is really through the incarnation and crucifixion that God's love for us comes to full fruition. Now in Christ we have a clear image of what God's character of benevolence is like. We see, through Jesus's actions and teachings, that God desires for us to act benevolently toward each other. Then the rest of the New Testament writers, and especially Paul, flesh out what it means to be disciples of Christ and live benevolently in the world. So we can look at Jesus's life and teachings as the clearest examples of God's love, and we can and should read the rest of Scripture in light of Christ's witness. Furthermore, through the resurrection we are indwelt by the Spirit, who testifies on Christ's behalf (John 15:26). Christ and the Spirit are linked, and it is through the Spirit that we know the loving character of Christ.

Today we are led by the Spirit to love God and one another and to live benevolently. This pneumatological emphasis on love is central to a renewal ethics. In his book *Spirit of Love*, Amos Yong points out that while Pentecostals often understand the gift of the Spirit as empowering the Christian life through spiritual gifts and empowered mission,[4] the Pentecostal movement at its inception understood the reception of the Spirit as an infilling of divine love.[5] Yong cites firsthand accounts from the Azusa Street Revival—the symbolic birthplace of the Pentecostal movement—that state again and again that the fresh outpouring of the Spirit manifested divine love.[6] Consider, for instance, the words of Frank Bartleman, eyewitness and chronicler of the revival: "Divine love was wonderfully manifest in the meetings. The people would not even allow an unkind word said against their opposers or the churches. The message was the love of God."[7] William Seymour, the initiator of the Azusa Street Revival, even modified one of the landmark doctrines of Pentecostalism, the

---

4. Amos Yong, *Spirit of Love: A Trinitarian Theology of Grace* (Waco: Baylor University Press, 2012), 40.

5. Yong, *Spirit of Love*, 62.

6. Yong, *Spirit of Love*, 62–64.

7. Frank Bartleman, *Azusa Street* (New Kensington, PA: Whitaker House, 1982), 51.

"doctrine of initial evidence," to account for divine love. This doctrine, which claims that the gift of tongues is the initial physical evidence of the baptism of the Holy Spirit, was developed by Seymour's predecessor, Charles Parham, in 1901 at his Bible school in Topeka, Kansas.[8] While Seymour at first circulated Parham's doctrine, he modified it in the early years of the revival. In a 1907 issue of *The Apostolic Faith*—the Azusa Street Mission's periodical, which was widely distributed across North America[9]—Seymour wrote that initial evidence is "Divine love, which is charity. Charity is the Spirit of Jesus."[10] So while we should certainly understand the gift of the Spirit as one of empowerment, we cannot forget that it is the Spirit of love who empowers us to do God's work on earth.

Seymour's modification makes biblical sense if we consider how Paul talks about the gifts of the Spirit in 1 Corinthians 12–14. Chapter 12 begins with Paul talking about order in the church before discussing the role of spiritual gifts. Then chapter 13 defines love and states that any gift without love is worthless. Chapter 14 reverses the order of the topics in chapter 12, discussing the roles of spiritual gifts and church order. This passage follows a chiastic pattern where points A and B lead to C (the main point) and are then mirrored in reverse order by points B′ and A′. The central point of a chiasm is the focal point of the whole passage, and in the case of 1 Corinthians 12–14, the central point is chapter 13. So for Paul, *love* is the principal concern of church order and spiritual gifts. And it is divine love, which is the foundation of all the gifts including tongues, that is truly the initial evidence of Spirit baptism. Additionally, Roy Ciampa and Brian Rosner state that chapter 13 is also "at the heart of Paul's ethical thrust through this letter."[11] Paul's main point is that all spiritual gifts are to be done out of love and in service of the community, not for personal glory. As love is the basis of all spiritual gifts, so too should it be our motivation for life in the Spirit.

8. Vinson Synan, *The Century of the Holy Spirit: 100 Years of Pentecostal and Charismatic Renewal* (Nashville: Nelson, 2001), 3.

9. Adam Stewart, "Azusa Street Mission and Revival," in *Handbook of Pentecostal Christianity*, ed. Adam Stewart (DeKalb: Northern Illinois University Press, 2012), 46.

10. William Seymour, "Questions Answered," *The Apostolic Faith* 1, no. 9 (June–September 1907): p. 2, column 1. It should be noted that while historian Cecil Robeck argues that Seymour rejected the doctrine of initial evidence, Renea Brathwaite argues that he merely modified the doctrine to engage pastoral concerns about living a godly life. See Cecil Robeck Jr., "William J. Seymour and the 'Biblical Evidence,'" in *Initial Evidence: Historical and Biblical Perspectives on the Pentecostal Doctrine of Spirit Baptism*, ed. Gary McGee (Peabody, MA: Hendrickson, 1991); and Renea Brathwaite, "Tongues and Ethics: William J. Seymour and the 'Bible Evidence'; A Response to Cecil M. Robeck, Jr.," *Pneuma* 32 (2010): 203–22.

11. Roy Ciampa and Brian Rosner, *The First Letter to the Corinthians* (Grand Rapids: Eerdmans, 2010), 561.

Linking the gift of the Spirit to divine love is not novel to Pentecostalism, however. Augustine made that connection in the fourth century in his treatise *On the Holy Trinity*: "Wherefore, if Holy Scripture proclaims that God is love, and that love is of God, and works this in us that we abide in God and He in us, and that hereby we know this, because He has given us of His Spirit, then the Spirit Himself is God, who is love."[12] This course of thought has caused Frank Macchia to conclude that love through the Spirit is God's "supreme gift," which "gives us life and that more abundantly. . . . It is at the very essence of God's nature as well."[13] Yong contends that if we understand the Spirit as the Spirit of love that was poured out on all flesh (Acts 2), then we can see the church that formed at Pentecost as a gracious community of love. He sees a community of love functioning this way: "The love of God ignites love for God, expressed in the prayers and praises of the people directed to God, and generates neighborly love, seen in the generosity and solidarity of the people with each other, as well as with those who were added to the community on a daily basis."[14] While Yong is certainly right that this is what would mark a community of love, can we truly say that global Pentecostalism is recognized as such? Rather than portraying a descriptive analysis of Pentecostal social engagement, Yong seems to portray Pentecostal ideals or aspirations.

If the primacy of love is indeed the foundation of renewal ethics, then Pentecostals must consistently strive to better love God and others (as is true for all Christians). Christians generally agree that loving God is of utmost importance, but their commitment to love others is often betrayed by their actions. In the West, for instance, the media contains so many examples of Christians demonstrating hatred toward others that Christians are often known by their intolerance rather than by their love. This is in large part due to the politicization of Christian worldview that has taken place in the West. Let's consider again the topic broached at the introduction of this chapter concerning Christian worldview and national identity. Political parties often demonize their opponents in order to secure base support, so when Christians uncritically align themselves with a party's values, they often unwittingly begin to subscribe to the party's hateful rhetoric toward others.[15] Christians are then forced to negotiate the example of love demonstrated biblically in Christ and through the Spirit with the exclusionary politics of their party. It must be stated emphatically that

---

12. Augustine, *On the Holy Trinity; Doctrinal Treatises; Moral Treatises*, ed. Philip Schaff and Anthony Uyl (Woodstock: Devoted, 2017), 233.

13. Frank Macchia, *Baptized by the Spirit: A Global Pentecostal Theology* (Grand Rapids: Zondervan, 2006), 259.

14. Yong, *Spirit of Love*, 98.

15. What's worse is when those "Christian" voices begin to catalyze rationalizations for hatred.

any school of thought that rationalizes or even encourages the hatred of *any* people group is not from God. Not only do such discourses work against God's efforts of unity in the Spirit, but they betray the very heart of what it means to be a community of love.

Echoing Leviticus 19:18, Christ told us to love our neighbors as ourselves (Matt. 22:39; Mark 12:30; Luke 10:27), and in the Sermon on the Mount he radicalizes the commandment to love: "You have heard that it was said, 'You shall love your neighbor and hate your enemy.' But I say to you, Love your enemies and pray for those who persecute you" (Matt. 5:43–44). Who is your neighbor? Who is your enemy? These questions are not about proximity or cultural fit. Our *actions* toward each other determine if we make neighbors or enemies out of others. In the parable of the good Samaritan (Luke 10:25–37), Jesus does not define the neighbor as someone who shares a similar religious or ethnic identity (in this case, a Jewish priest or a Levite). The neighbor is the man who shows compassion toward the beaten traveler. Significantly, the one who demonstrates benevolence toward the beaten Jew is a Samaritan—the religious and ethnic other. The person who should have been the natural enemy of the Jew becomes his neighbor. If enemies are those who actively oppose us with hostility, then we too often make enemies out of those who should be our neighbors. Instead, Christ calls us to make neighbors out of our enemies.

If we continue to take Jesus at his word, then we will love even those who seek to harm us. This is where a renewal ethics really sets in. We shouldn't wonder *if* we should love our enemies; Jesus said we must! Renewal ethics concerns itself with *how* we should love our enemies even as we protect ourselves and others from them. First, we must pray for those who persecute us, just as Jesus says to do in the Sermon on the Mount. Jesus practices what he preaches as he prays for the Romans who crucify him (Luke 23:34). As we pray for our enemies, we still must negotiate what it means to follow our duties to protect those in our care (our families on a personal level and our communities on a social level) while still demonstrating love toward those who seek to harm us and those in our care. The Bible says we have a duty to look out for the interests of others (Phil. 2:4), provide for those in our households (1 Tim. 5:8), and contribute to the needs of others (2 Cor. 10:13). But we also know that ultimately God is our defender against evil (Ps. 18:2; 2 Cor. 4:8–18; 2 Thess. 3:3). While we cannot give a blanket answer for how to respond morally in times of hardship, suffering, or war, we *can* say that Christians should always ask, "What is the most loving thing to do in this situation?" If the Christian is truly seeking justice *and* benevolence, then he or she is taking Jesus at his word. Sometimes we must stand up against injustice, and other times we must learn to be content through personal hardships. We cannot say how the principle of benevolence will apply in every messy situation we encounter, but if our heart posture is one of love toward all, then we have demonstrated the Spirit of love. It is this Spirit of love that animates a renewal ethics.

Civic Awareness for the Renewal Christian

We can see how integral love is for our renewal ethics, but how does this translate to civic engagement? To what extent should Pentecostals be involved in social and political matters? Some have argued that Christians in general should passively stay away from any sort of civic engagement. This line of thinking takes its cues from **quietism**, a pejorative term that describes a form of Christian spirituality that sees passivity and the subdual of human effort as key to allowing divine action to take course. Quietists have no compulsion to engage in civic matters because they believe God will intervene. After all, they believe, doesn't Jesus advocate for a form of quietism when he says, "Give . . . to the emperor the things that are the emperor's" (Matt. 22:21)? It seems here that Jesus is saying we are to obey the laws of the land without pushback. But perhaps there's more to that passage.

If we read Matthew 22:21 in its immediate context, we see the Pharisees once again plotting to trap Jesus by asking if the Jews should pay taxes to Rome or not. If Jesus says no, the Pharisees will tell the Roman authorities that there's a Jewish rebel telling the Jews not to pay taxes. If Jesus says yes, the Pharisees will tell the Jewish people that Jesus isn't for them and is only a pawn of the Roman government. Jesus's response to this plot cleverly avoids their trap and reveals what God is really concerned about: "But Jesus, aware of their malice, said, 'Why are you putting me to the test, you hypocrites? Show me the coin used for the tax.' And they brought him a denarius. Then he said to them, 'Whose head is this, and whose title?' They answered, 'The emperor's.' Then he said to them, 'Give therefore to the emperor the things that are the emperor's, and to God the things that are God's'" (22:18–21).

When talking about civic obedience, we tend to quote only the first half of Matthew 22:21 as a mandate to pay taxes. But notice the second half of verse 21: "and [give] to God the things that are God's." This indicates what God really cares about: people! Because the coins bear the image of Caesar, they belonged to him. Likewise, what belongs to God is what bears God's image. Genesis 1:27 tells us clearly that humanity is *made in the image of God*, so what God cares about is humanity's return to God, not money or politics.

God's polity is a renewed reality, and its currency is love. This doesn't mean we should become quietists and completely step back from civic engagement. Rather, it puts our civic engagement in right perspective. The first and most important thing for God is to reconcile humans, the image bearers, to God. The church has been given the ministry of reconciliation (2 Cor. 5:18) and is tasked with reconciling to God and with others. Our civic engagement must be done with this in mind. Whatever we do and advocate for as Christians should work toward the ministry of reconciliation that God entrusts us with. Our task is not to become quietists, therefore, but to see how we can effectively and graciously get involved socially and politically in ways that motivate reconciliation.

Perhaps a better biblical image for how Christians are to engage the world can be found through the principles of salt and light that are conveyed in the Sermon on the Mount. Consider Matthew 5:13–16:

> You are the salt of the earth; but if salt has lost its taste, how can its saltiness be restored? It is no longer good for anything, but is thrown out and trampled under foot.
> You are the light of the world. A city built on a hill cannot be hid. No one after lighting a lamp puts it under the bushel basket, but on the lampstand, and it gives light to all in the house. In the same way, let your light shine before others, so that they may see your good works and give glory to your Father in heaven.

Here Jesus clearly demonstrates how his followers should engage the world. Saltiness refers to Christians being noticeably different (in a good way) and not conformed to the world. When Christians conform to their societies, they become indistinguishable from the rest of the world, losing their witness. Light refers to Christians who seek to serve their communities. As light, Christians create an alternate community that portrays love and hope to the weary and distraught.[16] These two principles, along with verses like John 15:19 and 17:14–16, give weight to the popular maxim of being "in the world but not of the world." This saying means that as created beings we are fully a part of the world, but God has called us to be different by testifying of God's love and reconciliation. As mentioned earlier, Christians are to be known by their love (John 13:35) and have been given the ministry of reconciliation (2 Cor. 5:18).

Since ethics deals with *right action*, it is not enough to simply believe in the principles of salt and light in a renewal ethics—these principles must be enacted. In their book *Kingdom Ethics*, David Gushee and Glen Stassen argue that the climax of Matthew 5:13–16 is the last verse, which talks about good deeds ("good works" in the NRSV). They write, "The climax clarifies the meaning-content of the salt and deeds. Doing good deeds is the content of being the salt of the earth and the light of the world. What makes the salt keep its saltiness

---

16. David P. Gushee and Glen H. Stassen, *Kingdom Ethics: Following Jesus in Contemporary Context*, 2nd ed. (Grand Rapids: Eerdmans, 2016), 201.

is the good deeds that show God's light to people."[17] A community of love is one that *acts* in love with deeds that demonstrate the principles of salt and light. Actions are formative in a renewal worldview; actions help shape worldviews just as worldviews affect actions toward others. More will be said about this in subsequent chapters. For now, it is enough to say that a Pentecostal's civic awareness must be steeped in love and must follow the principles of salt and light. This is what helps us maintain a right ethical posture toward others in the social sphere.

Political Engagement for the Renewal Christian

Finally, let's consider what constitutes a disposition of love in the political arena. In order to proceed naturally from the previous sections, we will need to ask what it means to love our neighbors and our enemies politically. How do we as citizens both of the kingdom of God *and* of our state engage in political affairs in a way that's loving and representative of our Christian commitments? Do we simply submit to our governments even when they are unjust? Can we resist the evils of our governments in ways that are loving? These questions will be discussed through our renewal ethics, which recognizes the primacy of love for moral action.

Romans 13:1–6 is regularly cited as biblical evidence that Christians are to submit to their governing authorities. After tumultuous elections, proponents of the victorious party often cite the latter part of verse 1 as biblical evidence intended to pacify the losing opponent's resentments: "For there is no authority except from God, and those authorities that exist have been instituted by God." The passage goes on to state that authorities only punish us if we've done wrong (v. 4), so we must do what is right. The government's God-given authority is also why in verse 7 Paul says to pay our taxes: "Pay to all what is due them—taxes to whom taxes are due, revenue to whom revenue is due, respect to whom respect is due, honor to whom honor is due." While this passage seems straightforward, some have argued that the context is indispensable for grasping its meaning. For instance, Mark Nanos argues that this passage is written to the newly converted gentile Christians. Nanos believes Paul is urging them to submit to synagogue authority. This is consistent with Paul's larger concerns for gentile Christians to adopt new Christian lifestyles discussed throughout 12:1–15:13.[18] Although Paul is certainly addressing gentile Christians, Nanos's interpretation

---

17. Gushee and Stassen, *Kingdom Ethics*, 200.

18. Mark Nanos, *The Mystery of Romans: The Jewish Context of Paul's Letter* (Minneapolis: Fortress, 1996), 295.

doesn't make sense of Paul's mandate to pay taxes. Taxes concern political, not religious, authorities. Perhaps Paul is making general claims about a believer's relation to authority. Paul seems to address the ideal and not the particular. Notice that Paul never mentions any government by name. Although he is speaking to Roman Christians, he never mentions Rome. He seems to indicate that God institutes authority in that we are allowed to govern ourselves, and since God is supreme, this authority can only derive from God.

We should also note that Paul does not say to *obey* authorities but says to *submit* to them. Submission means yielding to power, whereas obedience means following commands. If a person intentionally breaks an unjust law knowing the consequence of the crime and then willingly submits to the punishment, then he or she has still submitted to the government *via* civil disobedience. This is significant because sometimes authorities are evil and oppose God. Think about those countries that outlaw Christianity, institute slavery, or oppress marginal groups. Are Christians supposed to stand idly by and betray their own sense of biblical justice or, as in the case of martyrs, their faith? There are many instances where biblical heroes opposed their governments because the administrations were out of step with God's will: Moses (Exod. 3); Shadrach, Meshach, and Abednego (Dan. 3); Daniel (Dan. 6); Peter and John (Acts 5); and so forth. Even Paul was imprisoned for civil disobedience (Acts 16:16–40). These heroes of the faith did not demonstrate uncritical obedience to their governments but practiced civil disobedience as a form of submission to their governments. The same can be said of Christ, who at times broke Jewish laws or customs to the point that it led to his arrest and crucifixion.[19] We can conclude that Paul is telling us to respect authority in general but not to uncritically accept the laws of the government or to blindly defend their legitimacy.

If we read the verses immediately after Romans 13:1–7, we see that when Paul talks about submission, he's really concerned with how we demonstrate love toward one another. Verses 8–10 state, "Owe no one anything, except to love one another; for the one who loves another has fulfilled the law. The commandments, 'You shall not commit adultery; You shall not murder; You shall not steal; You shall not covet'; and any other commandment, are summed up in this word, 'Love your neighbor as yourself.' Love does no wrong to a neighbor; therefore, love is the fulfilling of the law." Here Paul links the great commandments of love to moral political action. The way Christian citizens demonstrate love toward society is through submission, even if it requires civil disobedience. As a disposition of love, believers should be good citizens, abiding by the rule

---

19. Two examples are when Jesus was caught eating on the Sabbath in Mark 2:23 and when he cleansed the temple in Matt. 21:12.

of law. We are not to needlessly become troublemakers. But if there are matters of biblical injustices, there is enough biblical evidence that demonstrates how to respond in love *and* resistance. The reason this topic is difficult is because Christians have to negotiate what it means to be in this world but not of it. What if the governments we are called to submit to oppose the will of God? How do we navigate this tension in a renewal ethics? To answer these questions, let's look at what it means to hold ultimate allegiance to God's kingdom while remaining a citizen of an earthly kingdom or state.

The Bible speaks of the kingdom of God and the kingdom of the world or Satan. The **kingdom of the world** is antithetical to God, morally opposing God's will for a fully reconciled reality. The **kingdom of God**, on the other hand, is a spiritual reality, inaugurated by Christ, where God reigns as king. This fully redeemed spiritual reality is consummated at the **eschaton**, the post-historic era where God reigns. Jesus inaugurated the kingdom of God during his earthly mission. Jesus described the kingdom's inauguration as a message that needs to be received (often by a radical change of relationship to others) rather than an actual event that needs to take place (Mark 4:11–20; 9:43–48; Luke 4:43–44; 8:10–15; 9:60–62; 18:28–30). And while the kingdom was hidden from the world (Mark 4:26–32), it was received by Jesus's followers (10:13–45). Yet Jesus also spoke of the kingdom as a future reality that is yet to take place. Jesus refers to blessings in this life *and* in the age to come (10:30), to the casting out of demons as the kingdom of God coming to the people (Matt. 12:28), and to an "age to come" (12:32) in the same context. Jesus tells the Pharisees that the kingdom is among them and refers to the Son of Man coming at an unexpected time in the same context (Luke 17:20–37). To bring these ideas together, theologian George Ladd sees the kingdom as being present but not fully consummated.[20] We await the "not yet" of the final "day," which manifests the kingdom of God in all its glory.

This means we are living in the time between the times—between the inauguration and the consummation of the kingdom of God. We can and should expect healing and miracles today since the Spirit being poured out on all flesh is part of the presence of the kingdom of God. But since the kingdom of God is not finally present, not all are or will be healed during this overlap. The blessings of the kingdom of God are available to those who enter the kingdom now, yet the blessings we receive now are just "firstfruits," a foretaste of what is to come when the kingdom is finally and fully manifested. Because we live in the overlap, there is already current victory over the spiritual powers. Satan

---

20. George Ladd, *The Presence of the Future: The Eschatology of Biblical Realism* (Grand Rapids: Eerdmans, 1974), 20.

still exists, but he and the other spiritual powers are defeated enemies under Christ. Since we are seated with Christ, we have authority over these powers. We don't have to claim this authority; it already exists. We can look forward to a future day when this world will truly be changed. This is an enduring hope, but we are not left without God's dynamic presence in the present. God's kingdom is evident now because the Spirit is active in and through us. While we await a final restoration, we must recognize that God's kingdom has already broken into the present.

The kingdom of God is presently transforming the world, so while things may seem grim and without hope, we are to be ready and to be actively doing good as ambassadors of God's kingdom message and reign. Second Corinthians 5:20 says that we are Christ's ambassadors and that God makes his appeal for reconciliation through us. Just as an embassy houses representatives of a sovereign country in a host state, the church is to represent the kingdom of God while inhabiting the kingdom of the world. In his book *A Pentecostal Political Theology for American Renewal*, Steven Studebaker argues that the Spirit of Pentecost is at work in our present age, working through every aspect of life, including political systems, to lay a foundation for a fully redeemed reality—the New Jerusalem.[21] Pentecostals find themselves caught between two worlds, the kingdom of the world, which is realized through whatever government is in power, and the kingdom of God.[22] The kingdom of God consists of God's people who demonstrate God's true polity, which should set an example for all other political systems. The kingdom of God gives us a vision of a world governed by peace and goodwill for all humans—a world of equity and justice for all humans, especially for the poor, marginalized, and dispossessed. The problem of Christian nationalism arises when we conflate the kingdom of God with the kingdom of the world, which allows the world to determine and undermine God's true polity of reconciliation.[23]

In our highly politicized, late modern world, Christians around the globe increasingly feel pressure to support particular political factions. We are often told that a specific party aligns more with a biblical worldview and that Christians

21. Steven Studebaker, *A Pentecostal Political Theology for American Renewal: Spirit of the Kingdoms, Citizens of the Cities* (New York: Palgrave Macmillan, 2016), 142.

22. This idea was brought to the theological forefront through Augustine's book *City of God*, which was an attempt to create an apologetic showing that Christianity was not bad for Rome. To make his point Augustine talked about two cities: the City of God, which is a regenerated remnant that reflects but is not identical to the church, and the City of the World, which is under the dominion and power of darkness. Augustine never said that the City of God was the church and the City of the World was the state, but ideas about the dichotomy between the church and a secular kingdom began here.

23. Studebaker, *Pentecostal Political Theology*, 4.

have a responsibility to advocate for that party's moral standards in society. In countries like the US, for instance, faith and national identity have collided and integrated so thoroughly that news channels have begun to recognize the "Evangelical vote" as a major determining factor for elections. But the truth is that no political party is Christian per se, and it's easy to spot both Christian and non-Christian ideals throughout the competing political systems.

The problem with Christians putting their hope in any political regime is that the kingdom of God is not reflected in any earthly political system, as Studebaker demonstrates. Rather, life in this world should be seen as life in Babylon. Studebaker contends that Babylon in the book of Revelation represents a desire for economic success and political ambition and thus refers to the "corrupt life in and of this world."[24] Every nation is "of this world," so a Christian's political response must be in contradistinction to its corruption. Jesus makes this point while on trial before the crucifixion: "Jesus answered, 'My kingdom is not from this world. If my kingdom were from this world, my followers would be fighting to keep me from being handed over to the Jews. But as it is, my kingdom is not from here'" (John 18:36). Christians must claim allegiance to the kingdom of God first and foremost and then must scrutinize whatever Babylon they inhabit. Scrutiny is critical observation—it judiciously examines the good and bad of what's happening. We have the right to call out what is wrong and to celebrate what is going well in our respective countries, but our posture must always be one of love. In Romans 12:9–18 Paul describes the marks of a true Christian:

> Let love be genuine; hate what is evil, hold fast to what is good; love one another with mutual affection; outdo one another in showing honor. Do not lag in zeal, be ardent in spirit, serve the Lord. Rejoice in hope, be patient in suffering, persevere in prayer. Contribute to the needs of the saints; extend hospitality to strangers.
>
> Bless those who persecute you; bless and do not curse them. Rejoice with those who rejoice, weep with those who weep. Live in harmony with one another; do not be haughty, but associate with the lowly; do not claim to be wiser than you are. Do not repay anyone evil for evil, but take thought for what is noble in the sight of all. If it is possible, so far as it depends on you, live peaceably with all.

With a posture of love, we must work toward goodness and justice, live peaceably and generously, and be patient in suffering. A renewal ethics recognizes that our true citizenship is in the kingdom of God and that we have an ambassadorship to the kingdom of the world. As such, we seek to expand the kingdom of God through Christian love.

24. Studebaker, *Pentecostal Political Theology*, 9–10.

The Spirit is constantly working toward renewal, so we must be aware of what God is doing in our midst. As Studebaker writes, "The Spirit of Pentecost is at work in Babylon bringing the renewal of the new creation, and laying the foundation of the New Jerusalem. That means that continuity between life in this world and the one to come triumphs over discontinuity."[25] Christians are to continue expanding the kingdom of God in Babylon. We are called to faithfully carry on the ministry that began with Christ and continues until his return. This means we cannot be swayed by the workings of the kingdom of the world; such workings inevitably lead to a Christian nationalism. Rather, we must let godly things define our politics. Political engagement in a renewal ethics is marked by Christian love that is oriented toward helping and caring for others. If we are guided by the commandments to love God and love others, we must ask what it means politically to love our neighbors. Relatedly, we must also ask what it means politically to love our enemies. Our political mission is to make the world less broken; this is how we usher in the kingdom of God, which Christ inaugurated. The Sermon on the Mount calls us to be peacemakers, and as we read in Romans 12:18, we are to live peaceably. So while the kingdom of the world glorifies war, we must stand against violence and war, affirming that God has called us to a ministry of reconciliation. The guiding value of love and the principles of salt and light must flow all the way from our personal moral living to our civic and political engagement.

Conclusion

Let's turn once again to the question posed at the start of this chapter: How should Christians vote? As you've likely noticed, we are not going to tell you what party to vote for. We recognize that our readers will come from different political contexts around the world, so any response that's too specific will be unhelpful. Broadly speaking, however, we suggest voting according to the value of Christian love and the principles of salt and light instilled by the Spirit and Scripture. Don't be pigeonholed into uncritically adopting one party's views. Make a list of guiding Christian principles and vote for the person who most closely reflects the kingdom of God in character (for their leadership) and through their policies. What are some of these guiding principles? We know the animating core of a renewal ethics is love, so think of the principle of *benevolence*, for example, as you envision a leader caring for both their own citizens and the citizens of other nations (your neighbors, in a sense). Think also of God as the giver of life, and vote for the person who sees how *life* as

25. Studebaker, *Pentecostal Political Theology*, 142.

a principle affects matters of human and reproductive rights as well as matters of war and punishment. Think of *grace* as a guiding principle that affects matters of prison reform and social rehabilitation, among others. Relatedly, think of biblical *justice* and how this affects policies around gender and racial equality. Finally, think of how a principle of *hope* affects civic realities in numerous areas, everything from education to climate change. A renewal ethics must think through all these principles and more in a way that is profoundly guided by the Spirit of love.

There will be times when Christians fall on both sides of a political issue and genuinely believe that their stance is the best way to love the vulnerable. In those situations, before we launch our critiques, we must first come to a deep understanding of both sides of the issue. A good way to know if you're understanding the rival position correctly is to try stating it in a way that its advocates approve of. So much can be solved when we understand the reasoning behind differing positions. We'll also realize that there is a lot of common ground between the two views, and legitimate compromises can usually be made. Finally, we must treat the advocates of the other position with dignity and respect even when we disagree with their reasoning. At this point, we can vote according to our values and principles, understanding that for society to be more just and loving, our love must shine forth even in disagreement.

As mentioned in this book's introduction, our triperspectival approach connects the active (body) with the emotional (soul) and the mental (mind). Goodness, we argue, is the foundational basis for right actions that emerge from and influence our experiences and beliefs. A renewal worldview integrates all three facets of holistic formation; actions affect worldview just as they are shaped by worldview. The guiding value for a renewal ethics is Christian love that is demonstrated in our moral living and in our civic and political engagements. Now that we've established the general disposition of a renewal ethics, we can begin to trace the historical foundations of Christian ethics in the next chapter.

Study Questions

1. How should we define Christian love?

2. How can the principles of salt and light determine a Christian's civic engagement?

3. What are some practical ways you can expand the kingdom of God in Babylon through civic and political influence?

6

A Historical Survey
of Goodness and Ethics

Key Words

Deontological ethics: *A normative ethical theory that locates moral norms on rules or duties.*

Divine command theory: *A deontological theory that bases moral good and obligation on God's commands.*

Ethics: *The reflective activity of discerning moral content.*

Eudaimonia: *The highest good, a complete happiness that denotes human flourishing.*

Morality: *The actual contents of good and evil.*

Normative ethics: *A field of ethics that seeks to determine frameworks for prescriptive moral behavior or character.*

Teleological ethics: *A normative ethical theory that locates moral norms on good consequences.*

Telos: *An intended goal or purpose.*

Virtue ethics: *A normative ethical theory that emphasizes the centrality of virtuous character over action.*

D o you long to live a beautiful life? If so, you must have some understanding of the moral good since the good is presupposed in the beautiful. Since all humans desire a good and beautiful life, however defined, ethical formation is necessary. In fact, we can't run away from ethics. Questions of right and wrong beliefs and actions surround us every day. Before we can move further, then, we must clarify some central terms. While "ethics" and "morality" are often used interchangeably, there are technical differences. **Morality** refers to the actual contents of good and evil. The judgment "Murder is wrong" pertains to morality. **Ethics** refers to the reflective activity of discerning moral content. This discerning process deals with moral prescriptions. Unlike fields of study that *describe* moral beliefs and actions, such as anthropology or sociology, ethics is a field of study that seeks to *prescribe* moral beliefs and actions. The difference is like the difference between receiving a medical diagnosis and receiving a prescription. A diagnosis describes medical issues, whereas a prescription seeks to heal them. This difference represents the fact-value dichotomy. Relatedly, just because something *is* the case (description) does not mean that it *ought to be* the case (prescription). As parents have sometimes been known to ask their children (using a bit of hyperbole), "If all of your friends jump off a bridge [description], does that mean you should jump too [prescription]?"

Normative ethics refers to a field of ethics that seeks to determine frameworks for prescriptive moral behavior or character. There are three major approaches to normative ethics. The first two are ethics of action: **deontological ethics** locates moral norms on rules or duties, and **teleological ethics** locates moral norms on good consequences. Deontology requires obligation to perform moral duties without regard to intentions, motives, or consequences. Teleology requires pursuing the best consequences of an action. An act would be good even if it violates a seemingly good moral norm, such as the duty to tell the truth, as long as its consequence or end result promotes the greater good. The third approach to normative ethics, known as **virtue ethics** (sometimes called "aretaic ethics," from the Greek *aretē*, often translated as "virtue"), emphasizes the centrality of virtuous character over action. The most important facet of this approach is the development of virtuous character, and moral action is a derivation of character.

The following historical survey covers central figures and their ideas. The first and second sections introduce ancient ethics: the Greek formulations of virtue ethics and the holistic ethics of Hebraic thought. We then consider two predominant ethical systems of modernity: utilitarianism and Kantian deontological ethics. We won't be covering important subjective theories that deny the existence or the stability of moral truths. Renewal ethics is not purely objective, however, as if mind-independence of moral truths is the highest goal we seek. Rather than accepting a clear objective-subjective dichotomy, renewal ethics will follow the holistic patterns of Hebraic ethics and will include elements of the various historical theories we cover here.

Ethics in the Greek Tradition

Although philosophy may seem overly abstract and impractical, ethics is one of philosophy's most practical fields. For many ancient philosophers, the philosophical enterprise itself had an ethical dimension because the goal of philosophy is to discover and pursue the good life. The good life is both aesthetic and moral. An unjust life, for example, cannot be considered a good life. Plato and Aristotle did much to establish and advance theories of the good, virtuous life. They were not merely interested in establishing the methods for determining right action because the virtues were fundamental to action. Without the virtues, neither individuals nor communities can function well. As you will see below, virtues also had an objective quality. They were not contingently determined by individuals or cultures. Although virtue ethics has been criticized for being relativistic, it was not intended to be so by Plato and Aristotle.

Plato and Justice

For Plato and his teacher, Socrates, the good is a transcendental that acts as the precondition for all knowledge, and justice is the complete virtue, which arises from a harmonious relationship between the virtues. Plato introduces us to Socrates in his *Republic*, a philosophical work written in dialogues. In one part, Socrates vigorously debates the Sophist Thrasymachus. As a Sophist, Thrasymachus does not believe in the transcendence of the good. For Thrasymachus, justice is the advantage of the strong: might makes right. The powerful determine what's right and punish transgressors. Socrates asks what happens when the powerful mistakenly create laws that, rather than harming transgressors, harm the general populace. Is it just to follow the rules of the strong if they disadvantage the common people? Having been caught in an inconsistency, Thrasymachus reveals that power is more important than justice and injustice. Although the powerful might be disadvantaged at times, overall the powerful benefit more than the just because the unjust are willing to use any means to prosper. Thrasymachus thus doubles down, saying that might makes right. As a Sophist who does not believe in objective morality, Thrasymachus easily considers injustice as virtue and justice as vice.[1]

Socrates recognizes this confusion between virtue and vice, and he gets Thrasymachus to agree that the just seek to outdo the unjust, whereas the unjust seek to outdo everyone. Thrasymachus also agrees that, unlike the just, the unjust are knowledgeable and good. However, these agreements lead to Thrasymachus's defeat. Socrates compares a musician with a nonmusician.

1. Plato, *Republic*, trans. G. M. A. Grube (Indianapolis: Hackett, 1992), 14–20.

One is an expert; the other is not. One has knowledge; the other does not. In tuning an instrument, the musician does not seek to outdo another musician, but he does seek to outdo a nonmusician. (After all, how embarrassing would it be if a nonmusician's instrument was better tuned than a musician's?) The nonmusician seeks to outdo both the musician and other nonmusicians. The same goes for any expert and nonexpert. It's only the nonexpert (i.e., the one who is vicious/unjust) who seeks to outdo everyone. Socrates establishes that the expert (i.e., the one who is virtuous/just) has knowledge, while the nonexpert lacks knowledge. Since having knowledge is wise, and being wise is good, it is the just who are wise and good. The unjust are ignorant and bad. Socrates thus demonstrates that *justice*, rather than the advantage of the strong, is the true virtue. Importantly, he defines virtue as the excellence of the soul, signifying that only the virtuous can live a good life because they are ruled by an excellent soul. The opposite is true for the one ruled by a vicious soul.[2] With this turning to the soul, Plato sets up his famous argument for justice as the harmony of the tripartite soul and state.

Three parts compose both the person's soul and the state, and two opposite parts seek to gain dominance: the *rational* and the *appetitive*. The rational represents the right use of reason. The appetitive represents bodily desires. The middle, spirited part represents the neutral (but active and emotional) elements that differ from base bodily desires. Reason must govern the appetites through the spirited part. A hierarchy thus exists between the three parts. Reason ought to govern the appetites with the spirited.[3] The virtues make this harmonious relationship possible: *moderation* governs the appetites; *courage* governs the spirited part; and *wisdom* governs the rational. When this harmony occurs, justice is present. The state is but a bigger representation of the tripartite soul. In it, the merchant class (appetitive), soldiers (spirited), and rulers (rational) all have a role to play. For Plato, the just state is one in which each class of people performs their tasks rightfully and does not interfere with the functions of other classes. Justice is thus the complete virtue, and these four (moderation, courage, wisdom, and justice) represent the classical cardinal virtues.

The Form of the Good

For Plato, the good represents the highest reality and is present in every instance of good in this world. The good is universal and more real than the particular. The good belongs to the world of the Forms, a world of abstract universals that is more real than our world of physical matter. Matter is but

2. Plato, *Republic*, 24–31.
3. Plato, *Republic*, 115–20.

a copy of the Forms, just as a picture is a copy of the real object. To know the Forms is to know truth through abstract, universal reason. Importantly, the Form of the Good is the highest Form, which acts like the sun that shines its light on all things to make them knowable.[4] All truths thus have a tinge of the good. Therefore, the Form of the Good has absolute independence and reality.

Since it is necessary that the Form of the Good exist, the Form of the Good is more fundamental than divinity. In *Euthyphro*, Socrates meets Euthyphro, who is waiting to prosecute his own father for killing his servant, who had killed another servant. Euthyphro is incredulous that his father and family consider him impious for prosecuting his father. Socrates thus asks Euthyphro for the definition of piety and establishes the working definition of piety as what all the gods love and impiety as what all the gods hate. From this definition, Socrates offers the (in)famous Euthyphro dilemma: "[Is the good] beloved by the gods because it is [good], or [is it good] because it is beloved of the gods?" Some things are loved because they are the kinds to be loved. Others turn out to be kinds to be loved because they are loved.[5] In the former, the goodness of the thing invites its loving. In the latter, the act of loving makes the thing good.

In contemporary language, the Euthyphro dilemma asks, "Is something good because it is independently good apart from what God believes, or is something good because God says it's good?" If the latter is true, then the good is subject to the arbitrary whim of God since whatever God commands is good,[6] equating to divine moral relativism. If the former is true, then God is subject to an independent good. God's morality is dependent on God's response to this greater (moral) reality.

Aristotle's Virtue Ethics

Aristotle further developed Plato's philosophy of virtue in his *Nicomachean Ethics*, named after his son Nicomachus. His virtue ethics is based on *telos*, an intended goal or purpose. Thoughts and actions "aim at some good."[7] Everything that exists has a dominant purpose at which it is aimed. In nature, the

---

4. Plato, *Republic*, 189.

5. Plato, "Euthyphro," trans. Benjamin Jowett, Internet Classics Archive, accessed June 7, 2022, http://classics.mit.edu/Plato/euthyfro.html.

6. For instance, Richard Dawkins and the so-called New Atheists have taken up this view. Dawkins, upon (erroneously) reading the acts of God in the Old Testament, has described God as "a petty, unjust, unforgiving control-freak; a vindictive, bloodthirsty ethnic cleanser; a misogynistic, homophobic, racist, infanticidal, genocidal, filicidal, pestilential, megalomaniacal, sadomasochistic, capriciously malevolent bully." Richard Dawkins, *The God Delusion* (New York: First Mariner Books, 2006), 51.

7. Aristotle, *Nicomachean Ethics*, trans. David Ross (New York: Oxford University Press, 2009), 1.

sun's purpose is to provide light. Among human creations, a chair's purpose is to hold a person's body. Fulfilling these purposes is good, and hindering them is bad.

What of human purpose? We in the West may think individualistically about our purpose. My purpose is to have a good job and a happy family. My purpose is to have a personal relationship with Jesus. For Aristotle, the purpose of each kind is dependent on one's nature. By nature, humans are rational, political animals; we inhabit social spaces and relationships and use reason.[8] Our good is thus social, and the ultimate social goal is *eudaimonia* or happiness.[9]

The English term "happiness" seems hedonistic and does not convey the fullness of Aristotle's meaning. Happiness is not wanton pleasure, wealth, or even honor. A better description of *eudaimonia* is a life lived well,[10] which occurs socially and not in isolation; so happiness is social flourishing. *Eudaimonia* should thus be defined as the highest good, a complete happiness that denotes human flourishing. The flourishing life is the ultimate good for which we must aim. Importantly, social flourishing is intrinsically connected to virtue: "Happiness is an activity of soul in accordance with perfect virtue."[11] Without virtue, happiness is impossible. The virtuous person who has achieved happiness is complete and self-sufficient. Some ends, like pleasure, wealth, and honor, do not qualify as happiness because we pursue them in order to be happy. They're intermediate goods. Beyond them is something greater that we desire, which we pursue as our ultimate goal. Happiness is this complete, self-sufficient good because it lacks nothing.[12]

Aristotle divides the soul into irrational and rational parts. The rational part of the soul is subdivided into intellectual and moral virtues. The intellectual virtues strictly possess reason and pertain to excellences of the mind, such as open-mindedness, intellectual courage, and wisdom. The moral virtues pertain to moral character, such as courage, moderation, and compassion, and they are rational because they listen to reason.[13] Achieving happiness requires cultivating both types of virtues in our lives, although we'll focus on the moral virtues here.

What is virtue? First, it is an excellent disposition or character of the soul. As excellent character, it makes us good and helps us function well.[14] Vice is the opposite of virtue. Even though our Western culture promotes vices like

8. Aristotle devotes significant attention to the topic of friendship in *Nicomachean Ethics*.
9. Aristotle, *Nicomachean Ethics*, 5.
10. Aristotle, *Nicomachean Ethics*, 5.
11. Aristotle, *Nicomachean Ethics*, 19.
12. Aristotle, *Nicomachean Ethics*, 10–11.
13. Aristotle, *Nicomachean Ethics*, 21.
14. Aristotle, *Nicomachean Ethics*, 29.

hubris and aggression as means toward personal fulfillment,[15] vice actually "frustrates the ends for which an agent aims or . . . actively harms the agent."[16] Thus, virtue and vice are terms that have to do with success. We cannot be courageous, for example, unless we succeed at practicing courage. We do not become a coward unless we successfully and continuously give in to cowardice.

Second, virtue is not a trait we are born with. We are born with different capacities for passions and actions, but virtue is not a capacity. Virtue develops through habitual activity. We become what we do. If we act in moderation, we will become moderate. If we act justly, we will become just. Virtue and vice develop through habit. A habitual liar can tell a truth, but one action does not make him a truthful person; it is an accident of his lying character. Habit is a consciously chosen activity over a prolonged period. Virtue is thus voluntary action chosen by persons who know what they are doing. Any action that occurs outside of firm character is accidental.[17] Since virtue arises from firm character, how can we start becoming virtuous? We must start somewhere. If a liar desires to change, he must begin to be truthful. The truth-telling at first is not virtuous because it doesn't arise from developed character; it merely resembles virtue.[18] Habitual truth-telling, however, will transform him into a truthful person.

Third, virtue is the golden mean between the vices of excess and lack. For example, courage is the mean between recklessness (excess of courage) and cowardice (lack of courage). The middle, however, is not objectively fixed but contextually determined. For example, if given the choice of eating two eggs or ten, one shouldn't necessarily eat six eggs. Six eggs might be too little or too much depending on the eater's exercise level.[19] Unlike virtue, vice does not have a mean. According to Olli-Pekka Vainio, there are thus "two sides to Aristotle's virtue ethics. On the one hand, ethics cannot be fitted into a formula (because the middle way varies according to the situation), but, on the other hand, some acts are always wrong irrespective of the situation (because they are bad by nature)."[20] There is no appropriate context for committing a vice. Adultery, for example, is always wrong.

Aristotle provides an important and practical ethical theory. In our late modern era, especially in the US, the debate on moral issues plays out predominantly along deontological and teleological lines. This phenomenon is

---

15. A quick look at popular entertainment suffices as evidence.

16. Craig A. Boyd and Kevin Timpe, *The Virtues: A Very Short Introduction* (Oxford: Oxford University Press, 2021), 5.

17. Aristotle, *Nicomachean Ethics*, 27–28.

18. John M. Frame, *The Doctrine of the Christian Life* (Phillipsburg, NJ: P&R, 2008), 95.

19. Aristotle, *Nicomachean Ethics*, 30.

20. Olli-Pekka Vainio, *Virtue: An Introduction to Theory and Practice* (Eugene, OR: Cascade Books, 2016), 24–63.

evident with each mass shooting. Lenient gun control advocates primarily stand behind the principle that people should have access to guns and argue that this principle is both legal and moral since gun ownership allows citizens to stand up against tyranny (deontological). Even if guns kill people, responsible gun owners do not partake in mass shootings and actually deter or stop them (teleological). Advocates of stronger gun control argue that the proliferation of guns leads to more gun violence, whether through purposeful acts or by accidents, and they contend for thorough background checks to limit gun violence (teleological).[21] Virtue ethics focuses instead on character development for the goal of social flourishing, and it reminds us that policy changes alone do not lead to better, more just societies. As a practical ethics, it reminds us that merely knowing the good is not enough. We must implement virtuous habits that contribute to social flourishing.

Virtue ethics, however, does not provide guidance on how to act in each circumstance, expecting that the virtuous person will have the requisite virtues to know how to act rightly in each circumstance. Aristotle admits that it is difficult to know how to act "to the right person, to the right extent, at the right time, with the right motive, and in the right way."[22] The virtuous person will deviate from the golden mean at times because of this lack of moral clarity. And even as virtue is rational activity, Aristotle confesses that knowing how much to deviate from the golden mean without incurring moral guilt comes by way of perception, not reason.

The Holistic Ethics of Hebraic Thought

Contemporary popular Christian ethics seems to revolve around either personal conduct or political policies. Part of the reason for this focus has to do with the narratives that drive our imagination—they are shaped by a gospel that emphasizes personal forgiveness and relationship and by theology that encourages this individualistic dimension. Hebraic ethics, by contrast, lacks this individualistic dimension. It also largely lacks the political component because it arose outside the realities of contemporary nation-states. Hebraic ethics, presented here through the motif of the kingdom of God, is primarily communally focused and places great emphasis on embodied concerns that arise from social sins. The gospel of this kingdom, then, is about not merely the forgiveness of personal sins but also the reversal of oppression and corruption that results from sin's cosmic effects. Especially compared to the modern ethical theories that we will

21. Scott B. Rae, *Moral Choices: An Introduction to Ethics*, 4th ed. (Grand Rapids: Zondervan, 2018), 417–20.
22. Aristotle, *Nicomachean Ethics*, 36.

cover later, it is not reductively deontological or teleological; neither is it merely *aretaic*, or related to virtues. It recognizes that the complexity of moral reality requires attending to all three ethics as perspectives of the whole moral reality.

The Material Kingdom

The Jews of Jesus's time who grew up with the Old Testament lacked the theological imagination to entertain the idea of a spiritual heaven. Jesus did not introduce a radically new idea that is disassociated from the Hebraic worldview. "The Kingdom of God is a Jewish idea, through and through, rooted in the embodied drama of Israel and God's relationship with Israel."[23] Isaiah, who spoke about God's coming reign as king over Israel and the world, strongly informed Jesus's ideas about the kingdom, prompting Peter Gosnell to declare Isaiah the ethical bridge between the Torah and the Gospels.[24]

For Isaiah and Jesus, the divine king comes to establish righteousness in the world. Their vision highlights God's intervention "to rescue those who are being crushed by unjust power."[25] God's kingship offers holistic salvation that redeems "spiritual" sins *and* injustice that people experience in their lives. The Jews were a people who lived under centuries of foreign oppression due to their idolatry and the injustice they performed against their own people, which led to "severe hardship as God's disciplinary intervention for their misbehavior, inflicted with a parent-like design to get them back on track."[26] Isaiah brought forward God's accusations against these social sins of Israel, which serve as the backdrop for our understanding of Isaiah's messianic prophecies. The kingdom of righteousness and justice intends to deliver people from their plight.

God's deliverance is made possible because the Davidic king has returned to Israel. King Jesus is the Spirit-anointed man who proclaims holistic salvation. We witness Jesus's self-understanding of his ministry when he announced its inauguration in his hometown, as recorded in Luke 4:14–20. In Luke's account, Jesus, empowered by the Holy Spirit, goes to the synagogue of Nazareth and is given a scroll from none other than Isaiah. The passage he reads states,

> The Spirit of the Lord is upon me,
>   because he has anointed me
>   to bring good news to the poor.

23. David P. Gushee and Glen H. Stassen, *Kingdom Ethics: Following Jesus in Contemporary Context*, 2nd ed. (Grand Rapids: Eerdmans, 2016), 5.

24. Peter W. Gosnell, *The Ethical Vision of the Bible: Learning Good from Knowing God* (Downers Grove, IL: IVP Academic, 2014), 30.

25. Gushee and Stassen, *Kingdom Ethics*, 5.

26. Gosnell, *Ethical Vision of the Bible*, 156.

He has sent me to proclaim release to the captives
    and recovery of sight to the blind,
    to let the oppressed go free,
to proclaim the year of the Lord's favor. (vv. 18–19)

Jesus's kingly work does not allude to our popular understanding of the gospel but describes the dominant biblical theme of care for the oppressed and suffering. The oppressed and suffering (e.g., widows, orphans, and the poor) acutely experience the injustices of life. Mere confession of belief without living for the kingdom betrays Jesus's good news and indicates the same type of empty belief that even demons share (James 2:14–19). The kingdom is not some future spiritual destiny but something we perform today. Mere belief is never a substitute for faithful action.

We don't want to mislead readers into accepting a dichotomy between faith and works, as if we are recommending a gospel of "works righteousness." Hebraic thought integrates faith and works as two sides of the same coin. Realizing the kingdom by performing "justice, peacemaking, healing, community building, and deliverance"[27] is not purely a human endeavor. If kingdom building is purely human work, then we replace God's central role and place ourselves and our works at the level of divinity. As much as the gospel of hard work is written into the DNA of the US, we cannot equate our efforts with God's work. Just as Jesus was able to usher in the kingdom only through the power of the Holy Spirit, our work is possible only because we participate in God's own performance of kingdom building.[28]

We must know what the kingdom is like in order to work for its advancement. Isaiah is again helpful, providing us with seven marks of the kingdom that we, as imitators of Jesus, are to perform for its advancement. These seven marks appear repeatedly in Isaiah and picture divine salvation in holistic terms. They are "deliverance/salvation, justice, peace, healing, restoration/rebuilding of community, joy, and the experience of God's presence."[29] They clearly reflect tangible good news for downtrodden people who have suffered under the heavy yoke of the Romans and their own kind, the Jewish elites. Their presence in our lives signifies kingdom presence. Are we not commanded to make disciples for this kingdom? Therefore, kingdom ethics is a form of deontological ethics called **divine command theory**, which holds that moral good and obligation are dependent on God's commands.

27. Gushee and Stassen, *Kingdom Ethics*, 13.
28. Gushee and Stassen, *Kingdom Ethics*, 13.
29. Gushee and Stassen, *Kingdom Ethics*, 10.

Israel's primary sins were not personal, private sins but social sins. Social sins are especially potent because they dig their roots deep into the fabric of society and its imagination. People who benefit from social sins can even become blind to them, as was the case with the Jewish leaders.[30] The good news, while offered to everyone, is especially pertinent for the marginalized because it has tangible implications for this life. The good news is good because it rights both internal sins and "external, physical wrongs."[31] Scripture, especially in prophetic books like Isaiah, is "notorious for emphasizing certain themes that are often grouped under the banner of 'social justice.'"[32] While this emphasis does not signal favoritism on God's part, it reveals that God is most concerned with the suffering: "Jesus is a messianic restorer of broken people, first."[33] Therefore, Jesus consistently demonstrates through his dealings with people that the kingdom of God reverses the role of the downtrodden, just as his glorification reversed his humiliation on the cross.[34]

This message is threatening to those who benefit from social sins, which explains why Jesus was crucified as a political prisoner. A mere gospel of forgiveness and love would never have resulted in his crucifixion. Jesus threatened the religious-political elites by preaching the dawn of a new kingdom and the return of its king, who would overturn the sinful patterns of both persons and society. "To proclaim a just reign of God is to attack unjust power structures in God's name, and thus to bring the wrath of those powers on one's head."[35] It's clear why Jesus said his followers must carry their cross. His death as "King of the Jews" meant that his followers who work for the kingdom of God would become potential targets of the same cross of our king.

Since God's kingdom reverses the corruption of sin in the personal and social order, God brings wholeness to the world. We become agents of this wholeness, God's *shalom*, when we follow God's command to live justly and to care for both soul and body. Seeking the kingdom's advancement and our own wholeness by obeying God's commands shows that Hebraic ethics is also teleological. We shouldn't follow God's commands out of rote obedience. God promises rewards to those who seek the kingdom of God (Matt. 6:33), and pursuing God's will ought to lead to communal flourishing and wholeness.[36]

---

30. Gushee and Stassen, *Kingdom Ethics*, 15.
31. Gosnell, *Ethical Vision of the Bible*, 213.
32. Gosnell, *Ethical Vision of the Bible*, 165.
33. Gosnell, *Ethical Vision of the Bible*, 214.
34. Gosnell, *Ethical Vision of the Bible*, 192.
35. Gushee and Stassen, *Kingdom Ethics*, 16.
36. Frame, *Doctrine of the Christian Life*, 101.

Just Righteousness

Social justice is a contested topic in our day. Yet among the myriad of impor-tant ethical themes in Hebraic thought, especially for the prophets, one of the most important is justice: "hardly any concept appears so often" in Scripture.[37] It shows up in sixteen out of seventeen passages about kingdom deliverance in Isaiah.[38] Importantly, Hebraic thought parallels justice with "righteousness." Many of our readers may understand righteousness as denoting standards of personal moral worth, often defined by what one does *not* do as much as by what one does: someone is righteous, for example, if he or she does not listen to secular songs and has a fervently praying spirit.

The two Hebrew terms for righteousness, *tsedaqah* and *mishpat* (including its Greek equivalent, *dikaiosynē*), do not indicate such individualistic, moralistic meaning. *Tsedaqah* indicates a concrete normative standard that a relation-ship or situation demands. We live righteously by responding rightly to what a relationship or situation demands. *Mishpat* broadly refers to legal right or proceedings. Christopher J. H. Wright argues that the words overlap in many ways, but *mishpat* refers to concrete acts that specific situations call for in order to conform to the demands of *tsedaqah*.[39] David Gushee and Glen Stassen define the terms similarly, but they give a pithier translation of *tsedaqah*: "delivering-justice and community-restoring justice."[40] Justice calls for the restoration of the wronged. Hence, righteousness delivers justice to the wronged and restores what has been broken. Often, "justice" and "righteousness" appear together in Scripture. Like "law and order" and "health and safety," when "righteousness and justice" appear as a pair, they form "a *hendiadys*—a single complex idea expressed through the use of two words."[41] Together, the meaning they create is close to the English equivalent of "social justice." However, they refer more to concrete action, a just life, than to an abstract concept or ideal.[42]

Justice work "is the kind of thing that gets a prophet killed."[43] Jesus stands in a long line of prophets who were killed for pursuing justice. However, Jesus's resur-rection, glorification, and Spirit endowment make kingdom realization possible. The kingdom of God brings deliverance to body and soul, to humans and non-humans alike. Corruption from sin touches all areas of creation, and God works

37. Gushee and Stassen, *Kingdom Ethics*, 126.
38. Gushee and Stassen, *Kingdom Ethics*, 131.
39. Christopher J. H. Wright, *Old Testament Ethics for the People of God* (Downers Grove, IL: IVP Academic, 2004), 256–57.
40. Gushee and Stassen, *Kingdom Ethics*, 127.
41. Wright, *Old Testament Ethics*, 255.
42. Wright, *Old Testament Ethics*, 257.
43. Gushee and Stassen, *Kingdom Ethics*, 130.

to overturn this corruption by righting wrongs, enacting *mishpat* to conform to *tsedaqah*. We are called to participate in this kingdom building by imitating Jesus's call to pursue just righteousness. Social justice is not an anti-Christian concept. The discomfort that some feel about it may come from the concrete contents that various groups add to the abstract concept of social justice, but social justice as a concrete way of life is a central moral imperative for Christians.

While differences may exist between various understandings of social justice, there are enough similarities to make those who benefit from or are blind to social sins uncomfortable. This discomfort is not merely, or even primarily, an ideological consequence but stems from character. Our affective character and the narratives we identify with have great power in directing the formation of our beliefs. Therefore, leading a life of just righteousness is not only deontological and teleological; it also requires virtue, for an unjust person cannot lead a consistently just life. One who loves idolatrous pleasures and enthrones himself on the seat of moral autonomy desires neither God's kingdom nor the pleasures of submitting to the kingly authority of Jesus. The Beatitudes (Matt. 5:1–12) describe the character traits of kingdom citizens; practicing them will greatly form our character.[44] However, they're not optional for Christians. If we don't enact them in our lives, we become like salt that has lost its saltiness and light that is hidden (vv. 13–16). May it not be! Practicing them will be fruitful because we will gain the eyes to see and ears to hear, and our hearts will be directed toward God and others. We will know God and discern God's voice better because we will conform more and more to the image of Christ. This is the virtue perspective of kingdom ethics.

Consequences or Duty? The Great Modern Debate

As we leave behind the holistic ethics of Hebraic thought, which involves all elements of deontological, teleological, and virtue ethics, we arrive at the influential ethical theories that have greatly shaped contemporary ethical imagination. First, we will survey utilitarianism, the teleological theory that Jeremy Bentham authored and that his student John Stuart Mill modified. We will then look at the work of Immanuel Kant, a pivotal figure who did much to isolate the objective good in deontological ethics. Reacting strongly against utilitarianism, Kant argued that the good is not based on positive consequences but on moral duty as discerned by reason alone. His theory is supremely objectivist as he leaves behind every form of subjective intention and desire.

---

44. Chap. 2 of Gushee and Stassen's *Kingdom Ethics* provides a short but important explanation of the Beatitudes.

Utilitarianism

Utilitarianism is a type of teleological ethics that determines the moral worth of an action by the good consequences it may realize: the end *does* justify the means. Hence, teleological ethics is often called *consequentialism*. The utilitarian principle is "the greatest good for the greatest number of people." Even without knowledge of utilitarianism, anyone familiar with democracy will recognize that utilitarianism undergirds it. The good of each person counts equally, and the good of the majority determines the right course of action.

The founder of utilitarianism was the British philosopher Jeremy Bentham, an eccentric fellow whose mummified body is still on display at University College, London, per his instructions in connection with his significant charitable giving to the university. For Bentham, humans are motivated by the "Great Happiness Principle," which defines happiness and unhappiness in terms of pleasure and pain.[45] We all seek pleasure and avoid pain. Moral action is action that increases pleasure and minimizes pain. Like the votes in a democracy, pleasure and pain are quantifiable measures. In defining moral worth in terms of pleasure, Bentham viewed morality hedonistically, and his "hedonistic calculus"—made up of intensity, duration, certainty, nearness or remoteness, fecundity, purity, and extent—measured the units of pleasure and pain in order to determine the moral worth of an action.[46]

There is something rather inhuman about Bentham's approach and the notion of quantifying pleasure and pain objectively, which seems nearly impossible. As anyone who has been asked to describe their pain level using the numerical pain scale can attest, pain is highly subjective. Pain that counts as an eight on a scale for one person might only be perceived as a five by another person. There is a subjective element to pain that can be different for everyone. Moreover, Bentham's model does not consider the quality of pleasure and pain but essentially assumes that they are of the same quality and can be easily quantified. For example, we can recognize that self-sacrifice is often painful, sometimes mortally so, but we consider it of high moral worth.

John Stuart Mill was a child prodigy and a student of Bentham, but he revised Bentham's utilitarianism, especially after he suffered a mental crisis partly due to the "impoverished conception of emotional life . . . in Benthamism."[47] He overcame his crisis chiefly through his discovery of Romanticism, which placed great emphasis on the affective, aesthetic dimensions of human life

---

45. John Stuart Mill, *Utilitarianism* (Auckland, New Zealand: Floating Press, 2009), 14.
46. Radoslav A. Tsanoff, *The Great Philosophers*, 2nd ed. (New York: Harper & Row, 1953), 506.
47. Nicholas Capaldi, *John Stuart Mill: A Biography* (New York: Cambridge University Press, 2004), 58.

over against the Enlightenment's cold rationalism.[48] A fundamental change Mill made to Bentham's utilitarianism was defining pleasure in terms of quality rather than quantity. In fact, he found it absurd to calculate pleasure only in terms of quantity.[49] Anyone who has heard the statement "It's apples to oranges" will recognize how qualitatively different pleasures can be. If pleasure is simply quantitative, then we are no better than animals that can be easily satisfied. Because we are higher rational beings, Mill famously stated that "it is better to be a human being dissatisfied than a pig satisfied; better to be a Socrates dissatisfied than a fool satisfied."[50] Mill thus rejected the simple hedonism of Bentham.

How can we differentiate between different qualities of pleasure? Mill's answers are rather simple and commonsensical. First, he says, on examining two types of pleasures that we have experienced, the one that most, if not all, of us consider the more pleasurable is the one that is qualitatively better. What happens if the majority desire base pleasures over "higher" pleasures? Surely, indulging in hours of streaming our favorite shows is more pleasurable than arduously mulling over life's deepest questions! Mill's answer, unfortunately, is elitist. He argues that our capacities for higher character and nobler feelings are easily eroded, especially by life circumstances, such as "unintellectual" occupations (or, in our contemporary society, endlessly scrolling through social media to detox from a stressful day). In this way, he reflects the elitism of Plato in preferring the "rational" over the "appetitive." As rational creatures, we can come to agree that the higher pleasures are more worthy by cultivating an intellectual life.[51]

Mill's second answer to the question of how to differentiate between qualities of pleasure is that if we decide that an act is preferable even if it brings a great amount of discontent, then we can consider it to be a higher quality of pleasure. Cases of self-sacrifice exemplify this second condition.[52] This example of self-sacrifice reveals the communal dimension of Mill's utilitarianism. What is most important is not the good of the individual. The principle of utility is concerned with the general welfare of all. "As between his own happiness and that of others, utilitarianism requires him to be as strictly impartial as a disinterested and benevolent spectator."[53] He sees Jesus's golden rule—that we treat others as we desire to be treated and love others as our neighbors—as a reflection of the spirit

---

48. Capaldi, *John Stuart Mill*, 66.
49. Mill, *Utilitarianism*, 16.
50. Mill, *Utilitarianism*, 19.
51. Mill, *Utilitarianism*, 19–20.
52. Mill, *Utilitarianism*, 16–17.
53. Mill, *Utilitarianism*, 31–32.

of utilitarianism. This concern for the general welfare of the whole leads Mill to view utilitarianism as the most beautiful ethical system. However, he does not require every moral decision to be concerned with the benefit of others. He recognizes that most of our moral decisions only concern individuals or those immediately involved. As long as these decisions do not violate the rights of others, then we can make decisions that benefit only the particular persons involved. However, he expects that such individual actions, when performed ethically along utilitarian logic, will lead to the cumulation of overall happiness.[54]

Utilitarianism has been popular because it is a simple theory. We need to be good predictors of consequences and determine whether our actions will promote the greatest good for the greatest number of people. Unlike deontological ethics, utilitarianism is flexible and better accounts for the complex variables of each ethical situation. It also does not require divine commands to determine moral action. However, as shown by Mill's admiration for Jesus's golden rule, Mill did not consider utilitarianism to be atheistic. He argued that "if it be a true belief that God desires, above all things, the happiness of his creatures, and that this was his purpose in their creation, utility is not only not a godless doctrine, but [it is] more profoundly religious than any other."[55] However, divine command theory is not required for utilitarianism, and God need not play any role in utilitarian judgments. Hence, utilitarianism is a popular option for secular liberal politics (that is, a political position that promotes individual freedom, not to be confused with any political party), which places fundamental importance on democratic principles. In a voting system, the majority determines the direction of the state, either directly or indirectly by proxy.

The Deontological Ethics of Immanuel Kant

Kant, a vocal critic of utilitarianism and of teleological reasoning in general, developed a deontological approach to ethics that sees duty as being for duty's sake. Kant believes utilitarianism fails to respect or acknowledge an individual's rights. Because utilitarianism looks at what produces the most pleasure for the most people, individual rights are unprotected and can easily be trumped on the basis of general welfare. For Kant, a person's individual rights must be protected because the person has inherent worth as a rational being. What defines us as human beings is our capacity to reason. We are free insofar as we are able to govern our will through reason. We can choose a reasoned position over our desires. For instance, if we are hungry but have chosen to abstain from food for the sake of spiritual discipline and clarity, we have reasoned to be governed

---

54. Mill, *Utilitarianism*, 32–34.
55. Mill, *Utilitarianism*, 39.

not by a law of nature or an inclination but by our rationally determined will. We have freely chosen to fast despite our body's yearning to eat.[56]

For Kant, freedom is not simply choosing what we want without any impediments or obstacles; it concerns our autonomy. The word "autonomy" comes from two Greek words, *autos* (the self) and *nomos* (the law). Acting autonomously, therefore, means acting according to a law that we have given ourselves through reason.[57] Our capacity to give laws to our wills comes from reason, which reveals another failure of utilitarianism: it fails to properly define morality or what morality is about. Bentham and Mill say morality is fundamentally just a calculus of pleasure and pain. But morality can't simply be about calculating what makes us happy or not. Being able to discern what we like or dislike does not mean we have a good understanding of moral right and wrong. The only way to determine right and wrong is to ask ourselves whether we're governed by the consequences of our actions or by reason.

If we are governed by consequences, as in utilitarianism, we have not identified the morality of an action, only it's social effectiveness. If, however, we determine through reason that something is right for its own sake, then we've discovered that it is actually morally good. Kant's notion of autonomous freedom animates his ethics, and the quality of a person's moral action is dependent on his or her enduring commitment to obey what has been discovered to be good. Although Kant was a professing Christian, Kant's ethics is predominantly nontheistic. God is an afterthought to our ability to discover the objective, universal duty. This is because our reason alone can discover the objectively good moral duty.

Kant is concerned with the universal good, which is untainted by particularities, such as the particularities of intentions, desires, and consequences. In their stead, he identifies good will as the "good without qualification." Even if an act of good will brings about a disastrous consequence, we can't fault a good will. Good will "is good in itself."[58] The "good" of a will is determined by its relation to reason. When the will is persuaded by its own inclinations and desires, such as the desire for happiness or pleasure, it fails to qualify as good. Even an altruistic will that enjoys bringing satisfaction to others is morally dubious.[59] A good will, then, is one that follows the dictates of reason and determines its duty through a command—Kant calls this command an *imperative*.[60]

---

56. Immanuel Kant, *Grounding for the Metaphysics of Morals: On a Supposed Right to Lie because of Philanthropic Concerns*, trans. James W. Ellington, 3rd ed. (Indianapolis: Hackett, 1993), 4.

57. Kant, *Grounding for the Metaphysics*, 44.

58. Kant, *Grounding for the Metaphysics*, 7.

59. Kant, *Grounding for the Metaphysics*, 11.

60. Kant, *Grounding for the Metaphysics*, 24.

Kant presents two types of imperatives: the hypothetical and the categorical. The hypothetical imperative is teleological and has an "if . . . then" structure that determines the effectiveness of an action based on its ability to obtain some desired good. The hypothetical imperative is morally problematic because it cannot deliver universal moral law due to the particularities of each situation and purpose. Universal moral commands are achievable only through reason, and reason dictates that a categorical imperative must follow this rule: "Act only according to that maxim whereby you can at the same time will that it should become a universal law."[61] By this, Kant means that a moral rule becomes a *categorical* imperative if we can universalize it without any contradiction or inconsistency.

Kant uses the form/matter distinction in his understanding of the categorical maxim. Like Plato and Aristotle, Kant views the form as the universal aspect of the categorical imperative. A maxim is universal because it refers to no purpose or consequence. Moral worth is dependent purely on the act of the will to perform the moral imperative. One who performs it is like a moral hero because he or she can gain nothing from it. Kant exemplifies this view in an illuminating scenario about one's desire for self-preservation. The act of self-preservation by people who desire to do so has no intrinsic worth. However, for the one who is depressed, has no hope for life, and desires death, yet chooses to live as a performed duty, has acted in a morally honorable way.[62] Unlike for Plato and Aristotle, matter for Kant refers to our end as rational beings. Due to our rational nature, reason dictates that we can never be means to some other end. We are ends in ourselves. Therefore, a categorical imperative is a universal rule, which always treats humans as ends in themselves rather than means to some other end.[63]

Kant provides several examples of the categorical imperative. Most famously, he asks whether a desire to break promises can become a categorical imperative. When we try to universalize the maxim that promises can be broken when convenient, we will find that the concept of promise becomes meaningless. If everyone can break promises, then there can be no such thing as promises. Categorical imperatives are universal rules that bind absolutely, without any exception. Kant even argues that we cannot tell a lie to save a life![64]

Kant's rational ethics seeks to secure universal duty through autonomous reason. God plays no actual role in determining the categorical imperative since all we need is reason. However, given that people may lack the motive to

61. Kant, *Grounding for the Metaphysics*, 30.
62. Kant, *Grounding for the Metaphysics*, 10.
63. Kant, *Grounding for the Metaphysics*, 41.
64. Kant, *Grounding for the Metaphysics*, 65.

live justly, we could postulate God's existence. The possibility of God's divine justice granting eternal happiness or punishment acts as an important moral motivation.[65]

Conclusion

Throughout this chapter, we surveyed important figures and theories, although the available space did not allow us to do justice to the complex history of ethics. However, examining the representatives allowed us to introduce key concepts and show how they represent these various normative ethical theories. A broad survey like this also helps us see a major shift that occurred between ancient and modern ethics. Ancient Greek ethics was often focused on virtues and *telos* without being consequentialist. In Hebraic ethics, we see the interplay of all three ethical theories. There is depth to these theories, unlike utilitarian and Kantian ethics, which are strictly one-dimensional. One cause for this shift is the primacy placed on the power of disembodied reason to discover objectively good action. The primacy of reason is especially true for Bentham and Kant; it is less so for Mill. This type of rationalism was not present in ancient Greece. Even though Plato denigrated all that belongs to the material world, he did not see virtue as purely ethereal, especially as it relates to the functioning of the state. He advocated for the merchant-appetitive class not to be eliminated but simply to be governed well by the rulers. For Aristotle, the virtues have both intellectual and moral dimensions, and their development through embodied actions is critical for achieving social flourishing. Disembodied reason, therefore, cannot have radical autonomy over our bodies lest we end up with a subhuman ethics.

Indeed, for Christians, our bodies were created good by God. *Being* good is as important as knowing the good, as the ancients remind us. Rote obedience to duty is morally dubious, as is the justification of any means used to obtain good consequences. We must discern moral principles while also recognizing how particular situations and consequences can inform the relevancy of those principles. Developing virtues, such as wisdom, allows us to become people who can discern the interplay between moral principles and particular situations and consequences. It also allows us to know how to navigate our complex and often unclear moral realities, both mentally and affectively, especially as those who are motivated by love for God and others—humans and nonhumans alike. As we shall see later, like Hebraic ethics, renewal ethics integrates deontological, teleological, and *aretaic* insights as perspectives of the whole ethical picture.

65. Frame, *Doctrine of the Christian Life*, 115.

It's also important to keep in mind that, as creatures of God, we must come under the authority of the good (God). The good, in our view, is not purely subjective; it represents the character of God, which is an objective reality apart from our determinations. The good is also not purely an object, since God is a subject who invites us to participate subjectively with the objective reality of God's moral life. This participation occurs not only in the spiritual realm but in God's good material creation. We are not mere spectators of the good but participants in this life. Knowing and being good eliminates the divide between subject and object. We are under God's authority and obey that authority as we participate in the good in this life.

Study Questions

1. Explain how the golden mean of virtue is contextually determined.

2. Describe the attributes of the kingdom of God according to the Isaianic view of Jesus.

3. How should we understand righteousness?

4. What are the essential concepts of deontological, teleological, and virtue ethics?

7

Contemporary Christian Ethics

Niebuhr, MacIntyre, and Hauerwas

Key Words

Christian realism: *An ethical and political theory that recognizes the tension of living a moral Christian life in a sinful world. It takes a dualist approach that sees individual (moral) behavior and social (political) behavior as being governed differently in contrasting realms.*

Common good: *The good we all share and seek together as we participate in the life of the community.*

Cruciformity: *Conforming ethically and spiritually to a self-sacrificial lifestyle like that of the crucified Christ.*

Discipleship: *The condition of being a follower of Christ and an active adherent to his teachings.*

Emotivism: *"The doctrine that . . . all moral judgments are nothing but expressions of preference, expressions of attitude or feeling, insofar as they are moral or evaluative in character."*[1]

Narrative ethics: *An approach to ethics that focuses on story for ethical deliberations.*

What would Jesus do?[2] This popular early 1990s slogan implies that a Christian's actions should be characterized by what Jesus says and does. Maxims like this are often so simplistic that they are unhelpful. How can you know what Jesus would do in any given situation, especially if you

---

1. Alasdair MacIntyre, *After Virtue: A Study in Moral Theory*, 3rd ed. (London: Bloomsbury, 2011), 13.
2. The phrase originated as the subtitle of Charles Sheldon's classic Christian novel *In His Steps* (1896).

don't already have a deep sense of who Jesus is and what he's like? But therein lies the beauty of this maxim—it *assumes* you already have a deep knowledge of Jesus. It assumes you already are his disciple. Christian ethics as a subset of ethics proper makes the assumption that adherents are already part of the tradition. A Christian ethics does not wonder *if* Jesus is Lord but asks, "*Since* Jesus is Lord, how then shall we live?" This is, essentially, what the question "What would Jesus do?" is asking. In the prior chapter we briefly explored the history of Christian ethics, and in this chapter we'll look at some major streams within Christian ethics today to see how they approach this question.

While this chapter offers a comparative account of popular late modern ethical systems within Christianity, it does not divide its comparison neatly along the lines of Catholicism, Eastern Orthodoxy, and Protestantism as was done in chapter 3, when we discussed theological aesthetics. There certainly is denominational variety in the thought of our representative thinkers (Reinhold Niebuhr came from the Reformed tradition, Alasdair MacIntyre is Catholic, and Stanley Hauerwas is Methodist), but their thought is not necessarily representative of their respective traditions. Rather, each thinker makes broad claims that traverse beyond denominational (or even religious, as in the case of MacIntyre) strictures. We will look at Niebuhr's sense of Christian realism, MacIntyre's recovery of the virtue tradition for modern ethics, and Hauerwas's turn toward narrative in his rendition of Christian virtue ethics. Together these representatives craft the necessary talking points for establishing a renewal ethics, which we'll discuss in the next chapter.

An Overview of Christian Ethics

As we saw in chapter 6, Christian ethics can be approached in many ways. In our late modern world, however, the field of Christian ethics has focused on virtue and narrative ethics. In recent years, there has been a great emphasis on moral and spiritual formation in hopes that Christians would reason morally *because* they are good and loving people. It is not that good moral actions make good people, but good people make good moral decisions. This line of thinking makes sense of Matthew 7:17–20, where Jesus shows that the moral agent's goodness is what produces good works and not vice versa: "In the same way, every good tree bears good fruit, but the bad tree bears bad fruit. A good tree cannot bear bad fruit, nor can a bad tree bear good fruit. Every tree that does not bear good fruit is cut down and thrown into the fire. Thus you will know them by their fruits." As we will demonstrate below, repeated good actions can positively form a person's moral agency through habituation, but ultimately it is the person's character that determines their actions.

One of the struggles virtue ethics sometimes faces is determining what exactly the desired virtues are. If virtues shift from age to age, and from culture to culture, how can we know whether an action is objectively good? Doesn't virtue ethics simply reduce down to relativism, where each agent or culture determines what is virtuous? The way Christian ethicists typically get beyond these challenges is by making Jesus the quintessential virtuous person on whom Christians model all moral action. As God incarnate, Jesus modeled the moral human life perfectly, so Christian virtue ethics looks at Jesus's life and teachings to discover what virtues are normative for Christian living. This is why the Sermon on the Mount—the longest record of Jesus's teaching—is often seen as the primary biblical source on which Christians can base their moral principles.[3] Indeed, the Sermon on the Mount offers tremendous moral insight, as Jesus addresses head-on what it means to be part of the kingdom of God.

We are formed morally, spiritually, and in every aspect of our lives as we embrace a cruciform life. **Cruciformity** refers to conforming ethically and spiritually to a self-sacrificial lifestyle like that of the crucified Christ.[4] Cruciformity should be the goal of any Christian ethics. Christianity isn't merely a set of beliefs or a philosophical approach to subscribe to. It is, as we've argued, a complete, holistic way of life that's predicated upon being conformed to the image of Christ (Rom. 8:29). If being Christlike *isn't* the goal of the Christian moral system, then it has fundamentally failed. Christian moral thinking is necessarily tied to **discipleship**, which is the condition of being a follower of Christ and an active adherent to his teachings. Being a disciple is more than being a student. It requires a full, lifelong commitment to take on the ways of Jesus. Discipleship is also heritable as disciples learn to live like Jesus and help others do the same.

While we can certainly find our moral model in Christ, moral formation for the Christian is active and requires a perpetual commitment to die daily to our old, sinful selves (Rom. 8:13; 1 Cor. 15:31; Gal. 2:20). This requires a concerted effort on our part to align holistically with God—mind, body, and soul. You might have heard that everything starts from the top, from the renewal of the mind. After all, Romans 12:2 states, "Do not be conformed to this world, but be transformed by the renewing of your minds, so that you may discern what

3. See David P. Gushee and Glen H. Stassen, *Kingdom Ethics: Following Jesus in Contemporary Context*, 2nd ed. (Grand Rapids: Eerdmans, 2016); William Mattison III, *The Sermon on the Mount and Moral Theology: A Virtue Perspective* (Cambridge: Cambridge University Press, 2017); Charles Talbert, *Reading the Sermon on the Mount: Character Formation and Decision Making in Matthew 5–7* (Columbia: University of South Carolina Press, 2004); and Jonathan Pennington, *The Sermon on the Mount and Human Flourishing: A Theological Commentary* (Grand Rapids: Baker Academic, 2017).

4. This concept was coined and championed by Michael Gorman. See Michael Gorman, *Cruciformity: Paul's Narrative Spirituality of the Cross*, 20th anniv. ed. (Grand Rapids: Eerdmans, 2021), 4.

is the will of God—what is good and acceptable and perfect." Here Paul seems to indicate that renewing the mind is what's most important as we seek to act according to God's will. We tend to forget, however, that in the preceding verse Paul states, "I appeal to you therefore, brothers and sisters, by the mercies of God, to present your bodies as a living sacrifice, holy and acceptable to God, which is your spiritual worship" (v. 1). Paul connects holistic worship with the renewal of the mind. He says that we are to "present [our] bodies as a living sacrifice," which refers both to our posture in worship and to our actions.

We often assume that if we can think Christianly, we'll act more like virtuous Christians. What if the opposite is true? If we read the first and second verses of Romans 12 in order, we'll see that offering our bodies in worship precedes renewing our minds. Maybe if we act in Christian virtue, we'll begin to think like Christians. This is precisely what James K. A. Smith says in his book *Desiring the Kingdom*. Smith contends that people are fundamentally desiring beings, and our actions are shaped by what we love and consider to be ultimate.[5] Many of our decisions are made at the affective or gut level. We do not necessarily think things all the way through before we act, but we act on what we *know* to be true almost instinctually. This gut-level decision-making is driven by what we deeply desire. Our hearts are already oriented toward an intended result, so our actions reflect what we already deeply hold. Good trees bear good fruit.

Smith also believes, however, that we can shape our desires through habitual practices. People are liturgical animals—"embodied, practicing creatures whose love/desire is aimed at something ultimate."[6] As liturgical animals, we are shaped by habitual practices. The things we do over and over shape what we ultimately desire—they shape us at the gut level. So if we repeatedly do destructive things, our desires will be shaped to yearn for destruction. If we do good, virtuous things, however, our desires will be shaped to want what's good. Habits, in a sense, train our hearts toward ultimate desires.[7] Shaping one's desires so that they conform to God's desires is what constitutes holistic disciple making. Smith writes, "Being a disciple of Jesus is not primarily a matter of getting the right ideas and doctrines and beliefs into your head in order to guarantee proper behavior; rather, it's a matter of being the kind of person who *loves* rightly—who loves God and neighbor and is oriented to the world by the primacy of that love. We are made to be such people by our immersion in the material practices of Christian worship."[8] Thus, good Christian

5. James K. A. Smith, *Desiring the Kingdom: Worship, Worldview, and Cultural Formation* (Grand Rapids: Baker Academic, 2009), 51.

6. Smith, *Desiring the Kingdom*, 40.

7. Smith, *Desiring the Kingdom*, 58.

8. Smith, *Desiring the Kingdom*, 32–33.

moral action flows out of a Christian's holistic formation. Through habituated, virtuous action, we shape our desires to conform to what God loves, and when this happens, good fruit naturally comes forth because we're good trees.

While Stassen, Gushee, and Smith give us a practical sense of how our Christian virtues are formed, we will spend the rest of this chapter exploring how Christians have supported these practical insights through moral systems, and how these insights apply to the social sphere. The three thinkers we engage below add something significant to Christian moral thought in the past century, and looking at their contributions broadly will help us determine what a renewal perspective of goodness might entail.

Niebuhr's Christian Realism

In the first half of the twentieth century, the Christian ethical theory that was perhaps most widely known was Christian realism. **Christian realism** is an ethical and political theory that recognizes the tension of living a moral Christian life in a sinful world. It takes a dualist approach that sees individual (moral) behavior and social (political) behavior as being governed differently in contrasting realms. When we separate moral and social behaviors, we are able to make political decisions based on a realistic notion of the current state of affairs while holding on to personal moral aims. Ethics governs the relationships between people, but politics, through power and coercion, governs the relationships between social groups. Since there are different realms of decision-making and moral deliberation, one can come to a political position that compromises or conflicts with his or her personal moral code. This is how someone can say, "I am personally against abortion, but I don't think the government should restrict a woman's rights over her own body." This is a realist position that separates personal morality (i.e., being personally against abortion) from political stance (i.e., believing that the government shouldn't restrict a woman's rights). Other examples include, "I personally do not want a gun in my house, but I think we have a right to bear arms," and "I believe homosexuality is a sin, but I don't think there should be a law restricting who can get married." This sort of reasoning is common, which indicates how tremendously influential Christian realism has been within Christian circles for the past hundred years.

The person most associated with Christian realism was theologian, ethicist, and public intellectual Reinhold Niebuhr. In the early 1900s, Niebuhr served as a Protestant pastor in Detroit before taking a teaching position at Union Theological Seminary in New York. Although Niebuhr began his career subscribing to pacifism, during World War II he actively sought to persuade Christians to

stand against Hitler and support American war efforts.[9] Witnessing the atrocities of World War II, Niebuhr converted from Christian idealism to Christian
realism because pacifism proved to be an unrealistic response to true crisis.[10]
His new realist approach to ethics and politics opened the door for Christians
to responsibly engage in war and conduct violence, but only under particular
circumstances. This sense of realism has influenced many Christian American
politicians since. Christian realists seek to navigate the complex political system through a realistic balance of their Christian convictions and the actual
state of affairs.[11]

Niebuhr best articulates his views on Christian realism in his classic work
Moral Man and Immoral Society. He starts by demonstrating the differences between individual and group ethics. Individuals can be sympathetic toward others
and can overcome their own egoism, but social groups cannot. Niebuhr writes,
"In every human group there is less reason to guide and to check impulse, less
capacity for self-transcendence, less ability to comprehend the needs of others
and therefore more unrestrained egoism than the individuals, who compose
the group, reveal in their personal relationships."[12] As the book title suggests,
humans strive to be moral, but society does not. People have limits in their sympathy and rationality, however. Inevitably, people will become unreasonable,
and this compounds and becomes increasingly negative when we move from
the individual to society.[13] The group is bound together not by moral reasoning
but by a mere common purpose or impulse. These impulses can be good, evil,
or morally neutral. Aryan supremacy, for instance, was the common impulse
that bound the Nazis together. This impulse asserted itself through political
power, which paved the way for countless evil actions to follow. The group's actions were governed politically through force, not morally through conviction.

Nevertheless, a Christian *should* follow Christ's commandment to love others
individually, and this looks like charity toward anyone he or she comes into

9. Colm McKeogh, *The Political Realism of Reinhold Niebuhr: A Pragmatic Approach to Just War*
(London: Palgrave Macmillan, 1997), 20.

10. Niebuhr's early concept of Christian idealism saw divine love as the highest ideal. Since love
is heedless and self-sacrificial, it ought to never harm anyone. Niebuhr's early views adopted an
apolitical Christian pacifism. See Colm McKeogh, "Reinhold Niebuhr's Christian Realism/Christian
Idealism," in *The Realist Tradition and Contemporary International Relations*, ed. W. D. Clinton (Baton
Rouge: Louisiana State University Press, 2007), 191–92.

11. Some of the politicians who have been influenced by Niebuhr's general approach to ethics
and politics include Jimmy Carter, Martin Luther King Jr., Dennis Healey, and Barack Obama. See
Richard Harries and Stephen Platten, eds., *Reinhold Niebuhr and Contemporary Politics: God and
Power* (Oxford: Oxford University Press, 2010).

12. Reinhold Niebuhr, *Moral Man and Immoral Society: A Study in Ethics and Politics* (Louisville:
Westminster John Knox, 2013), xxvii.

13. Niebuhr, *Moral Man and Immoral Society*, 35.

contact with. Politically, however, the love of others looks like justice for all, which isn't equivalent to the biblical command to love others. Cornel West summarizes Niebuhr's position well: "The Christian command to love thy neighbor is not reducible to the collective quest for justice. Justice is what love looks like in public, but justice is never identical to love. There is a basic difference between the morality of individuals and the morality of groups."[14] So, Niebuhr would say, Jesus extends a pure ethic of love and nonviolence, but this perfect morality is not practical in our immoral society. Jesus's perfect love is a high ideal, but this ideal must be moderated by an ethics of realism when applied socially. Niebuhr says that Jesus's ethic of love only deals with the vertical dimension, the connection between the will of God and the will of humans, and does not deal with the "immediate moral problem of every human life—the problem of arranging some kind of armistice between various contending factions and forces."[15] It does not, in other words, address the horizontal dimensions of political and social ethics. But on this point, one of Niebuhr's most famous adherents, Dr. Martin Luther King Jr., disagrees: "He [Niebuhr] fails to see that the availability of the divine Agape is an essential affirmatim [sic] of the Christian religion."[16] For King there is the horizontal application of love in Jesus's ethics. King did not extrapolate on this further in his essay, but one could look at his social activism and see that a commitment to reconciliation might be what love beyond justice looks like on a social level. This is the position we adopt and will expound on further in the next chapter.

Niebuhr, if we return to his thinking, sees the nations as intrinsically selfish. Because groups never come into contact with other groups the way individuals do, they can never truly sympathize with or have deep understanding of the interests of other groups. He writes, "Since both sympathy and justice depend to a large degree upon the perception of need, which makes sympathy flow, and upon the understanding of competing interests, which must be resolved, it is obvious that human communities have a greater difficulty than individuals in achieving ethical relationships."[17] Rather than functioning on reasoned action, nations act in accordance with the will of the many within their group. This sort of social unity is gained through power, so the dominant power drives the group's actions, which results in inequality.[18] Nations then try to rationalize

14. Cornel West, foreword to Niebuhr, *Moral Man and Immoral Society*, xi.

15. Reinhold Niebuhr, *An Interpretation of Christian Ethics* (New York: Living Age, 1956), 45.

16. Martin Luther King Jr., "Reinhold Niebuhr's Ethical Dualism," May 9, 1952, The Martin Luther King Jr. Research and Education Institute, Stanford University, accessed June 25, 2022, https://king institute.stanford.edu/king-papers/documents/reinhold-niebuhrs-ethical-dualism/. King's essay contained a possible transcription error—i.e., "affirmatim" should read "affirmation."

17. Niebuhr, *Moral Man and Immoral Society*, 85.

18. Niebuhr, *Moral Man and Immoral Society*, 89–90.

their selfish motivations through hypocrisy, elevating their self-interests to the status of "universal values" and then demanding allegiance from their citizens.[19] This is the irredeemable state of society, which inevitably results in clashes between nations.

If nations are this corrupt, how can they ever achieve justice? Here Niebuhr decisively breaks with pacifism and argues that justice can come through revolution and by political force. Niebuhr argues that violence is not intrinsically immoral, because the only thing that is intrinsically immoral is ill will.[20] Violence is not always enacted out of ill will (self-defense, for instance, is not an act of ill will), so we must learn when and how it is morally acceptable to use violence. The ends *sometimes* justify the means, and a just nation establishes an appropriate balance between ends and means. In this way, violence and revolution *can* be permissible if they result in a just social system.[21] Furthermore, democracy can correct some of the inequalities that arise out of an economic system, but this can only be done gradually through a collaboration between social classes.[22] The end goal is to create a more just society, so to achieve this goal, the realist uses any means necessary through a delicate balance. While the Christian lives morally in a corrupt society, the society can become more just through a realist polity.

There are aspects of Niebuhr's critique that seem irrefutably true. The world is corrupt, and Christians have caused problems by forcing moral ideologies onto secular publics. But much of what Niebuhr says should be scrutinized. Can a Christian really believe that Jesus's ethic of love *can't* be applied socially? This seems to limit the power of the gospel, as King pointed out. The task of a renewal ethics is to, like Niebuhr, take a realistic look at our state of affairs, but then to see how the renewal tradition speaks to Jesus's ethic of love *both* individually *and* socially. We'll argue in the next chapter that love applied socially equates not to mere justice but to reconciliation. While Niebuhr pulls away the curtain and shows us the hard task of ethics, we will look at MacIntyre and Hauerwas next to see how their ethical systems can help ground a renewal ethics.

MacIntyre and the Virtue Tradition

Alasdair MacIntyre's classic book *After Virtue* is commonly acknowledged as one of the most important works on ethics in late modernity. Although MacIntyre

19. Niebuhr, *Moral Man and Immoral Society*, 95. This is also one of Niebuhr's main points in *Irony of American History*.

20. Niebuhr, *Moral Man and Immoral Society*, 170.

21. Niebuhr, *Moral Man and Immoral Society*, 179.

22. Niebuhr, *Moral Man and Immoral Society*, 203.

is a devout Catholic, his work does not extend a Christian ethics but is written for the general public. Yet it is important for our discussion because it is perhaps the greatest modern source for Christian virtue ethics, which became an important contrast to Christian realism. MacIntyre's weighty critiques of modern ethical systems and his construction of a contemporary virtue ethics are regularly picked up and expanded by Christian ethicists, as is evident in Stanley Hauerwas's thought, discussed below. So in this section, we'll briefly discuss MacIntyre's critiques of modern ethics and discuss his solution for revitalizing virtue ethics in our late modern age.

After Virtue offers a way of understanding morality that moves beyond modern liberal individualism and toward a "shared deliberation enabled by virtue."[23] MacIntyre first makes his case by offering a damning critique of modern moral thinking, which he deems broadly to be weak and groundless reductions of previously held Christian moral principles. The West was once deeply rooted in Christian ethical systems (e.g., the divine command theory of nominalists like Ockham, the natural teleology of Aquinas) but has since come to reject the philosophical and theological groundings of these systems while selectively keeping some of their practices and moral rules.[24] What's left is a disjointed set of pseudo-Christian rules that a person can follow. Christopher Lutz puts it well: "Inasmuch as it [modern morality] cannot justify its moral claims, those moral claims are exposed as the selectively Christian, and sometimes un-Christian morality of an arbitrary post-Christian ideology."[25] Modern morality struggles to validate its moral rules and practices as justifiable in any sense beyond personal preference.

Today the West has generally adopted an emotivist approach to morality, in which the individual is the sole arbiter of moral insight. MacIntyre defines **emotivism** as "the doctrine that all . . . moral judgments are *nothing but* expressions of preference, expressions of attitude or feeling, insofar as they are moral or evaluative in character."[26] The phrase "nothing but" is important in MacIntyre's definition. While all moral reasoning has a subjective element, since personal agents are the moral actors, emotivism reduces moral thinking to *only* personal preference. The problem here is that this sort of thinking is individualistic and anti-communal, and MacIntyre (indebted to his Marxist roots) believes that a person is morally accountable to his or her community.[27] In stark contrast to Niebuhr, MacIntyre believes communities have a sense of the

23. Christopher Stephen Lutz, *Reading Alasdair MacIntyre's "After Virtue"* (London: Continuum, 2012), 8.

24. Lutz, *Reading Alasdair MacIntyre's "After Virtue,"* 78.

25. Lutz, *Reading Alasdair MacIntyre's "After Virtue,"* 32.

26. MacIntyre, *After Virtue,* 13.

27. MacIntyre, *After Virtue,* 147.

common good, and his idea of the common good is not merely an aggregation of individual moral positions. Rather, the ancient sense of the **common good**, which MacIntyre seeks to recover, is the good we all share and seek together as we participate in the life of the community.[28]

Because modern liberalism[29] is ill-equipped to address or solve moral and political issues, perhaps we should hark back to an ethical system that looks at human action and the virtues that should be cultivated to produce appropriate moral reasoning. For MacIntyre, this was accomplished by the virtue ethics of Aristotle. What makes Aristotle's ethics so appealing to MacIntyre is that it's guided by a *telos*, or ultimate aim. The *telos* for Aristotle is not something that can be conquered but an aim that constructs our whole life.[30] As you may recall from chapter 6, Aristotle's *telos* is *eudaimonia*, a happiness that connotes human flourishing.[31] When there is an established ultimate aim such as *eudaimonia*, then rules become practical and actionable in order to achieve those aims. When people have a concrete idea of what the good life entails, they can scrutinize their moral actions. If their actions lead to their intended outcomes, they're acting out of virtue; if they do the opposite, they're acting out of vice.

Modern moral philosophies are problematic because they want to give moral agents total sovereignty while binding them to traditional moral rules. They establish moral rules without establishing what the agent will gain by following them.[32] There is no end goal, just purposeless rules that are said to be moral. The choices we are left with are either to agree with modern ideology and reject teleology, making ourselves the only moral arbiter whose moral decisions are guided by our own will to power, or to come back to teleology as a way of recovering a virtue ethics that aims for the good life.[33]

For MacIntyre, recovering virtue ethics means retrieving a social teleology. The ancient Greeks were part of a heroic tradition that believed that a community's notion of human excellence was the goal for human action.[34] The

28. Lutz, *Reading Alasdair MacIntyre's "After Virtue,"* 29.

29. "Liberalism" here refers not to a political party's leanings but to a secular, materialist sense of individual freedom (liberty) and the human rights that are to be protected by law.

30. MacIntyre, *After Virtue*, 204.

31. Aristotle, *Nicomachean Ethics*, trans. Drummond Percy Chase (Mineola, NY: Dover, 1998), 13.

32. Lutz, *Reading Alasdair MacIntyre's "After Virtue,"* 96.

33. MacIntyre frames these two logical responses to our modern dilemma as following Nietzsche or Aristotle. Nietzsche famously rejected every semblance of Christian morality, proclaiming that God is dead (see Friedrich Nietzsche, *Beyond Good and Evil*, trans. Walter Kaufmann [New York: Vintage, 1966]; Friedrich Nietzsche, *On the Genealogy of Morals*, trans. Walter Kaufmann and R. J. Hollingdale [New York: Vintage, 1967]; and Friedrich Nietzsche, *The Antichrist*, in *The Portable Nietzsche*, trans. Walter Kaufmann [New York: Penguin Books, 1982]) and that the modern agent's motivation for morality must be the will to power alone.

34. Lutz, *Reading Alasdair MacIntyre's "After Virtue,"* 108.

Greek term *aretē* comes from the Homeric poems and, as we saw in chapter 6, is typically translated as "virtue," but it has to do with human excellence of any kind.[35] For heroic societies, "the exercise of a virtue exhibits qualities which are required for sustaining a social role and for exhibiting excellence in some well-marked area of social practice."[36] In other words, virtues demonstrate a person's excellence within a community. A moral education is thus needed to help us grasp and desire those actions that make us better and more virtuous people. MacIntyre believes we should adopt this sense of communal virtue formation for our modern context.

One difference between MacIntyre and Aristotle is that Aristotle saw his sense of virtue as universally true, whereas MacIntyre understands virtue formation to be historically tied to an ongoing tradition.[37] A modern sense of training in the virtues understands its place in history, acknowledging that there are competing worldviews that coexist. Each community maintains its own narrative and its own sense of excellence, so virtues will differ from community to community. This does not equate to relativism, but it does acknowledge pluralism. It's pluralistic in the sense that it recognizes a plurality of competing narratives, each with its own normative practices and set of virtues. It's not relativistic, however, because it never states that each community has an *equally valid* sense of the world or that the truth is true only to them. It's impossible to stand at a point of narrative neutrality to determine which view is correct; this is not the same as saying that every narrative tradition is correct.

MacIntyre also notices a paradox concerning virtues: "Only insofar as we have already arrived at certain conclusions are we able to become the sort of person able to engage in such enquiry so as to reach sound conclusions."[38] In other words, if a person desires to live a virtuous life, the society the person is a part of must have already elevated certain characteristics as being virtuous. This means that a moral judgment was already made by the society, a judgment with which the person implicitly agrees since he or she chooses to model his or her life accordingly. MacIntyre acknowledges this paradox as something inevitable. Virtues are formed out of communities and traditions—a person does not come to an understanding of virtues in isolation because they are born socially out of community. Thus, a "rational teaching authority" is needed to establish and extend the moral habits deemed to be virtuous in a society's moral inquiry.[39] The teacher is part of the tradition and passes down its precepts

35. MacIntyre, *After Virtue*, 143.
36. MacIntyre, *After Virtue*, 218.
37. Lutz, *Reading Alasdair MacIntyre's "After Virtue,"* 112.
38. Alasdair MacIntyre, *Three Rival Versions of Moral Enquiry: Encyclopaedia, Genealogy, and Tradition* (Notre Dame, IN: University of Notre Dame Press, 1990), 63.
39. MacIntyre, *Three Rival Versions*, 63.

to new constituents. The student doesn't blindly follow the traditions of the community but "rescrutinizes" a community's values so they genuinely become his or hers.[40] This accounts for changes in social thinking, as what is deemed virtuous shifts and changes over time. One can always trace the genealogy of the virtue, observing its adaptation and revision.

MacIntyre's ethical system, as noted above, isn't a *Christian* ethics per se, but it does give Christian ethicists some great points to consider. MacIntyre provides a legitimate critique of the individualistic emotivism of modern ethics and paves the way for an ethical system that's focused on teleology, communal accountability, and virtue formation. A renewal ethics can take each of these points from MacIntyre and apply them directly to a renewal worldview. Just as MacIntyre recognizes that there are many different traditions with their own moral virtues, we can look at the renewal movement as a formational tradition. The renewal *telos* is to be Christlike and Spirit-filled, so Pentecostals are habituated into community-formed practices that cultivate renewal virtues and help believers accomplish that *telos*. The virtues that make up a renewal perspective on ethics will be discussed further in the next chapter.

Hauerwas and Narrative Ethics

Many forms of modern ethics look at moral concerns as rational problems to be solved, but this makes ethics merely a branch of decision theory.[41] Instead of just looking at ethics as a set of decisions, we can look at the narrative that forms us into the moral people we want to be.[42] Story connects us to each other and gives us a sense of belonging. Hearing other people's stories helps us grow as we empathize and identify with them. Rather than observing universal moral rules or principles, we can gain ethical insight from the stories we listen to and claim as our own. This sort of thinking has led to the fairly recent development of narrative ethics.

Narrative ethics is an approach to ethics that focuses on story for ethical deliberations. It sees a person's narrative as being tied to a larger community's story. As such, a person's moral reasoning is inextricably linked to his or her narrative context. The narrative ethicist would say that a person's moral life follows the form of a story. A person's context influences even the structures from which he or she reasons. Paul Simmons puts it well: "Story is basic, theories

40. MacIntyre, *Three Rival Versions*, 201.
41. Stanley Hauerwas and David Burrell, "From System to Story: An Alternative Pattern for Rationality in Ethics," in *Why Narrative? Readings in Narrative Theology*, ed. Stanley Hauerwas and L. Gregory Jones (Grand Rapids: Eerdmans, 1989), 163.
42. Hauerwas and Burrell, "From System to Story," 167.

and processes are derivative. The formation of character as well as the shape of moral discourse, central paradigms, images and metaphors depend upon the narrative to which they belong."[43] In other words, the events experienced and choices made are interpreted through an overarching life story.

As we'll see, the field of narrative ethics is rooted in the virtue tradition, so MacIntyre is a major dialogue partner to many narrative ethicists. This is certainly the case for Stanley Hauerwas, who's arguably the most respected proponent of Christian narrative ethics.[44] In his classic book *A Community of Character*, Hauerwas constructs a Christian social ethic that's rooted in the Christian narrative. He argues that Christian morality only makes sense as a continuation of the overarching Christian story. Like MacIntyre, Hauerwas believes it's not possible to come to ethical convictions without a teleological end in sight. Since ethical principles should be those that help us become the people or society we want to be, Christian convictions should support the vision for what kind of community the church desires to be.[45] The church should strive to reflect the kingdom of God, and the basis of a Christian ethics should be to affirm that God has called Christians to take up God's story and help expand the kingdom of God on earth. The church is not the kingdom of God, but it can exist and function in such a way that it makes the kingdom of God visible to others.[46]

For Hauerwas, the Christian narrative must be the basis for a Christian social ethics. As he writes, "The social significance of the Gospel requires the recognition of the narrative structure of Christian convictions for the life of the church."[47] The church is a "story-formed community," and Jesus "determines the story as the crucial person in the story."[48] Being part of the kingdom of God requires taking up Christ's story and learning to follow him. In other words, it requires discipleship. Cruciform discipleship, for Hauerwas, is tied to being fully integrated into God's community: "To be a disciple is to be part of a new community, a new polity, which is formed on Jesus's obedience to the cross. The constitutions of this new polity are the Gospels. The Gospels are not just the depiction of a man, but they are manuals for the training necessary to be

43. Paul Simmons, "The Narrative Ethics of Stanley Hauerwas: A Question of Method," in *Secular Bioethics in Theological Perspective*, ed. Earl Shelp (New York: Kluwer Academic, 1997), 159.

44. Hauerwas, the longtime Duke University professor, was named "America's Best Theologian" by *Time Magazine* in 2012.

45. Stanley Hauerwas, *A Community of Character: Toward a Constructive Christian Social Ethic* (Notre Dame, IN: University of Notre Dame Press, 1981), 1.

46. Stanley Hauerwas, *The Peaceable Kingdom: A Primer in Christian Ethics* (Notre Dame, IN: University of Notre Dame Press, 1983), 97.

47. Hauerwas, *Community of Character*, 9.

48. Hauerwas, *Community of Character*, 43.

part of the new community. To be a disciple means to share Christ's story, to participate in the reality of God's rule."[49] Because Jesus is the prime actor of the story, we can look to him as our ultimate moral model. It is through Christ that we are grafted into God's larger narrative, and as the prime actor, Christ perfectly demonstrates virtuous human action. Thus, our Christian virtues are necessarily rooted in Christ's witness.

Sometimes the virtue tradition appears too individualistic as it calls for individual moral agents to better themselves by training in the virtues. Hauerwas, however, reminds us about the social character of the virtues. He writes, "The individual virtues are specific skills required to live faithful to a tradition's understanding of the moral project in which its adherents participate."[50] In other words, virtue formation helps situate us into our community's moral project. The moral project of the Christian tradition is to live a cruciform life that expands the kingdom of God on earth, so Christian virtues help us pursue goals that are both individual and communal.

Moral formation also occurs by submitting to the Bible. In fact, the willing submission to scriptural authority is a significant way the church contrasts itself with the world, which desires freedom from all authorities. While many Christian ethics see the Bible as a foundational rule for moral formation, Hauerwas sees scriptural authority in a different light. Hauerwas believes Scripture can act as a moral guide but should not be seen as providing a rigid morality to follow. The Bible isn't a mere rule book of moral standards; rather, it "provides the resources necessary for the church to be a community sufficiently truthful so that our conversation with one another and God can continue across generations."[51] Because the Bible points to Jesus, it points to truth. When Christians try to live in faithfulness to the biblical witness, they are living in faithfulness to the truth.[52]

A major goal of Christian ethics is to form individuals and communities in such a way that the church becomes a witness of the kingdom of God to the world. Accordingly, then, a Christian ethics is by nature a social ethics.[53] When the church acts in a truly loving and gracious way that's totally indicative of Christ, then it becomes a desirable alternative community in our violent, fractured world.[54] It is only when the world longs to be like the church that the church can help shape the world's *telos*. Unfortunately, however, the church's

---

49. Hauerwas, *Community of Character*, 49.
50. Hauerwas, *Community of Character*, 115.
51. Hauerwas, *Community of Character*, 64.
52. Hauerwas, *Community of Character*, 66.
53. Hauerwas, *Peaceable Kingdom*, 97.
54. Hauerwas, *Peaceable Kingdom*, 6.

witness is jaded and variegated. The church struggles to demonstrate a clear vision of the kingdom of God because it is internally ravaged by moral conflict.

As discussed in chapter 5, the church gets so caught up in the political realm that it lets political matters seep into its identity. Instead of being an alternative community in the world, the church more frequently links up with a political party and helps extend a political agenda. The way the church should be involved politically is by setting a powerful example of what the kingdom of God looks like in the world, not by adopting a party's ideals and merging them with the Christian faith. As Hauerwas writes, "The gospel is a political gospel. Christians are engaged in politics, but it is a politics of the kingdom that reveals the insufficiency of all politics based on coercion and falsehood and finds the true source of power in servanthood rather than dominion."[55] The church is an alternative to the world's polity when it advocates for peace instead of war, love instead of hate, service instead of power, contentment instead of control, and belonging instead of ostracization. At its best, it acts politically by demonstrating Christ's polity, the polity of the kingdom of God, not by perpetuating the polity of an earthly kingdom. For Hauerwas, the call to make the kingdom of God visible in the world requires living peaceably through Christian love in a world ravaged by sin.

Hauerwas's narrative approach to ethics can be adopted and adapted for a renewal ethics. Further developing the virtue tradition, Hauerwas highlights the role of the community in moral formation as we're grafted into a community's narrative. Taking this approach, we can evaluate the renewal tradition and see how the Acts 2 narrative of the universal outpouring shapes our moral reasoning. Hauerwas sees the kingdom of God as the *telos* of a Christian social ethics, and a renewal ethics can add to this view by clarifying that it is the Spirit who enables the kingdom's eschatological future to break into the present. The kingdom of God is already here and not yet fulfilled, so when we experience the Spirit of Christ at work in the world, we're experiencing a foretaste of the kingdom where Christ reigns supreme. Such a narrative approach to ethics fits perfectly in a renewal worldview that advocates for holistic formation.

Conclusion

As we briefly consider the thought of three of the past century's most influential ethicists, we can see how a renewal ethics might begin to form and fit within a renewal worldview. Niebuhr's Christian realism helps us recognize the atrocities going on around us and call out the futility of weak religious

---

55. Hauerwas, *Peaceable Kingdom*, 102.

ideology when it comes to solving the world's most pressing issues. While it fails to show the true extent and power of Jesus's ethic of love, it does give us the vocabulary for dealing with moral and social issues. MacIntyre shows us that ethical systems fail when they do not have a true *telos* guiding their moral actions. We can retrieve a social teleology that helps us envision the types of people we want to be and the type of nation we want to be a part of. Finally, Hauerwas shows us that the narrative nature of moral reasoning avoids the ethical compromises that can occur in Christian realism. Acting according to a *telos* that's rooted in the kingdom of God allows us to become a true witness in the world, both individually and socially, through the church.

As we move ahead in crafting a renewal ethics, we will apply the Acts 2 narrative of renewal to our own version of narrative ethics. We will see how the universal outpouring of the Holy Spirit affects our holistic formation and commissions us to carry out the ministry of reconciliation around the world. This Spirit formation radicalizes Jesus's ethic of love by empowering us to train in virtue as we conform to Christ's image and work in the power of the Spirit to bear witness all over the world. We will take a realistic look at the state of our world and will avoid pie-in-the-sky ideological proclamations, but we will fully recognize Christ's ethic of love to be foundational for all Christian living.

Study Questions

1. How does being a disciple differ from just being a student?

2. According to Niebuhr, what does it mean to take a realist approach to individual and social ethics?

3. Explain why MacIntyre believes modern ethical systems have failed.

4. How does a narrative approach to ethics flow out of the virtue tradition?

+ 8 +

A Renewal Perspective on Goodness, Ethics, and Civic Engagement

Key Words

Euangelion: *Translated as "gospel" or "good news"; its central message is the kingdom of God.*

Gnosticism: *A late first-century movement that saw the body and the material world as evil and believed that salvation is attained through gaining secret gnosis (knowledge).*

Graded absolutism: *The ethical theory that moral conflict can be resolved by choosing the higher moral principle.*

Justice: *The fair and equitable treatment of people in a society.*

Reconciliation: *The end of any estrangement between God and others that was brought about by sin.*

Repentance: *The act of changing one's mind and behavior to realign with God's purpose.*

What's the difference between *doing* good and *being* good? Or to pose this question another way, can we separate our moral decision-making from our virtuous character? We have argued throughout part 2 of this book that such a separation is not really possible. Because we're holistic beings, our virtuous characters are inextricably linked to whatever methods we use to make moral decisions. We're embodied and narratively contextualized, so our modes of reasoning and operating are bound up with our individual experiences and communal interpretations of events. Right actions emerge from and influence our experiences and beliefs. We've thus advocated for a triperspec-tival approach to morality in a renewal worldview. Looking for a *telos* to guide our renewal ethics, we called Christian love the cardinal virtue that situates every other virtue. *Our love guides our right actions, and our actions animate our goodness.* This chapter teases out what exactly this approach entails, first by looking at what the renewal narrative tells us about loving God and others, and then by considering what it means to live peaceably in a reconciled reality.

We'll begin by outlining the guiding narrative of the renewal movement. This gives us a basis for our ethical system before we discuss what sorts of narrative-specific virtues extend moral formation in a renewal ethics. We will see how the Spirit equips, empowers, and forms us morally to live virtuously in the kingdom of God. Then, returning to the notion of Christian love discussed in chapter 5, we will explore what it means to call love the chief virtue of a renewal ethics. We'll apply our triperspectival approach to ethical reasoning and recognize reconciliation as the appropriate *telos* of a renewal social ethic. This chapter ties together all the threads from chapters 5, 6, and 7 to present a renewal ethics that supports a renewal worldview.

The Narrative of Renewal Ethics

The general Christian narrative often revolves around salvation in terms of what Jesus did on the cross. The cross and resurrection are, after all, the pivotal moments of our justification. By Christ's sacrifice we are forgiven, which opens the door for us to reenter the kingdom of God. Salvation in a renewal narrative, however, comprises more than merely the removal of condemnation (justifica-tion); it also comprises ongoing cruciform discipleship. Living a life of renewal means we're living a holistic, Spirit-filled life. Jesus didn't die on the cross so that we'd simply acknowledge he's God or recognize we are forgiven—he died so that we could be fully reintegrated into God's family. Jesus didn't launch a philosophical movement but inaugurated a kingdom that began at the incar-nation and then was proclaimed throughout Christ's ministry, unlocked at the cross, and universalized at Pentecost. The story of renewal looks at salvation in a fuller sense that moves beyond mere justification to life in the Spirit.

Can the essence of the gospel be distilled down to Jesus's vicarious death leading to our everlasting life with him if we believe in and confess his lord-ship? If so, it's interesting that Jesus never made this distillation an essential part of his message. In fact, he never commanded people to believe that he will die for their sins so that they can have a personal relationship and eternal life with him. Rather, the central message of the *euangelion*, translated as "gospel" or "good news," is the kingdom of God. When we ask our students how they understand the kingdom, many reply that it is a spiritual heaven that will be their eternal home upon their death (the resurrection is rarely ever mentioned).

This understanding of the gospel and kingdom encourages the belief that the purpose of life is to believe in a message about God that has not been made available to everyone, which will allow us to leave this dying world behind to live blissfully in a spiritual realm with God. Not only does this view differ from the gospel Jesus preached; it's also closer to the heretical view called **Gnosticism**, the late first-century movement that saw the body and the material world as evil and believed that salvation is attained through gaining secret *gnosis* (knowledge). Whether it's Gnostic or not, the popular theology of personal "believe-ism" does not afford much raw material to develop an ethics that is relevant to our involvement in the world, let alone one that is faithful to the gospel of Jesus Christ. Rather than teaching easy believe-ism, Jesus taught that the kingdom of God (or heaven) is realized through him.

King Jesus returned to restore a kingdom that vanquishes evil through acts of mercy, justice, and sacrificial love, which his followers are to imitate. When we realize that Jesus's ministry is as critical to the gospel as his crucifixion because it depicts the intrusion of God's kingdom in this world, we can see how the Christian life is not merely individualistic and private. For we must seriously consider the moral imperative to advance the kingdom as imitators of its king. If we disregard that Jesus's central mission was to preach the coming kingdom that aims to bring holistic salvation, we will simply perpetuate an easy believe-ism that justifies sinners without any sacrifice. We must then wonder why a theology with only a crucified messiah would require the bulk of the Gospels, which have very little direct connection to his crucifixion. If our redemption requires only Jesus's death, then Jesus could have been simply caught and executed (as a baby) by Herod. But God's plan was to preserve Jesus (hence, the angel warning Joseph of Herod's plan in Matt. 2:13–15) so that Jesus could grow up and, through his ministry, teach us what it truly means to be a Spirit-saturated human who is living in and advancing the kingdom of God.

For Pentecostal theologian Frank Macchia, Christ's story doesn't climax with the cross and the ascension. Rather, looking at the whole narrative arc of Christ's life and ministry, Pentecost is the natural climax because it is where "the Spirit Baptizer [Christ] pours forth the Spirit on all flesh and incorporates us into himself—into the life and mission of the triune God."[1] This marks the birth of the church and the transfer of the kingdom-building ministry of Christ to the church. Since *only God can give God,* Pentecost fully and finally affirms the

---

1. Frank Macchia, *Jesus the Spirit Baptizer: Christology in Light of Pentecost* (Grand Rapids: Eerdmans, 2018), 64.

deity of Christ our Lord. Pentecost also shows that the Christian life constitutes not simply believe-ism but our full incorporation into the life in the Spirit and citizenship in the kingdom. Macchia puts it well: "His entire journey, from his incarnation to his crucifixion and resurrection, creates the means by which he incorporates all flesh into his life in the Spirit, his life with the Father. Mediating a river of the Spirit for others on behalf of the Father reveals Christ's very identity and mission."[2] A renewal ethics thus reflects on what it means to live a holistic life in the Spirit. To get a sense of what virtue formation looks like in a renewal ethics, we will consider its narrative-specific virtues next.

The Narrative-Specific Virtues of the Kingdom

Leading a just and righteous life is not merely deontological or consequential; rather, it requires the formation of virtues toward an intended *telos*. An unjust person cannot lead a consistently just life. One who loves idolatrous pleasures and enthrones himself on the seat of moral autonomy desires neither God's kingdom nor the pleasures of submitting to the kingly authority of Jesus. The Beatitudes (Matt. 5:1–12) describe the character traits of kingdom citizens. They show what sorts of virtues form us into God's vision of faithful citizenship.

The poor in spirit are blessed because they recognize that the world has failed them, so they throw themselves wholly into the care of God, who delivers them. To those who put God as their one and only point of trust, God promises to give the kingdom.

God blesses those who mourn. Mourning doesn't mean always being dour and gloomy. On the contrary, we see joy as an important theme throughout Scripture! But those who mourn are blessed because a contrite heart is necessary for repentance. They see their personal and communal sins and have a desire for change. God promises them comfort. One who does not see the need for mourning requires no comforting.

God blesses the meek. The meek are not doormats, inviting others to step all over them. Rather, they have subjugated their autonomy and completely surrendered themselves to God, becoming God's willing vessels. Unlike the zealots who sought to expel the Romans through military victory, those who have surrendered to God in meekness become vessels of peace—a worthy endeavor that is not for the faint of heart or for doormats—just as God is the God of peace (Rom. 15:33). To the meek, God promises the earth.

Blessed are those who hunger and thirst for just righteousness because they will be filled with it. As God restores the broken to wholeness through overturn-

---

2. Macchia, *Jesus the Spirit Baptizer*, 27.

ing injustice and evil, God will deliver wholeness and flourishing to those who seek just righteousness. This is God's promise; this is the way of the kingdom.

The merciful are blessed because they imitate God in acts of deliverance. God demands justice, mercy, and faithfulness, which make up the "weightier matters of the law" (Matt. 23:23). Just as God shows mercy to us, we are to imitate God by showing mercy to others. When we do, God promises that we will be shown mercy.

The pure in heart are blessed because they will see God. The heart is the central part of the human being. The heart is either directed toward God or toward idols. People's speech exposes what's in their hearts (Matt. 15:11). A heart devoted fully to God will have a consistency of faithful worship and care for others and not of self-glorification. Those who have postured themselves fully toward God will see God.

God blesses the peacemakers because God is a reconciler who sent Jesus, the Prince of Peace, to reconcile fallen humanity with the creator. The radicality of this reality is that God made peace with enemies. When we fight for peace, especially on behalf of those who lack the fullness of *shalom* in their lives, we imitate God and are called God's children.

Finally, those who fight for just righteousness will inevitably face persecution. Their fiercest critics may even come from within their own group. When people benefit from social sins, they are strongly motivated to maintain the status quo. However, loyalty to Jesus and his just kingdom takes precedence over earthly power and authority. Citizens of the just kingdom who struggle for its advancement will receive God's kingdom.[3]

Practicing the Beatitudes habitually forms our character. We will gain the eyes and ears to see and hear, and our hearts will posture toward God and others. We will know God and discern God's voice better as we are led by the Spirit and become conformed more and more into the image of Christ. This is the virtue perspective of kingdom ethics. But enacting the Beatitudes is also necessary because they aim for the consequence of realizing *shalom* in the world. They are thus not optional for Christians. They are deontological commands to be performed. Failure to practice them renders us as salt that has lost its saltiness and light that is hidden (Matt. 5:13–16).

The Beatitudes provide us a road map for understanding virtue formation for any kingdom ethics, and when we understand them through the lens of Pentecost, it's clear that these virtues lead to holistic life in the Spirit. The Spirit poured out on all flesh universalizes the justifying gift of the cross and guides

3. David P. Gushee and Glen H. Stassen, *Kingdom Ethics: Following Jesus in Contemporary Context*, 2nd ed. (Grand Rapids: Eerdmans, 2016), 27–36.

and forms us in Christ's image. If you recall, in chapter 5 we said that the guiding value of a renewal ethics is Christian love, so all the virtues discussed above spell out ways to love better. For the rest of this chapter, we'll explore how the central value of love and the virtues of the kingdom guide our moral formation (loving God) and our civic and political engagements (loving others). We will also explain how to engage in ethical triperspectival reasoning.

Loving God and Making Ethical Decisions

"And now faith, hope, and love abide, these three; and the greatest of these is love" (1 Cor. 13:13). Christians have long considered faith, hope, and love as the theological virtues that complement the four cardinal Greek virtues of wisdom, justice, courage, and temperance. Among these, love is the chief of the virtues because it represents the essence of God and the end for which all things exist. Craig Boyd and Don Thorsen explain beautifully: "The love of God is the reason for all that exists; it animates all creation. . . . The aim of ethics can be seen as a call to love others since God is love and calls all people to loving relationships with one another."[4] For Christians, and Pentecostals specifically, love must be the driving force of ethics. We must not only use love as the lens through which we reflect ethically on our moral reality; we must also embody love as a dispositional virtue inculcated in us through en-graced habit.

Spirit Baptism and Love

Love has two dimensions. It is the work of God's grace, on the one hand, and it is our habituated work, on the other. Although we need both God's grace and our own work in order to love, grace takes precedence because love is impossible without it. Love belongs first and foremost in the will and not in the emotions. Love must be directed by God because human loves and emotions are erratic and too easily misdirected due to the corrupting effects of sin. To truly love, our hearts must be directed to good as such—to God—which is only possible through divine aid. This en-graced love makes our participation in God's love possible, thereby allowing us to love God and love our (sometimes hated) neighbors.[5]

For Pentecostals, Spirit baptism is this en-gracing moment. Spirit baptism is not merely an empowering event for mission and for the renewal of the

4. Craig A. Boyd and Don Thorsen, *Christian Ethics and Moral Philosophy: An Introduction to Issues and Approaches* (Grand Rapids: Baker Academic, 2018), 174.

5. Boyd and Thorsen, *Christian Ethics*, 179.

church. As Macchia powerfully states, "Spirit baptism is a baptism into the *love of God* that sanctifies, renews, and empowers until Spirit baptism turns all of creation into the final dwelling place of God."[6] The timing and language of Spirit baptism need not deter us here. Renewal Christians the world over will have different understandings of Spirit baptism, but the central idea is the same: the Spirit works to baptize creation into the love of God because God's love expressed through Jesus "has been poured into our hearts through the Holy Spirit" (Rom. 5:5). Both the beginning and end of creation is the love of God as mediated through the Spirit. Loving God and loving people both begin with the Spirit's work in us.

Loving God requires our formation into Christ's image through the work of the Spirit. We can tend to think of this work in private terms within the context of the worship service: we allow the Spirit to move our hearts toward God as we passionately seek after God in the pews and at the altar. While encountering God in worship settings is an important aspect of the renewed life, the moral dimension of our transformation requires our interaction with others in different settings.

Loving God and loving people are perspectivally integrated as two sides of the same coin. If we don't love God, we will lack the fullness of divine grace to heal our will to love properly. If we don't love people, then we must question our response to God's grace and our love for God. Living in freedom through Christ requires serving others humbly in love (Gal. 5:13). The rest of Galatians 5 is critical here:

> For the whole law is summed up in a single commandment, "You shall love your neighbor as yourself." If, however, you bite and devour one another, take care that you are not consumed by one another.
>
> Live by the Spirit, I say, and do not gratify the desires of the flesh. For what the flesh desires is opposed to the Spirit, and what the Spirit desires is opposed to the flesh; for these are opposed to each other, to prevent you from doing what you want. But if you are led by the Spirit, you are not subject to the law. Now the works of the flesh are obvious: fornication, impurity, licentiousness, idolatry, sorcery, enmities, strife, jealousy, anger, quarrels, dissensions, factions, envy, drunkenness, carousing, and things like these. I am warning you, as I warned you before: those who do such things will not inherit the kingdom of God.
>
> By contrast, the fruit of the Spirit is love, joy, peace, patience, kindness, generosity, faithfulness, gentleness, and self-control. There is no law against such things. And those who belong to Christ Jesus have crucified the flesh with its

6. Frank Macchia, *Baptized in the Spirit: A Global Pentecostal Theology* (Grand Rapids: Zondervan, 2006), 60 (italics added).

passions and desires. If we live by the Spirit, let us also be guided by the Spirit. Let us not become conceited, competing against one another, envying one another. (vv. 14–26)

Participating in the grace of the Spirit develops the fruit of the Spirit, which are virtues or positive character traits.[7] As virtues, they require our habitual practice. We must arduously practice love, joy, peace, patience, kindness, generosity, faithfulness, gentleness, and self-control, and with the grace of the Spirit, we will become people who embody these virtues. Through them, we will better love people and thus love God.

Virtues are interpersonally directed, as evidenced by the context of the passage. We express them toward others. When we do, we fulfill the entirety of the law. Contrarily, when we develop vices, we create dangerous interpersonal, social conditions.[8] The passage even warns that vicious people will not inherit the kingdom of God. This warning is unsurprising given that the described vices are not conducive to creating social flourishing (*eudaimonia* or *shalom*), which is the goal of the kingdom. Personal transformation, which includes moral transformation, is necessary for loving God and loving people. Therefore, just as Spirit baptism takes central precedence in a renewal worldview, personal transformation motivated by the love of the Spirit must also take center stage. Loving God requires this trinitarian transformation into the image of Christ through the baptism of the Spirit, which turns us into the dwelling place of God.

Triperspectival Ethics

Loving God is perspectivally related to loving people. Ethical decisions that impact this love saturate our everyday lives, so we must learn to make right ethical decisions. The personal and moral transformation discussed above falls under virtue ethics. However, renewal ethics is not synonymous with virtue ethics. As mentioned in the Beatitudes section above ("The Narrative-Specific Virtues of the Kingdom"), deontological and teleological perspectives are necessary for a holistic ethics. Our triperspectival approach considers the three ethical theories not as separate and opposing theories but as perspectives of the whole of our moral reality. While this theory is motivated by John Frame, the kingdom ethics of David Gushee and Glen Stassen is also appropriately triperspectival. They state,

7. The list does not exhaust the virtues in Scripture. See D. S. Dockery, "Fruit of the Spirit," in *Dictionary of Paul and His Letters*, ed. Gerald F. Hawthorne, Ralph P. Martin, and Daniel G. Reid (Downers Grove, IL: InterVarsity, 1993), 317–18.

8. James Montgomery Boice, "Galatians," in *The Expositor's Bible Commentary*, ed. Frank E. Gaebelein (Grand Rapids: Zondervan, 1976), 10:496.

The difference between deontologists, teleologists, and characterologists [that is, virtue ethics] . . . pertain[s] to what they base their moral norms on, or, as we are saying here, the *mode* in which they reason: obligation to do right, pursuit of a good end, or embodying God's character.

We believe a Jesus-centered ethic takes divine commands seriously and is vigorously deontological. But it understands the mandates and teachings of Jesus to be gracious and authoritative *invitations to become people (characterological) who do the will of God (deontological) and participate in the coming of the kingdom of God (teleological)*. Christians are to "go . . . be reconciled to your brother or sister" (Mt 5:24) because we are obligated to obey Jesus's command (deontological), because this breaks the cycle of relational brokenness and brings about peace (teleological), and because this fits the nature of the Christ who heads the church (characterological).[9]

The triperspectival ethics we promote is not strictly Pentecostal. Frame, Gushee, and Stassen are not Pentecostals. However, as we argue below, renewal ethics is properly triperspectival.

The logic of Pentecostalism has always been triperspectival. As Steven Land has argued, Pentecostalism is a triperspectival spirituality that integrates right beliefs and practices in the affections. The affections are the integrating core, but they do not have primacy since they themselves get expressed by the beliefs and practices.[10] This relationship is a continual spiral that involves each element and defines Pentecostal spirituality. Its ethics is similarly triperspectival, even if Pentecostals have not consciously used a triperspectival method.

Deontologically, Pentecostals have always taken God's commands seriously, placing principles in the driver's seat of ethical decisions. Teleologically, the return of Jesus motivates missional end-times kingdom work, which occurs through the Spirit-empowered life. This life motivates not only individual healing but also healing of the social body by empowering the marginalized.[11] *Aretaically*, the desire to become a holy people motivates moral choices. Obeying God's commands, working for the kingdom, and becoming a holy people are not disparate and competing ethical goals. Renewal ethics operates through these interrelated works.

Borrowing from Frame, we can envision triperspectival ethics as the interrelationship between normative/deontological, situational/teleological, and existential/virtue perspectives.

---

9. Gushee and Stassen, *Kingdom Ethics*, 79–80.

10. Steven J. Land, *Pentecostal Spirituality: A Passion for the Kingdom* (Cleveland: CPT, 2010), 1.

11. See Darío Andrés López Rodríguez, "The Redeeming Community: The God of Life and the Community of Life," in *Toward a Pentecostal Ecclesiology: The Church and the Fivefold Gospel*, ed. John Christopher Thomas (Cleveland: CPT, 2010), 80–82.

Figure 8.1

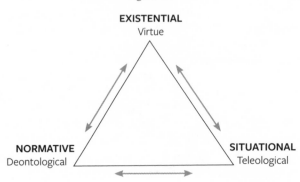

EXISTENTIAL
Virtue

NORMATIVE   **SITUATIONAL**
Deontological   Teleological

As the lines of figure 8.1 indicate, we can't have one without the other. We must consider how each perspective informs the other two, and no perspective is more important than the others. Therefore, we can enter into triperspectival examination from any perspective.

The situational perspective considers the best possible consequences of our actions.[12] It also examines how each situation contextualizes the relevancy of moral principles and virtues to determine which ones are applicable and more important. The normative perspective considers the relevant moral principles and obligations. We must ask how Scripture informs our situation.[13] However, we must also consult the whole of divine revelation, not just Scripture, especially when Scripture is not definitive on the matter.[14] The existential perspective involves our own moral development in practicing our ethical decisions. This perspective drives us to ask, "How must I change if I am to do God's will?"[15] It also involves the necessity of moral development in order to "read" the moral situation with wisdom and clarity and discern how norms and situations relate to one another. In all this, we must always remember that our ethical reasoning occurs within our social locations. Ethical reasoning and action are best done within intellectually and morally virtuous communities that help uncover blind spots and provide guidance in love and wisdom.

12. John M. Frame, *The Doctrine of the Christian Life* (Phillipsburg, NJ: P&R, 2008), 33.
13. Frame, *Doctrine of the Christian Life*, 33–35.
14. We must remember that understanding Scripture is itself perspectival. The "clarity" of our understanding of Scripture may be due to our own biases. In interpreting Scripture, we recommend consciously consulting the four aspects of the Wesleyan Quadrilateral: Scripture, reason, tradition, and experience. Even the most "literal" understanding of Scripture is informed by reason, tradition, and experience. Since our theological reading of Scripture is always already perspectivally informed by the Wesleyan Quadrilateral, we should become aware of this reality, be honest about it, and do it better.
15. Frame, *Doctrine of the Christian Life*, 34.

The key to triperspectival ethics is recognizing the complexity of our moral context. Much of our moral reality is not black and white. Given this dynamic nature, we shouldn't be surprised that moral principles will sometimes not be universally binding. Some principles will be universally applicable while others will not, but universality is always context dependent and never absolute (i.e., unqualified)—in other words, they may not be universal as such, but no situation or virtue warrants their violation. For example, we are confident that torturing babies out of desire for depraved pleasure is a universally condemnable principle. Adultery is another universal evil. The universal applicability is their context. No situation seems to provide sound reason for their moral approval.[16] The virtuous or vicious will impacts the quality of the principles' actualization. Universal moral truths are thus never absolute and unqualified. They are not mere objective facts for subjective recognition. We are always already involved in the determination of universal moral rules as ethical beings. Similarly, other principles are not universal because particular situations condition their importance and relevance.

Several scriptural examples help illustrate the dynamic nature of principles, which we will note in parentheses throughout these examples. First, consider the famous example of Rahab and the Jewish spies. Two principles are in conflict in this story: telling the truth and saving lives. If it's universally wrong to lie, Rahab should not have lied. Yet, not only is she excused for her lying, but she is one of the four women in Jesus's genealogy (Matt. 1:5) and is included in the "hall of faith" (Heb. 11:31) for giving sanctuary to the spies.[17] According to Norman Geisler, conflict of moral principles can be solved by **graded absolutism**, the theory that unavoidable moral conflicts can be resolved by choosing the higher moral principle.[18] In Rahab's case, the principle of saving lives is more important than telling the truth. The situational/teleological context determines the greater value of this principle, and an existential/virtuous (e.g., compassionate) person should choose to save lives by lying rather than telling the truth that will lead to certain death. Graded absolutism thus runs on triperspectival logic.

16. Perhaps we can imagine a "trolley" type of scenario in which a person must either torture a baby for pleasure or refuse and let a psychopath detonate a nuclear bomb in a crowded city. However, this context does not apply to the moral norm against infant torture since uncoerced pleasure from torture and coercion to seek pleasure from torture are different. Therefore, the universal applicability against this torture is context dependent in that there seems to be no context that allows for torturing babies for pleasure.

17. Rahab is esteemed for welcoming and giving lodging to the spies. However, part of this act included the deceptive act of hiding and lying about their whereabouts. If she had brought them in only to reveal their locations by telling the truth, her reception wouldn't have been welcoming.

18. Norman L. Geisler, *Christian Ethics: Options and Issues* (Grand Rapids: Baker Academic, 1989), 116–17.

Although Sabbath-keeping is a deontological principle of the Ten Commandments, Jesus forcefully teaches that the Sabbath was made for humans as a blessing (Mark 2:23–28).[19] Rigid, purely deontological Sabbath-keeping does not follow the spirit of the law that was given as a blessing to people. The situation/teleology determines the applicability of Sabbath-keeping, and its violation is warranted in certain circumstances.[20] The context of people's personality can even influence the form of Sabbath-keeping. Introverts often rest by having alone time. Extroverts, on the other hand, often recharge by spending time with others. For couples with opposite personality traits, how they keep the Sabbath will look different and should be negotiated.[21] Without recognition of these different contextual elements, Sabbath-keeping will look unyielding and oppressive to many who don't identify with the parameters of Sabbath rest as dictated by the cultural elites.

A dispute about the place of Jewish law for gentile Christians arose in the early church, as recorded in Acts 15. In this passage, some Jewish Christian leaders from the Pharisees insist that gentile Christians must be circumcised and follow Mosaic law. Upon hearing the testimonies of Peter, Paul, and Barnabas about how gentile Christians received the Holy Spirit and had their hearts purified by faith, James and the Jerusalem Council conclude that gentile Christians are not required to keep the entire Mosaic law. The council uses their virtue of wisdom to discern the life-setting of gentile Christians and the situational/teleological goal for their decision to create a set of short deontological rules that gentile Christians should follow: "to abstain only from things polluted by idols and from fornication and from whatever has been strangled and from blood" (Acts 15:20). According to Charles Talbert, these laws were the bare minimum to allow Jews to interact with gentiles, harking back to the Levitical laws that applied to Jews and non-Jews who sojourned together (Lev. 17–18).[22]

Are these universally binding New Testament moral laws as opposed to the ceremonial and civil laws that pertained only to the religious matters of the old covenant and the governing of the nation of Israel? First, it's problematic to distinguish the laws so clearly. Some ceremonial and civil laws are moral.[23] Second, it seems that the Jerusalem Council was not stripping down the Mosaic

19. In the same text, Jesus also indicates that David's eating of the consecrated bread, which is unlawful, is condoned and not sinful.

20. Walter W. Wessel, "Mark," in *The Expositor's Bible Commentary*, ed. Frank E. Gaebelein (Grand Rapids: Zondervan, 1984), 8:638.

21. See A. J. Swoboda, *Subversive Sabbath: The Surprising Power of Rest in a Nonstop World* (Grand Rapids: Brazos, 2018), 77.

22. Charles H. Talbert, *Reading Acts: A Literary and Theological Commentary on the Acts of the Apostles*, rev. ed. (Macon, GA: Smyth & Helwys, 2005), 132–33.

23. Frame, *Doctrine of the Christian Life*, 213–17.

law only to its universal moral elements for the gentile Christians. Instead, they seem to have wisely considered the situation of all those involved in an attempt to promote the most important and relevant principles that were applicable to them at that point in time, which were to allow the association between gentile and Jewish Christians. The minimal laws were needed because the Mosaic law was preached every week (Acts 15:21), and the issue of purity would be at the forefront of every Jewish Christian's mind.[24]

We see this dynamic relativity of the promoted moral law concerning food sacrificed to idols in 1 Corinthians 8–10. Corinth was a diverse, mostly gentile city. Its church reflected this diversity and was mainly a gentile church.[25] Some gentile Christians were arguing that they could continually attend cultic meals in pagan temples since they *knew* that idols were nothing more than figments of human imagination. Shouldn't they have the freedom in Christ to continually attend a social gathering that would have no negative impact on them? Here, Paul is consistent with the prescriptions of the Jerusalem Council. He forbids eating meat sacrificed to idols because this action could lead fellow Christians astray. The "weaker" brothers and sisters were likely recent converts who viewed these cultic meals as idolatrous. Observing Christians attend these cultic meals tempted them to participate as well. It was a case of "mature" knowledge leading to the destruction of the weaker Christians. However, Christian ethics "springs not from knowledge but from love."[26] Our rights take a back seat to our obligations to others. Thus, Paul gave up his rights and privileges, even becoming weak like the weak, becoming "all things to all people" (1 Cor. 9:22).

Notice, however, that Paul's reason for this prohibition is not an attempt to maintain Jewish-gentile relationships. The reasons for the continual prohibition are due to the gentiles' overconfident belief that their participation in these cultic meals will not negatively affect them and that they will somehow be immune to the cultic setting of the meals and the darker reality behind the idols: demons (1 Cor. 10:18–21). Although the moral principle (refraining from food polluted by idols) remains the same as in Acts 15, the context that motivates the principle (situation, consequences, and virtue [love]) is different. Moreover, when the context changes to meat sacrificed to idols that is sold in the marketplace for consumption in a noncultic setting, Paul condones eating the meat. It's not even a matter of conscience.[27] And because eating meat sacrificed to idols in this context is irrelevant as to conscience, Christians can choose to

24. Talbert, *Reading Acts*, 133.
25. Gordon D. Fee, *The First Epistle to the Corinthians*, The New International Commentary on the New Testament (Grand Rapids: Eerdmans, 1987), 3–4.
26. Fee, *First Epistle to the Corinthians*, 363.
27. Fee, *First Epistle to the Corinthians*, 488.

exercise the freedom to eat *or* to limit the freedom if someone else's conscience may be violated, since "the one who has pointed out the sacrificial origins of this meat to a Christian has done so out of a sense of moral obligation to the Christian, believing that Christians, like Jews, would not eat such food."[28] Since eating the meat could offend the person's expectation of Christian behavior, the Christian is to refrain from eating it. Clearly, context greatly determines the application of the Jerusalem Council's moral imperatives.

Furthermore, from a virtue perspective, we shouldn't pit knowledge against love. The Corinthians are right that idols are nothing. But rather than using that knowledge as an excuse to do what they desire, they should, motivated by love, refrain from eating *while* discipling the "weaker" Christians who were seeking to gain greater knowledge so that they too could gain greater freedom.[29] Paul himself knows how to navigate the difficulties of applying the Jerusalem Council rules because of his mature knowledge and love in the faith.

Loving God requires our (moral) transformation. Because the virtues involved in our transformation are social, our transformation is not strictly a private reality. Loving God, therefore, requires loving people. Love in action does not occur simply by obeying inflexible universal laws. Christians must discern how to love their neighbors by making ethical decisions that lead to *shalom*, to wholeness and flourishing. We recommend the triperspectival method to assess the situation and possible consequences in discerning the most important and relevant moral principle to follow. Such discernment requires growing in the virtues to gain intellectual clarity and affective intelligence. Doing so more and more will lead to transformation into the image of Christ through the grace of the Holy Spirit as we grow in love of God and neighbor. A triperspectival method, as we have seen, does not prioritize deontological, teleological, or virtue perspectives. All are central to right decision-making.

We want to also remind you that the overarching narrative through which we pursue triperspectival ethical reasoning is the Pentecostal story, centrally revolving around the Acts account of the Spirit poured out on all flesh to transform creation into the dwelling of God. This divine involvement of love serves as the basis for our moral transformation. The diversity of many tongues (and with different tongues come different ways of thinking and being) and the

---

28. Fee, *First Epistle to the Corinthians*, 485.

29. Gaining knowledge would not change the prohibition against eating in temples, however, even if cultic meals were ancient equivalents to modern-day "restaurant outings." The cultic meals had enough pagan elements to be harmful to Christians—Paul likens these meals to the communion meal, except that they invoke participation with demons rather than with God—hence, he prohibits participation in these meals, even for those who were mature enough to know the larger truth. Fee, *First Epistle to the Corinthians*, 361.

growth of the diverse early church provide the rich context that allows us to recognize the complexity of our moral reality. They provide the theological underpinning for recognizing how the old principles are modified in the new context of a Spirit-baptized world. Since renewal Christianity encompasses so many different Christian traditions, however, triperspectival reasoning will look different to each renewal community due to the additional community-specific narratives that modify the narrative (and language) of Spirit baptism. The Spirit thus stands out as the root and motivator of a renewal worldview, albeit in a triperspectival way since the acts of the Trinity are one. A renewal worldview emphasizes the perspective of the Spirit just as another worldview may be motivated christologically or even bibliocentrically.

Loving Others in Civic and Political Engagements

According to Reinhold Niebuhr's Christian realism (as discussed in the previous chapter), when Christ's command to love others is applied socially, it emerges as justice. A renewal ethics, however, makes the foundational claim that loving others equates not merely to justice but to reconciliation. Many social ethics articulate methods for making a more just society, but the kingdom of God calls us to push toward reconciliation. While **justice** refers to the fair and equitable treatment of people in a society, the theological concept of **reconciliation** constitutes the end of any estrangement between God and others that was brought about by sin. Justice strives to treat people equitably, but reconciliation reunites strangers so that they might become a family. This view of reconciliation links up with the idea that salvation is more than justification (justice); it constitutes a life of cruciform discipleship (reconciliation). Reconciliation goes further than justice, making *it* the end result Jesus calls us to when he commands us to love. Thus, reconciliation with God and with others is the *telos* of Christian love. The goal of the kingdom of God is to expand by grafting people back into God's family, not merely to help people live equitably with each other. Justice should be a given in our world. Yet the reality is that our world is so full of injustice that we end up using a great deal of energy simply fighting for equity. Justice should be the *ground floor* of a good society, not an aspiration. In this way, justice is the prerequisite for reconciliation. Reconciliation without justice is an impossibility, for it is just righteousness (*tsedaqah*) through Christ and his people, through the Holy Spirit, that advances the kingdom of God.

A renewal social ethics sees this notion of reconciliation as normative because of the Acts 2 account of Pentecost. If Pentecost is the initial outpouring of the Spirit that *perpetually* flows, then we are filled and saturated by the Spirit of Pentecost today. The Spirit of Pentecost was poured out indiscriminately on *all* flesh, and this reconciling Spirit enables us to break down social walls and reconcile with each other. This is the point Pentecostal ethicist Daniela Augustine makes when she states that the Spirit's outpouring "primes it [the broken world] for reconciliation with God and neighbor, stirring up the human conscience . . . toward imaging the Trinitarian protocommunal life."[30] At Pentecost, the Spirit universalizes the reconciling effects of the cross, which not only confers our salvation to us but enables us to carry on God's kingdom purposes.

In Christ we are transformed, and as the church we are commissioned to walk in the Spirit and expand the kingdom of God. Paul calls this our "ministry of reconciliation" in 2 Corinthians 5:17–20: "So if anyone is in Christ, there is a new creation: everything old has passed away; see, everything has become new! All this is from God, who reconciled us to himself through Christ, and has given us the ministry of reconciliation; that is, in Christ God was reconciling the world to himself, not counting their trespasses against them, and entrusting the message of reconciliation to us. So we are ambassadors for Christ, since God is making his appeal through us; we entreat you on behalf of Christ, be reconciled to God." As Savior, Christ reconciles us back to God. And as Spirit baptizer, Christ empowers and commissions us with the ministry of reconciliation. Christian unity through reconciliation should be so evident that the church inspires the world to live in a way that practices reconciling love. Pentecost gives us a vision for human flourishing through reconciliation, and this happens through genuine forgiveness, which leads to the embrace of the other.

One powerful way some Christian ethicists have talked about reconciliation is through the image of embrace. Miroslav Volf, one of today's foremost public theologians, developed a social theology called a "theology of embrace" that sees oppression and marginalizing sin defeated through embrace.[31] Similar to how justice is not enough, mere political liberation is also not enough. Political liberation is needed when a corrupt regime is in power, but if this sort of liberation is the end goal, then whatever new power structure takes its place inevitably results in corruption, and the cycle of oppression continues.[32]

For this very reason, Samuel warned the Israelites against enthroning a king. If Israel chose to copy all the other nations and install a king as their ruler, the king would eventually oppress them, just as Pharaoh had oppressed them centuries before, Samuel said.

---

30. Daniela Augustine, *The Spirit and the Common Good: Shared Flourishing in the Image of God* (Grand Rapids: Eerdmans, 2019), 165.

31. Miroslav Volf, "Exclusion and Embrace: Theological Reflections in the Wake of 'Ethnic Cleansing,'" *Communio Viatorum* 35, no. 3 (1993): 269.

32. Volf, "Exclusion and Embrace," 108.

> These will be the ways of the king who will reign over you: he will take your sons and appoint them to his chariots and to be his horsemen, and to run before his chariots; and he will appoint for himself commanders of thousands and commanders of fifties, and some to plow his ground and to reap his harvest, and to make his implements of war and the equipment of his chariots. He will take your daughters to be perfumers and cooks and bakers. He will take the best of your fields and vineyards and olive orchards and give them to his courtiers. He will take one-tenth of your grain and of your vineyards and give it to his officers and his courtiers. He will take your male and female slaves, and the best of your cattle and donkeys, and put them to his work. He will take one-tenth of your flocks, and you shall be his slaves. And on that day you will cry out because of your king, whom you have chosen for yourselves; but the LORD will not answer you on that day. (1 Sam. 8:11–18)

Moses had liberated the Israelites from Egyptian enslavement and established a system that empowered judges and priests to govern their society. With God as their only king, the Israelites would not serve an earthly ruler. But eventually the Israelites clamored for a king, and God relented, giving them what they wanted. Within a generation the Israelites found themselves oppressed yet again under the rule of their king, Solomon. When mere liberation is the goal, the cycle of oppression stands undefeated.

Volf's point with this narrative is that political liberation must be seen as "nonfinal." While it's good to seek liberation from oppression and to create public policy that moves us toward being a more just society, these are moves toward a nonfinal reconciliation. *Final* reconciliation comes about with the consummation of the kingdom of God. Final reconciliation is found in the eschaton when we stand in glory with God and appreciate the eschatological new beginning that follows Christ's return. This theological notion of final reconciliation is rooted in God's perfect love and is not a "self-enclosed 'totality.'"[33] In God's kingdom we dwell in the love of God, and this is what enables us to be truly reconciled with God and God's creation.

Talking about reconciliation is relatively straightforward, but when we think about what final reconciliation entails, things start getting difficult. Final reconciliation requires a two-way forgiveness. Sin causes exclusion, and reconciliation brings about embrace. Forgiveness is the pivotal action that closes the gap between exclusion and embrace. Volf writes that forgiveness "heals the wounds that the power-acts of exclusion have inflicted and breaks down the dividing wall of hostility. Yet it leaves a distance between people, an empty space of neutrality, that allows them either to go their separate ways in what is sometimes

---

33. Volf, "Exclusion and Embrace," 109.

called 'peace' or to fall into each other's arms and restore broken communion."[34] One positive consequence of forgiveness is peace, but forgiveness also makes possible the better consequence of embrace. Sometimes abusers make embrace in this life inconceivable, but the victim can still attain a sense of inner peace through forgiveness.

The reason embrace is so difficult to achieve is because it requires forgiveness from both the perpetrators *and* the victims. We tend to think of perpetrators as the only ones who need forgiveness, but victims may need to forgive *themselves* for what happened. Abusers regularly assign false identities onto victims and strive to control their actions—for a victim to repent from this entails a categorical rejection of whatever distortions perpetrators have forced onto them.[35] Repentance does not mean the victim shares culpability with the perpetrator for the offenses committed. Victims are not guilty of any crime and do not need to apologize for any part of the sin that was committed against them. The theological sense of **repentance** refers to the act of changing one's mind and behavior to realign with God's purpose. It entails turning from sin, but also turning from ungodly things in general. If perpetrators convince victims to radically redefine themselves as worthless or deserving of violence and hatred, then the victims too need to repent in the theological sense. Changing their negative views about themselves and acting accordingly is to participate in the act of transformation Paul writes about in Romans 12:1–2.

Victims must turn away from any destructive, ungodly concepts of their own identities and turn fully back to God's embrace, which recognizes they are truly beloved children of God. Here Volf looks at Christ's example: "Instead of aping the enemy's act of violence and rejection, Christ, the victim who refuses to be defined by the perpetrator, forgives and makes space in himself for the enemy. Hence precisely as a victim Christ is the true judge: by offering to embrace the offenders, he judges both the initial wrongdoing of the perpetrators and the reactive wrongdoing of many victims."[36] Even as Jesus was being crucified, he forgave his perpetrators and rejected everything they tried to confer on him. Their spit, insults, and slanders would not define Christ's love for them. In so doing, Jesus paved the way for even their embrace. This is what it means to love your enemies.

So how does this concept of final reconciliation translate to the public arena? It's one thing to become the type of person who seeks and works toward recon-

34. Volf, "Exclusion and Embrace," 126.
35. Volf, "Exclusion and Embrace," 116.
36. Volf, "Exclusion and Embrace," 127.

ciliation; it's another thing to influence a whole society to do the same. While there are some actionable steps we discuss below, first we must acknowledge that we cannot force our ideals onto anyone, and we cannot strong-arm a society toward reconciliation. Love doesn't work through coercion. As we learned from Hauerwas in chapter 7, our job as the church is to become a witness of the kingdom of God to the world. When the church at large truly becomes the loving community Christ has called it to be, then it will become the alternative community the world can emulate. Our love for God and for others must become our witness to the world. Our love for God will only be made evident when we love others. Jesus tells us as much in John 13:35: "By this everyone will know that you are my disciples, if you have love for one another." The first step for bringing reconciliation to the public arena is to love fiercely and become the witness Christ has called us to be.

We can also let the vision of final reconciliation drive our public action. If reconciliation is our *telos*, then we must advocate for those things that produce reconciliation. We should absolutely support movements and legislations that make us a more just society, but we must remember that mere justice is not enough. As noted above in our discussion of the Beatitudes, when we stand for peace, we imitate God. Christ calls us to be peacemakers in the world, which means standing against policies and politicians that divide people, induce violence, and create a culture of death. If *peace* is a guiding principle for us, we must advocate for peace rather than war and social unrest. Christ calls us to mourn with those who have suffered injustices and says that we are blessed when we hunger for just righteousness. If *justice* is a guiding principle, then we must tear down our human-made social divisions and stand for economic, gender, and racial equality. Christ calls us to live graciously and to be merciful. If *grace* is a guiding principle, then we must strive for prison reform and rehabilitation. We must give immigrants a humane pathway toward citizenship. Christ says we are blessed when we treat each other with loving-kindness and when we are meek and pure of heart. If *benevolence* is a guiding principle, then we must find ways to improve our domestic welfare and foreign aid. Christ calls us to be hopeful in all things, even in persecution, so if *hope* is a guiding principle, then we must be *for* those things that promote human flourishing, such as education reform. We are not here to tell anyone what political party to vote for, but we believe our present reality and goal for renewal must be guided by principles that align with Christ's mission of reconciliation. Christ's vision for the kingdom hinges on his commands to love God and love others, as spelled out in the Beatitudes. In a renewal ethics, we must let Christ's vision of the kingdom drive our personal, social, and political decisions.

Conclusion

We are not ethical machines. We embody a particular narrative that is deeply immersed in the work of the Trinity and realized by the Spirit poured out on all flesh. The Spirit baptizes us into God's love to transform the entire creation into God's dwelling place through the inauguration and advancement of the kingdom of God. Having been Spirit baptized, we must work toward our transformation to live for justice and, ultimately, reconciliation. It's in reconciliation that we participate in the reality of God's love, which turns enemies into friends. Reconciliation is the picture of divine embrace, the baptism of love.

The dual work of loving God and loving our neighbors is perspectivally integrated. We can't have one without the other. To assist in this endeavor, we proposed a triperspectival method for renewal ethics. As we have shown, Pentecostals have practiced renewal ethics. Scripture bears its wisdom. It is part of our ethical worldview. Triperspectival ethics is an overt method to work out what we already believe and how we make decisions. Therefore, when we face ethical situations, we must consider the normative, situational, and existential perspectives. We are embodied beings who exist in complex, particular realities. Moral principles often do not apply easily in static ways. We must develop our intellectual and moral virtues in order to gain the mental and affective clarity required to assess the complex relationship between the relevant moral principles and situations.[37]

Study Questions

1. Explain Frank Macchia's description of Spirit baptism and how it relates to loving God and people.

2. Identify morally ambiguous situations in the Bible, such as in the case with Rahab, where violation of moral norms seems to be accepted without condemnation, even given positive moral worth. Try to think through the situation triperspectivally (i.e., integrating the deontological, situational, and existential perspectives) to resolve the moral ambiguity.

3. What does Volf mean when he says that final reconciliation comes as embrace?

37. For further reading and application, we highly recommend chapter 4 of Scott Rae's book *Moral Choices*. This chapter discusses the model for making moral decisions. Although Rae does not seem aware of triperspectivalism, his model provides a practical step-by-step guide that walks the reader through considering the interplay between moral principles, virtues, and consequences. See Scott B. Rae, *Moral Choices: An Introduction to Ethics*, 4th ed. (Grand Rapids: Zondervan, 2018), 109–25.

PART 3

✦ Renewing Truth ✦

9

Cultural Apologetics

How to Speak Truth to Culture

Key Words

Behavioral economics: *Economics informed by psychology that investigates how people actually make decisions.*

Christian apologetics: *The field of defending the faith from counterclaims to its veracity.*

Cognitive biases: *Predictable and common errors arising from heuristics.*

Cultural apologetics: *The "work of establishing the Christian voice, conscience, and imagination within a culture so that Christianity is seen as true and satisfying."*[1]

Disenchantment: *A worldview that does not recognize the supernatural.*

Enchantment: *A worldview that recognizes the world as infused with the supernatural.*

Heuristics: *Cognitive shortcuts for making quick judgments.*

The internet has brought the global world into our lives. The digital age is synonymous with the information age; a seemingly infinite amount of information awaits our searching and browsing eyes. The richness of human diversity is at our fingertips, and this has challenged local communities' norms, including those pertaining to beliefs about beauty, morality, and truth. Plainly speaking, people don't always believe the same things as we do. However, a

---

1. Paul M. Gould, *Cultural Apologetics: Renewing the Christian Voice, Conscience, and Imagination in a Disenchanted World* (Grand Rapids: Zondervan, 2019), 21.

pluralism of perspectives is often healthy. We are God's finite creatures, and different views help us recognize that we all see in limited perspectives—we only "see in a mirror, dimly" (1 Cor. 13:12)—per our creaturely design. Pluralism is thus an opportunity to practice Christian hospitality in which we take on the humble posture of Jesus our king, who, as the host of the universe, became guest to his own creation through incarnating as a human being in a Bethlehem manger. However, the dizzying variety of different interpretations can promote an anything-goes relativism (i.e., every claim to truth, however opposite, is true) or skepticism (i.e., no one can know truth, or people who believe differently can't know truth). That is, we can regard every different belief as individually true, becoming connoisseurs of every belief—whether comparative or contradictory—or we can view any contrary beliefs other than our own with suspicion.

Anything-goes relativism is prone to logical critique.[2] A test for an interpretation's truth is the interpretation's ability to match with the boundaries of reality. The world exhibits logical order. According to Aristotle's law of noncontradiction, a thing cannot both be and not be in the same sense and at the same time. For example, a woman cannot be pregnant and not pregnant at the same time; one can't be dead and alive at the same time. Relatedly, anything-goes relativism can't be both true (p) and false (q). If p is true, then it must accept that q is true. But to accept q is to accept the falsity of anything-goes relativism. Violating the law of noncontradiction thus leads to absurdity. It is logically absurd to believe that Jesus is both the God-man and a mere failed apocalyptic preacher. As C. S. Lewis once stated, Jesus is either a lunatic, a fiend, or God.[3]

Skepticism is a growing problem in our day. Due to the dizzying array of belief options that seem plausible to the unsuspecting, people may conclude that knowledge is impossible. However, there is a more insidious skepticism that is growing in our day that feeds on the underbelly of the digital age. Diversity of beliefs has made spreading misinformation easy. The digital age ushered in the misinformation age that has helped solidify our sectarianism, which views other ideologies with suspicion. The ideological other is seen as a dangerous outside force—an insidious evil and an existential threat to our way of life—that seeks to lead the faithful astray. Such skepticism, formed by misinformation,

2. We are intentionally using the term "anything-goes relativism" to distinguish it from culturally relative knowledge. By culturally relative knowledge, we mean that knowledge is conditioned by our social perspectives. This differs from "cultural relativism," which denies that culturally determined truths must reflect reality in some way. It's also important to note that anything-goes relativism is a bogeyman of those who fear interpretation. You'd be hard-pressed to find an actual anything-goes relativist. This sort of relativist is as mythical as the Chupacabra, Big Foot, and the Loch Ness Monster.

3. C. S. Lewis, *Mere Christianity* (New York: HarperCollins, 1980), 52–53.

is often impervious to rational critique because it views ideological difference with suspicion. Evidence and arguments are met with skepticism at best and outrage at worst. How can we communicate truth, especially the truth of the gospel, in a misinformation age?

In this chapter we argue that this issue is not only a rational, mental issue but an embodied one. Specifically, our posture toward different perspectives is an affective and kinesthetic issue as much as, if not more than, a rational one. However, this raises problems with **Christian apologetics**, the field of defending the faith from counterclaims to its veracity. We inhabit a world in which rational critique may have no effect due to the growing divisiveness, relativism, and skepticism that are motivated by the digital age. People are becoming more comfortable with contradictions as they are constantly surrounded by information and misinformation. This posture is primarily the product not of mental assent but of embodied training. In our digital age, we blur the line between reality and virtual reality through our use of technology. But we do more than merely use technology; we "indwell" it. That is, technology becomes a part of us that navigates our new reality and creates our identity, meaning, and purpose. It becomes an extension of us that changes who we are, just like a car can become an extension of a person that changes a normally calm person to an aggressive, reckless driver (or like how social media has shaped us to become oversharing jerks).[4] Such indwelling of technology creates a new hyperreality, and through it we can take on multiple identities and lives. How can the gospel, then, take root in such a social context? Traditional rationalistic apologetics does not seem able to shoulder the primary burden any longer. While the apologetics field should not abandon its traditional rationalistic approaches altogether, it does need to undergo a cultural shift.

Paul Gould has written an apologetics book that addresses this change in ways that are more faithful to our embodied selves and our concerns. The defense (and presentation) of the gospel need not necessarily be rationalistic, by which we mean addressing philosophical arguments leveled by philosophers and other "cultured despisers" and placing preeminence on propositional reason to confront barriers to faith. As we move through the following chapters on truth and knowledge, we will demonstrate the effects of psychology in the

---

4. In a fascinating interview, Keanu Reeves recounts explaining the premise of the film *The Matrix* to some teenagers. As he explained how the main character sought to know the real from the unreal world, one of the teenagers retorted, "Who cares if it's real?" This question gives insight to how people, especially the younger generation, are already enmeshed in a hyperreal world that has commingled reality with virtual reality. See Keanu Reeves, "Keanu Reeves and Carrie-Anne Moss on Making *The Matrix Awakens* with Epic Games," The Verge, YouTube Video, December 9, 2021, 18:55, https://www.youtube.com/watch?v=0OK80eljWrs&t=566s.

knowing process and then present Gould's cultural apologetics project as an example of an embodied approach to truth and knowledge that has great affinity with a Pentecostal worldview.

Forming Beliefs in an Age of Misinformation

We now inhabit the world of "fake news," to use a term made popular by former president Donald Trump. The trust we used to place in institutions and figures has eroded, and this erosion has served to fortify an us-versus-them mentality that rejects the view that other groups, especially those of our ideological opponents, have access to and possess truth. For some, the matter is even more extreme. Truth, rather than being discovered, is created. The audacity of this view was exemplified by one of George W. Bush's associates, who claimed that we, the US, are " an empire now, and when we act, we create our own reality."[5] To Christians who believe that God is truth, such a statement ought to seem scary and idolatrous. Yet many of our beliefs, practices, and affections are the products of our sociological context. "Social factors are essential to understanding the spread of beliefs, including—especially—false beliefs."[6] Indeed, we form many, if not most, of our beliefs on the basis of testimony.[7] Our social context, especially being in the midst of those who are ideologically like-minded, greatly contributes to our belief formation and judgment-making. While rationalistic apologetics can be helpful, developments in psychology, philosophy, and theology have demonstrated that placing primacy on propositional knowledge, in fact, misunderstands our nature as knowing selves. Since the philosophical and theological arguments for our embodied nature are covered throughout this book, the next sections will introduce the developments in psychology that inform how intuitions, not the kind of deliberative thinking that is associated with apologetics, primarily drive our belief formation.

Behavioral economics is, relatively speaking, the new kid on the block of economics. It is economics informed by psychology that investigates how people actually make decisions. Traditionally, economics has ignored fully embodied humans in its equation. Instead, it viewed people as rational optimizers; given the right information, people will make the most rational economic choice that optimizes their situation. They make their choices based on unbiased beliefs and are not influenced by unruly emotions. These rational optimizers are what behavioral economists call *homo economicus* or

---

5. Cailin O'Connor and James Owen Weatherall, *The Misinformation Age: How False Beliefs Spread* (New Haven: Yale University Press, 2019), 25.

6. O'Connor and Weatherall, *Misinformation Age*, 11.

7. O'Connor and Weatherall, *Misinformation Age*, 8.

"Econs."[8] However, flesh-and-blood humans are not Econs, "calculators with stomachs."[9] They are, as Dan Ariely states, predictably irrational.[10] In Richard Thaler's terms, they misbehave *a lot*.[11]

To prove this point, take some time to think about your home. Most of us likely own a lot of stuff, stuff that stretched, or broke, our limited budgets. We all know that saving money is the rational action, but our checking accounts reveal a different story. Our consumer decisions are often driven by emotional impulses rather than rational deliberations. Or consider a second illustration, one that may resonate for fans of long-suffering, rebuilding sports franchises. Come the trade deadline, many such fans predict a haul of draft picks brought in by the trade of a middling veteran or underperforming prospect, only to be disappointed by mid- or late-round picks. This disappointment results from the endowment effect, an emotive overvaluation of things people already possess over things they don't yet possess.[12] These are but two examples of widespread decision-making practices that highlight the insufficiency of the rationalist model and instead point to a picture of the fully embodied person. Even if the rationalist model is the prescriptively "right" theory to follow, behavioral economics describes how people actually behave and shows that our behaviors "are susceptible to irrelevant influences from their immediate environment. . . , irrelevant emotions, shortsightedness, and other forms of irrationality."[13] We are not as rational and in control of our beliefs and decisions as we think. This is because we are not primarily reflective beings.

In his influential book *Thinking, Fast and Slow*, the Nobel laureate Daniel Kahneman provides a picture of two mental systems at work. System 1 is automatic, quick, and often nonvoluntary. System 2 represents the familiar picture of deliberative mental effort. The rationalist model errs by assuming the operative primacy of system 2, not recognizing that the source of system 2's beliefs and choices is system 1.[14] System 1 is at work all the time, and system 2 is recruited only when effort is required. Under the operation of system 1, our belief formation and decision-making are on cruise control, and system 1 is

8. Richard H. Thaler, *Misbehaving: The Making of Behavioral Economics* (New York: Norton, 2015), 4–5.

9. Ken Evers-Hood, *The Irrational Jesus: Leading the Fully Human Church* (Eugene, OR: Cascade Books, 2016), 11.

10. Dan Ariely, *Predictably Irrational: The Hidden Forces That Shape Our Decisions*, rev. ed. (New York: Harper Perennial, 2010). Evers-Hood helpfully clarifies that the term "irrational" does not mean a real state of irrationality but merely indicates an opposition to the "rational" primacy of Econs. Thus, the term acts as a heuristic to understand our embodied way of thinking as opposed to deliberative thinking. Evers-Hood, *Irrational Jesus*, xvi.

11. Thaler, *Misbehaving*, 4.

12. Thaler, *Misbehaving*, 18.

13. Ariely, *Predictably Irrational*, 318.

14. Daniel Kahneman, *Thinking, Fast and Slow* (New York: Farrar, Straus & Giroux, 2011), 20–21.

effective in helping us navigate the world. However, given that our beliefs are on cruise control, system 1 can lead us to err in the name of efficiency. System 2 can catch these errors once trained, but it is impractical and impossible to always operate in reflective mode. In fact, it is easy to deplete the energy of system 2, making us prone to empty persuasions and error.[15] As cognitive faculties, systems 1 and 2 are efficient at what they do, but they are not perfect. Kahneman thus suggests that we must allow both systems to operate according to their capacities, which allow for errors to occur, but to limit these errors by learning to recognize their occurrences.[16]

Ken Evers-Hood finds behavioral economics theologically and ministerially helpful. Learning under Dan Ariely at Duke University, Evers-Hood found similar dynamics between traditional and behavioral economics in ministry. Like traditional economics, ministers often concern themselves with the prescriptive question about how Christians ought to believe and behave. Like Econs, rationalist Christians can be "'theologicons': idealized, entirely rational church leaders and members unswayed by emotion, unaffected by behavioral blindspots, and able to renew their minds without serious attention to their brains or bodies."[17] Given that they are relating with embodied human beings, ministers must be aware of the descriptive reality of how people actually believe and behave. This prescriptive-descriptive dichotomy is a reason why a "great many new pastors feel as if they were prepared [in seminary] for a church that does not exist."[18] Prescriptively, we know that we should save money. Descriptively, many people lack an adequate emergency fund. Similarly, Christians ought to care about theologically important matters but often care more about church-specific traditions. Ministers relate with fully embodied beings, not brains on sticks, and must take into consideration how embodied, emotive beings behave. Importantly, ministers must recognize that actual behavior is not necessarily wrong. The behavior can be the proper functioning of our full humanity that helps us navigate our world efficiently.

Using the biblical characters Esau and Jacob, Evers-Hood assigns system 1 to the hot-blooded, emotional Esau and system 2 to the calculating Jacob. Esau

15. Kahneman, *Thinking, Fast and Slow*, 81. The psychologist Roy Baumeister demonstrated that mental exertion leads to glucose usage by the nervous system. A rather disturbing experiment that seems to confirm system 2's rational limitations involved testing the rate of parole requests by a panel of judges in Israel. While only 35 percent of parole requests were approved throughout the day, the rates varied depending on the time of the day and meal breaks. After a meal, when the brain was resupplied with glucose, parole was granted 65 percent of the time. The rate dropped steadily with time, reaching close to zero right before the next meal. Kahneman, *Thinking, Fast and Slow*, 43–44.

16. Kahneman, *Thinking, Fast and Slow*, 28.

17. Evers-Hood, *Irrational Jesus*, 71.

18. Evers-Hood, *Irrational Jesus*, xv.

doesn't care about the irrational choice of giving up his birthright for a mere bowl of stew. System 1 is impulsive and acts on emotions. Jacob knows how to gain the birthright through conniving, which takes great mental processing. System 2 is self-interested and seeks to maximize utility.[19] Jacob and Esau represent how our beliefs and decisions are impacted by our mental systems. Again, there is no necessary antithesis between the two systems. They often work well together, and they are part of being human. Evers-Hood even makes the controversial but cogent argument that we must understand Jesus as operating with the two systems, even with its errors and mistakes, if we are to take seriously Jesus's full humanity. To admit that Jesus made mistakes is not to be heretical but to understand that Jesus was truly like us in every way, for finitude and limitations are not necessarily sin.[20] What, then, are these mechanisms of system 1 that, while efficient in many ways, lead us to error?

System 1's automatic processing acts quickly because it relies on patterns that serve as shortcuts for making judgments. Behavioral economists have coined the term "heuristics" to describe these cognitive shortcuts. **Heuristics** are efficient because they allow us to process the whole of our experienced reality without our conscious reflection about it. Evers-Hood identifies four important heuristics. First, the *availability heuristic* refers to the likelihood or unlikelihood of an event based on how available the event appears to our mind. This availability can be based on the frequency of reminder or the level of emotional impact an event has on the mind.[21] Think of plane crashes. Statistically, they are rare events, but they are emotionally charged. News outlets continuously cover a plane crash for days, making it readily available to the mind, compared to the lack of coverage of car crashes. Such availabilities can lead to irrational fears of flying. Second, the *anchoring heuristic* refers to any element that anchors our mind and can be used as a standard for relating to similar elements. A salesperson can anchor the negotiation range by setting a high starting price. This anchor acts to deter a buyer from making a "disrespectful" first offer. One's view of whether a school is theologically liberal or conservative is based on the person's previous anchoring context.[22] Third, the *representativeness heuristic* refers to stereotyping. Stereotypes help us make quick judgments, sometimes to everyone's detriment. Finally, the *affect heuristic* refers to the great impact emotions play in our decision-making.[23] Many people recognize that strong emotions can lead them to make foolish

19. Evers-Hood, *Irrational Jesus*, 19–20.
20. Evers-Hood, *Irrational Jesus*, 41–50.
21. Evers-Hood, *Irrational Jesus*, 22.
22. Evers-Hood, *Irrational Jesus*, 23–25.
23. Evers-Hood, *Irrational Jesus*, 25–27.

choices.[24] However, high passions also fuel many of our important endeavors, even when our reflective deliberations caution us about the risks. Without our emotions, we will be unable to distinguish between our most important and mundane objectives and values.

Clearly, while these heuristics help us navigate the world quickly, they make us more prone to errors. Predictable and common errors that arise from heuristics are what behavioral economists call **cognitive biases**, which are "blind spots that are hardwired into us."[25] Evers-Hood presents five common cognitive biases. First, *confirmation bias* leads us to affirm beliefs that we hold and to discount contrary beliefs. This bias is prevalent due to the ease of finding information that confirms our beliefs. Second is *loss aversion*, according to which the pain we feel for losing something is doubly greater than the positive feeling we have from gaining that thing. Loss aversion explains why people don't like change. Change brings about the loss of stability, and this is painful, even if what people are changing from is not good. Third, *status quo bias* leads us to accept the default decisions made by others. People who are busy are especially vulnerable to this bias since it's easier to follow the crowd rather than exert mental energy by going against the grain. Fourth, *optimism bias* leads us to be more optimistic about our abilities than necessary. Because we tend to be overconfident in this regard, we are drawn to people who feed this bias and ignore those who challenge us. Finally, *framing bias* or framing effect shows that the manner of presenting the same information can have great impact on how people choose.[26] For example, if the survival rate of a surgery is 90 percent and death is 10 percent, framing the option based on the death rate will tend to lead patients to opt out of the surgery due to loss aversion, whereas framing it in terms of success will tend to promote electing the surgery.

Behavioral economists have shown that heuristics and biases, our system 1, are the primary drivers of our mental and active lives. System 2 can correct the errors of system 1, but its activities represent a fraction of our belief formation

24. Dan Ariely has shown us the great extent to which our emotions can direct our decisions. He ran an interesting and disturbing experiment in which he recruited male college students to answer questions about sexual activities in states of nonarousal and arousal. Some of the more controversial questions included, "Can you imagine being attracted to a 12-year-old girl?" "Can you imagine getting sexually excited by contact with an animal?" "Would you keep trying to have sex after your date says 'no'?" and "Would you slip a woman a drug to increase the chance that she would have sex with you?" These specific questions pertained to pedophilia, bestiality, and sexual assault. The scale of answers ranged from "no" (0) to "possibly" (50) to "yes" (100). The rates for these questions in a nonaroused state were 23, 6, 20, and 5, respectively. In a state of sexual arousal, the same students answered at a rate of 46, 16, 45, and 26. Ariely, *Predictably Irrational*, 136–37.

25. Evers-Hood, *Irrational Jesus*, 31.

26. Evers-Hood, *Irrational Jesus*, 32–39.

and decision-making. Behavioral economics demonstrates that we are primarily intuitive, pre-reflective beings who are impacted more by our embodied conditions than by our reflective ideas.

Similarly, the moral psychologist Jonathan Haidt has further demonstrated the primacy of intuition for judgment-making. Intuition refers to the quick and automatic judgments and decisions we make every day;[27] it is system 1 processing. Haidt uses the metaphor of an elephant and its rider to describe the relationship between system 1 (elephant) and system 2 (rider). The size of the elephant relative to the rider makes clear the primacy of intuition over reflection. Importantly, part of intuition is affect, which is "small flashes of positive or negative *feeling* that prepare us to approach or avoid something."[28] These feelings sometimes do not rise to the level of emotion because they are too quick. However, "almost *everything* we look at triggers a tiny flash of affect,"[29] so any activity of the rider (system 2) is dependent on the elephant (system 1). As such, affective reactions can narrowly frame the judgment options for the rider without the rider's awareness.

Solomon Asch provides another famous example of how system 1 greatly influences people's beliefs without system 2 kicking in to direct them. In an experiment, Asch asked people for their comments on the personalities of two individuals.

- Alan: intelligent, industrious, impulsive, critical, stubborn, envious
- Ben: envious, stubborn, critical, impulsive, industrious, intelligent

The order of these same personality traits tends to anchor people to think more positively about Alan than Ben, even though the traits are the same.[30] The first words initiate different affective intuitive judgments, influencing the elephant, not the rider, as the primary judgment-maker. Haidt thus states, "The bottom line is that human minds, like animal minds, are constantly reacting intuitively to everything they perceive, and basing their responses on those reactions. Within the first second of seeing, hearing, or meeting another person, the elephant has already begun to lean toward or away, and that lean influences what you think and do next. Intuitions come first."[31] Like behavioral economists, Haidt rejects the myth of rationalist primacy, even claiming that

27. Jonathan Haidt, *The Righteous Mind: Why Good People Are Divided by Politics and Religion* (New York: Vintage Books, 2012), 53.

28. Haidt, *Righteous Mind*, 65 (italics added).

29. Haidt, *Righteous Mind*, 65.

30. Kahneman, *Thinking, Fast and Slow*, 82. Kahneman is summarizing Asch here.

31. Haidt, *Righteous Mind*, 69.

"anyone who values truth should stop worshipping reason."[32] In this way, he rejects the rationalist model of moral judgment, according to which moral judgments are the product of moral reasoning; one reflects on an ethical issue and then pronounces a moral judgment.[33] In its place, Haidt developed the social intuitionist model of moral judgment.

The social intuitionist model reverses the order between reason and judgment, placing judgment prior to reason. That is, rather than reason determining a judgment, reason comes after judgment to justify the decision. From whence do moral judgments come? Intuition. To give this theory a test, think about the morality of the following situation: Imagine that you are a doctor in whose care are five patients in dire need of organ transplants. In the lobby of your office, a homeless, but otherwise healthy person is taking a nap. Would it be moral for you to drug him, harvest his organs, and donate them to the patients? Most likely (and hopefully!), you would have instantly judged the immorality of such an action without having to reflect first before rendering judgment. Only when asked the reasons for your judgment would you provide them. In this way, reasoning acts more like a lawyer who defends the client (moral judgment) than a judge seeking the truth.[34]

Haidt admits that reflection can change intuition and judgment, but this occurs rarely.[35] Are we then mere captives to our intuitions? Although he had previously agreed with David Hume's belief that we are bound by our passions, Haidt admits that the elephant and rider better represents the relationship between intuition and reflection. Unlike a captive who cannot question the captor, the rider is like a lawyer who represents a client. While in the service of the client (elephant), the lawyer (rider) can direct the client. Where reflection exercises its muscle is not in individual reflection but within social relationships; hence, the name *social* intuitionist model. When we are in the presence of people with whom we have good relationships, their moral intuitions, judgments, and arguments can change our intuitions and arguments.[36] Among friends and family, we let our guard down. We mimic their behaviors. Our interests and beliefs begin to merge, and even when they are different, we empathize and make room for such differences. Sometimes, this room involves sharing arguments that we take seriously, making possible the change of intuitions and judgments. These changes are possible because we care about

32. Haidt, *Righteous Mind*, 104.

33. Jonathan Haidt, "The Emotional Dog and Its Rational Tail: A Social Intuitionist Approach to Moral Judgment," *Psychological Review* 108, no. 4 (2001): 814.

34. Haidt, "Emotional Dog."

35. Haidt, *Righteous Mind*, 54.

36. Haidt, *Righteous Mind*, 79–80.

our groups.[37] Inversely, the same arguments used by ideological opponents (that is, opposing groups) can have no effect due to affective walls we raise as defense. The emotive influence on reflection is clear. If we want to persuade others, establishing collegial relationships is paramount.

Both behavioral economics and moral psychology reveal the power of pre-reflective intuition and automatic processing on our reflective abilities and directions. If this is how the human mind operates, then we must seriously consider reforming the aim of apologetics. Historically dominant apologetics methods have all tended to focus on persuading people toward the propositional truths of the gospel through reflective deliberations. Leaning on the findings of psychology, apologetics must consider the heuristics, biases, and social factors that play critical roles in judgment-making and belief formation. The next section presents Paul Gould's cultural apologetics project, which takes us toward this step.

Cultural Apologetics and Recovering the Christian Voice

Echoing Robert Webber's argument that Christians will have to contend with growing secularism, Paul Gould states that "the West is becoming increasingly post-, sub-, and anti-Christian," leading to greater hostility to the gospel.[38] This cultural shift does not bode well for Christians, especially rationalistic apologists, given the findings in psychology covered above. If reflection acts more like a lawyer that justifies the judgments of affective intuition, and if arguments are effective mostly within positive relationships, then growing hostility against Christianity will make the rationalistic apologetics enterprise more difficult as it aims to persuade people, even with indefeasible arguments and evidence. Some of the previously mentioned heuristics and biases are relevant here.

The growing vices of anti-intellectualism and scandals in certain visible sectors within Western Christianity feed the negative stereotyping within people's representativeness heuristic. Christians' continual claim to moral high ground can impact people's affective heuristic by encouraging incredulity and anger. Christianity then becomes not only an ideological opponent but a threat to their way of life, as they do not want to live according to moral standards that even Christians can't seem to meet, let alone desire. Therefore, culture wars become battlegrounds for the preservation of people's ways of life, which is greatly motivated by loss aversion. In such strained relationships, confirmation bias can run rampant, which further strengthens people's estimation of their own views (optimism bias). Due to sin's corrupting effects on the world, people are already

37. Haidt, *Righteous Mind*, 100.
38. Gould, *Cultural Apologetics*, 18.

defaulted to suppressing the truth of God, which is clearly revealed in the world
(Rom. 1:18–20). But Christianity's failure to testify to the beauty, goodness, and
truth of God only strengthens this suppression. The worldview of secular non-
Christians, here defined in terms of Charles Taylor's second notion of secularism
(which denotes nonreligious/spiritual identity), is often **disenchanted**.[39] A disenchanted worldview strips the world of the supernatural so that reality cannot
accommodate beings such as spirits, God, mythical creatures, and the like. An
enchanted worldview, on the other hand, recognizes that reality is infused with
the supernatural.[40] Even those who reside in majority religious communities can
become more easily disenchanted due to their ready access to other disenchanted
communities, whether in person or on the internet. In these secular communities, people are biased toward the status quo of a disenchanted worldview.

In this cultural context, Gould asserts a need for **cultural apologetics**, which
he defines as the "work of establishing the Christian voice, conscience, and
imagination within a culture so that Christianity is seen as true and satisfying."[41]
It aims to understand how a culture operates, and it offers a vision of, while
seeking to create, a world that is enchanted and desirable due to its realization
of the beautiful, good, and true.[42] Why is it that we are moved by spectacular
images and sounds of beauty, by brave and compassionate acts of goodness,
and by astonishing truths of the universe? God has created us to long for the
beautiful, good, and true because to long for them is to long for God, who *is*
Beauty, Goodness, and Truth.

Our delight and praise in witnessing the instances of beauty, goodness, and
truth are a testimony to our God-directed nature. Augustine's famous statement
is appropriate: "Man is part of your creation, and longs to praise you. You stir
us up to take delight in your praise; for you have made us for yourself, and our
heart is restless till it finds its rest in you."[43] Cultural apologetics seeks to help
people recognize that their delight in beauty, goodness, and truth is really a
delight in God. Therefore, Gould encourages cultural apologists to work as
artists, prophets, and intellectuals who can help awaken people's imagination, conscience, and reason and show how these three transcendentals are
grounded in the triune God.[44] Only focusing on the truth and rationality of

39. See chap. 1 under "Secularity and the Social Imaginary."
40. Pentecostals, on the contrary, have an enchanted naturalist worldview, according to which
the natural world is infused with the Spirit and experience with the Spirit is normal and expected.
James K. A. Smith, *Thinking in Tongues: Pentecostal Contributions to Christian Philosophy* (Grand
Rapids: Eerdmans, 2010), 97–98.
41. Gould, *Cultural Apologetics*, 21.
42. Gould, *Cultural Apologetics*, 22–24.
43. Augustine, *The Confessions*, ed. and trans. Philip Burton (New York: Knopf, 2001), 5.
44. Gould, *Cultural Apologetics*, 29.

Christianity ignores the other deep longings with which humans were created. Cultural apologists must aim to show how beauty and goodness are icons to divine reality just as truth is.

The moral vices exposed to the public by prominent Christians who claim to be agents of God's truth and moral purity are anything but ironic. When Christians demonstrate an ugly and unjust life, solely relying on truths of Christianity to bear witness to God is like relying on a one-legged stool to stand. Without the recognition that God is beautiful and good, the heart cannot perceive the truth of God because such truth is not desirable. Gould states, "What we find, in Scripture and in life, is that it is possible for two people to look at the same object or event and *see and understand it differently*."[45] This problem of perception is a worldview problem that is specifically tied to the imagination.

A disenchanted imagination cannot perceive the clear truths of God in creation. Even Christians can tend to divide reality into sacred and secular spheres, looking to Jesus in the realms of spiritual and moral knowledge and turning to other authorities in different realms of knowledge, such as science and pop culture.[46] From such a disenchanted perspective, God becomes more and more irrelevant as other fields of knowledge encroach upon spiritual and moral knowledge. This does not necessarily mean that people no longer believe in God, but it suggests that God only remains relevant in consumeristic fashion as just another product designed for personal enjoyment and fulfillment. However, a world devoid of a transcendent God is banal and ultimately unfulfilling. Again, if we have been made for God, then any substitute for God will not make wholeness possible. Yet, because God created this world, transcendence peeks through the disenchantment, and the cultural apologist's goal, with the help of the Holy Spirit, is to help direct the imagination toward these clues by "cultivating spiritual perception" to reenchant it once more.[47]

The first step toward re-enchantment is to reawaken the innate desires for transcendence, to recognize that disenchantment is an ultimately failing project that leaves us unable to grasp that which is greater than ourselves. Disenchantment leads us on a never-ending quest for momentary pleasures to temporarily appease, or even deaden, this desire for something greater. It's a suffocating existence, which can lead to what Charles Taylor calls the "nova effect," a new way of being and believing born out of the desire to escape a purely immanent way of seeing the world.[48] Thus, interest in "the occult, the

---

45. Gould, *Cultural Apologetics*, 40.
46. Gould, *Cultural Apologetics*, 33.
47. Gould, *Cultural Apologetics*, 83.
48. James K. A. Smith, *How (Not) to Be Secular: Reading Charles Taylor* (Grand Rapids: Eerdmans, 2014), 14–15.

paranormal, and the spiritual" are on the rise in our secular culture.[49] According to Taylor, this phenomenon represents the third pluralistic secularism, in which religious or spiritual beliefs can thrive but experience the "cross-pressure" of multiple belief options.[50] The cultural apologist thus must tap into this innate, even if cross-pressured, desire for transcendence and demonstrate the futility of pursuing idols that promise fulfillment.

The second step is to "return to reality" by participating with Jesus in seeing and delighting in the world, as he does, and by inviting others into this participation. When we see this world through an enchanted worldview, we can see it truly as it is, as a harbinger of transcendence. The world becomes alive and sacred rather than flat and meaningless, the by-product of ultimate chance. This means that the mundane is no longer mundane. The ordinary becomes a conduit of beauty, goodness, and truth. The Spirit beckons us to open our eyes and catch glimpses of God in the glistening of the sun, the warmth of a mother's touch, or even the "holy" moment of death. And when we delight in this transcendence-infused world, participating in the God of beauty, goodness, and truth, our invitation for others to join and delight in God becomes more plausible. Our participation in the divine reality of beauty, goodness, and truth is thus the prerequisite for fashioning us as icons of God.[51] For how can we invite others to fulfill their desires for transcendence when we find our desires too easily met with cheap counterfeits? As C. S. Lewis powerfully states, "We are half-hearted creatures, fooling about with drink and sex and ambition when infinite joy is offered us, like an ignorant child who wants to go on making mud pies in a slum because he cannot imagine what is meant by the offer of a holiday at the sea."[52] We cannot share what we don't have or experience.

The hidden forces of system 1 greatly impact our ways of relating to the world, including our beliefs about it, our affective postures toward it, and our responses to it. Although this system is efficient, it can mislead us in many ways, which is why we need to gain knowledge about how it operates in order to become more cognizant of its influence in our decision-making and knowing. As it relates to cultural apologetics, we must recognize that rational apologetics

---

49. Gould, *Cultural Apologetics*, 61. "Nones," those who identify as atheists, agnostics, religiously unaffiliated, or loosely affiliated, have been growing and, as of 2021, make up 29 percent of US adults (Gregory A. Smith, "About Three-in-Ten U.S. Adults Are Now Religiously Unaffiliated," Pew Research Center, December 14, 2021, https://www.pewresearch.org/religion/2021/12/14/about-three-in-ten -u-s-adults-are-now-religiously-unaffiliated/). Many Nones identify as spiritual but not religious and participate in "religious" practices like praying and meditation (Linda A. Mercadante, "Spiritual Struggles of Nones and 'Spiritual but Not Religious' (SBNRs)," *Religions* 11, no. 10 [2020]: 5).

50. Smith, *How (Not) to Be Secular*, 14, 23.

51. Gould, *Cultural Apologetics*, 85–86.

52. C. S. Lewis, *The Weight of Glory: And Other Addresses* (New York: HarperOne, 1980), 26.

ignores the realities that hidden cognitive, emotional, and social forces impact our rational deliberations, and we must work toward situating rational apologetics alongside, or perhaps even under, the significantly important axiological dimensions of apologetics. The meaningfulness of beauty and goodness, especially through their mindful presentation based on the insights of behavioral economics and moral psychology, can open others up to the truth in ways that rational apologetics may be unable to accomplish by itself.

Conclusion

Cultural apologetics recognizes that humans are not mere thinking things. It is not enough to demonstrate through rational means the truth of God's existence. In our disenchanted age, even establishing the truth of God and eliciting theistic belief may be met with apathy. If the self is primarily directed toward fulfilling one's own desires, then so what if God exists?[53] The apologist faces an uphill battle even in establishing the plausibility of Christianity's rationality due to heuristics and biases built up in response to the missteps of Christendom. Therefore, demonstrating gospel truth must come in tandem with demonstrating its beauty and goodness. By appealing to the innate desires for transcendence by embodying it in our lives, we as cultural apologists can help break down the barriers to gospel allegiance. Therefore, a Christian worldview on truth must place equal prominence on beauty and goodness. They are triperspectival in nature and in value. Truth must be not only believed but lived out. God is Truth as such, so participating in God's truth is good, and living out this good life is beautiful. Truth is thus embodied and holistic, and we will explore this view further as we consider a renewal worldview on truth in chapter 12.

Study Questions

1. Explain the difference between system 1 and system 2 thinking.

2. Explain the role of rational reflection in making moral judgments, both private and social, according to Jonathan Haidt's social intuitionist model.

3. Using the social intuitionist model, explain how confirmation bias can occur within social groups, and outline how Christians can use this model for positive dialogue about controversial matters.

4. What is the prerequisite for cultural apologists who seek to invite others to "return to reality"?

53. Gould, *Cultural Apologetics*, 53.

10

A Historical Survey
of Truth and Knowledge

Key Words

A posteriori: *Relating to knowledge based on experience.*

A priori: *Relating to knowledge gained independent of experience.*

Fideism: *Faith that is devoid of rational explanation.*

Forms/Ideas: *The universal, unchanging essence of things.*

Substance: *Anything that has form and matter.*

In a fascinating exchange between Jesus and Pilate in John 18:33–38, Jesus testifies to the truth of his kingly rule and vocation, which Pilate summarily dismisses with the terse reply, "What is truth?" (v. 38). The skeptical Roman is already under judgment in Jesus's kingly testimony. For Jesus is tracing back to the Hebraic idea that it is God who reveals and hides truth, and only the ones who listen to the right authority—"Everyone on the side of truth listens to me"—will have ears to hear. That Pilate does not know truth means that he has not listened to the right authority about truth. How could he? The Roman conception of the obtainment of truth is influenced by Greek philosophy, not Hebraic thought.

Pilate's question represents a clash of worldviews about truth and how truth is known. This clash owes much to the Greek worldview, since Western philosophy, including that of the Romans, was only made possible by the Greeks who came before them. This impact was pithily captured by the British philosopher Alfred North Whitehead, who once quipped that European philosophy was just a series of footnotes to Plato.[1] Although he wasn't the first to ask questions about some of these topics, Plato set the agenda of philosophy by asking and providing formidable answers, often through the mouth of Socrates, to big questions concerning metaphysics, epistemology, axiology, and political philosophy, among others. In this chapter, we will briefly survey this "footnote," describing what the historical traditions have said about truth and knowledge. The story begins with the birth of Western philosophy through Plato and Aristotle and quickly moves to the Enlightenment.

The Greek Quest for Philosophical Knowledge

If Thales of Miletus lived in our times, he would be called a Renaissance man. But given that he predated the Renaissance by almost two thousand years, he would have to settle for the title of "father of Western philosophy." Thales was not only a philosopher but an engineer, a geographer, an astronomer, and a mathematician. As for philosophy, Thales launched this project by providing a philosophical explanation to the question about ultimate reality. He and others who came after him until the time of Socrates are called pre-Socratics, and their two philosophical goals were to discover the root of ultimate reality and to find unity and order in a world of diversity and change. Their answers to the questions aren't as important as their contributions to the beginning of philosophy. For example, the Milesian philosophers proposed water (Thales), the unbounded infinite (Anaximander), and air (Anaximenes) as the root of ultimate reality. Heraclitus argued that change was ultimate and proclaimed that we can't step into the same river twice. Parmenides, on the other hand, reasoned that no change actually exists. Heraclitus and Parmenides can be seen as anticipating the later empiricist and rationalist traditions in philosophy. While their explanations of ultimate reality are no longer taken seriously, their significance lies in providing reasoned arguments devoid of religious explanations.[2] Rational *logos* replaced the religious *mythos*. Importantly, the purpose of rational inquiry was to know ultimate reality.

1. Alfred North Whitehead, *Process and Reality: An Essay in Cosmology*, ed. David Ray Griffin and Donald W. Sherburne (New York: Free Press, 1979), 39.

2. Prior to Thales, reality was explained by the activity of the gods, as exemplified in the poems of Homer and Hesiod. It is unsurprising that philosophy began in Miletus. Miletus was a rich commercial city in which trade and ideas from Egypt and the eastern Mediterranean regularly came into fruitful contact.

A little over a hundred years after the birth of Western philosophy, the Sophists came to prominence. The Sophists were traveling teachers of rhetoric who often displayed their rhetorical power in public to recruit students and occasionally acted as rhetorically gifted diplomats. Their views on ultimate reality, however, contrasted with the pre-Socratics who came before them. The Sophists believed that truth was relative. Neither religion nor philosophy could deliver stable truth. Their vocation explains their view: rhetoric was critical for obtaining power in government, so the Sophists were clever rhetoricians who were more concerned about power and persuasion than truth. Due to their wide travels, they encountered a variety of beliefs that acted as evidence that truth was not universal. Two prominent Sophists were Protagoras and Thrasymachus. According to Protagoras, "Man is the measure of all things."[3] In other words, humans determine truth. Since there is no objective truth, achieving power and success was most important. Whereas Protagoras made a metaphysical claim about truth, Thrasymachus made a moral claim about the nature of justice, which appears in Plato's book *The Republic*, arguing that justice is "in the interest of the stronger."[4] Simply, might makes right.

Against the relativism of the Sophists arose Socrates, a remarkable man of great intellectual depth whose thoughts are passed down only by the writings of his pupils, as was also true of Jesus. Socrates's purpose was to obtain truth, and he claimed that he didn't know anything. Instead, he saw philosophy as a midwife that helps birth wisdom through the arduous method of questioning, popularly known as the Socratic method. Because Socrates never wrote anything, we must turn to his student Plato to encounter the first robust theories of truth and knowledge, theories that continue to influence us today.

In his famous analogy of the cave, Plato argued that we live in a world of illusions. This "cave" is but a copy of the real world, which resides outside the cave. What we consider to be reality in the cave is only shadows reflected on the walls. When we escape the cave and enter the real world, we can see reality as it is, especially as the sun makes seeing or knowing possible. This analogy describes Plato's dualistic metaphysics. Our world, the world of matter, is a copy of the world of the **Forms** or **Ideas**, which are the universal, unchanging essence of things. The world of matter is filled with particular things that change. The world of the Forms is abstract and universal. It is "spiritual" since it is immaterial, just as our mental ideas are abstract. This real world contains the true nature of things and acts as the unifying order of all things. We can discern the fixed nature of chairs in a world full of different types of chairs

3. Radoslav A. Tsanoff, *The Great Philosophers*, 2nd ed. (New York: Harper & Row, 1953), 31.
4. Plato, *Plato's Republic*, trans. G. M. A. Grube (Indianapolis: Hackett, 1974), 12.

because we know the universal Form of "chairness" in our minds. We can obtain such knowledge, despite the variances in our world, because the Form of the Good directs our vision. Objective, mind-independent truths thus exist in a transcendent reality that impresses itself upon our world.

But if we don't reside in the world of the Forms, how can we know the objective nature of things? According to Plato, we have once resided in and beheld the world of the Forms. Knowledge in this world is just the recollecting of the memories of our past. Plato thus believed in reincarnation and the transmigration of souls. In Plato's work *Meno*, Socrates explains the possibility of this innate knowledge by leading an uneducated enslaved boy through a series of questions that allow the boy to solve a geometrical problem. Such rational guidance makes remembering possible.

Reason reigns supreme for Plato and Greek philosophy. According to Plato, the human soul is composed of three parts. The appetitive part are the bodily desires, which lure us to their fulfillment. The rational part connects us to the world of the Forms through abstract reasoning. It is the gateway through which we can overcome our fleshly desires of this world to obtain knowledge of the Forms. The spirited part of the soul is the emotive, active part, which should be used by reason to moderate bodily desires toward the good and true. Whereas the appetitive part seeks to ground us in the things of this world and make us ignorant of the Forms, we can use abstract reason to transcend this illusory world to behold reality as such. Sense perception, contra reason, can't be trusted since it observes the illusory world. Plato's metaphysics, therefore, proposes a rationalistic soteriology, a salvation from this world made possible through the use of abstract reason. This idea isn't so ancient after all. Christians who denigrate the entirety of "the world" as fallen in contrast to "heavenly" things follow Plato's dualistic metaphysics. Even though such theology is often expressed in anti-intellectual traditions, many of those traditions also reflect Plato's rationalistic epistemology by placing primacy on sermons. Spiritual formation, they believe, occurs primarily through the renewing of the mind (Rom. 12:2) by gaining biblical knowledge, and action necessarily proceeds from belief.

Aristotle, Plato's student, made an equally impressive and lasting impact on philosophy and theology. But against Plato's "Form-above-matter" dualistic metaphysics, Aristotle espoused an integrated "form-in-matter" metaphysics.[5] A **substance** is anything that has form and matter. A substance can only exist because its whatness, the essence that determines a thing's nature, is contained in itself, not in some abstract reality in another realm.

---

5. Due to this "naturalizing" of the forms, I do not capitalize it when describing Aristotle's view.

Aristotle's view, called hylomorphism, has greater explanatory power than Plato's view in accounting for order and causation within a world of change. In Plato's view, Forms that exist in matter can't adequately explain how change and motion occur in relation to the eternal, unchanging Forms. If the forms exist *in matter*, as in Aristotle's view, then what happens with the form in matter can explain change. A chair can lose its form in its destruction. A form can also guide change within matter based on its innate potentials. The form of an oak tree resides in the matter of an acorn, and the form draws the changes within the acorn to actualize its innate potential. Such changes are only possible because of the form residing in matter. All substances, with the exception of the Prime Mover, a pure substance with no matter (more on this below), have these potentials for possible actualization that are determined by their forms, and change is just the process of matter fulfilling its potentiality in actualization.

This movement of potentiality to actuality must begin somewhere. Without some absolute beginning, there would be an infinite regress of movements that make explanation and knowledge impossible. As many parents recognize, young children tend to ask "why" to every explanation. At a certain point, however, answers must stop because one has arrived at the explanatory terminus (and at one's wits' end!). As Ludwig Wittgenstein once stated, "If I have exhausted the justifications, I have reached [the explanatory] bedrock and my spade is turned. Then I am inclined to say: 'This is simply what I do.'"[6] Without this terminus, we can always ask for more explanations, and we will never achieve knowledge. Therefore, Aristotle argued that an ultimate cause, called the Prime Mover, initiates the movement from potential to actual without being caused itself. It is pure substance with no matter and thus has no potentiality for change. The Prime Mover explains change but is itself not subject to change. It is the Uncaused Cause, the first mover. However, this godlike figure, for Aristotle, is impersonal. It can't interact with the world, for such interaction would bring about change in itself, disqualifying it as the Prime Mover. Therefore, while Aristotle accounts for mind-independent, transcendent reality, such reality is impersonal, unlike all Christian worldviews, which understand ultimate reality as finally grounded in the personal figure of God.

How can we know the forms? For Plato and Aristotle, the location of the forms dictated their epistemology. Due to the abstract transcendence of the Forms, Plato valued abstract reasoning, such as mathematics and Socratic dialogue, as supreme modes of knowledge. Sense perception cannot deliver

---

6. Ludwig Wittgenstein, *Philosophical Investigations*, ed. P. M. S. Hacker and Joachim Schulte, trans. G. E. M. Anscombe, P. M. S. Hacker, and Joachim Schulte, 4th ed. (Malden, MA: Wiley-Blackwell, 2009), §217.

knowledge, only beliefs, since observation interacts with matter, which is merely a copy of reality. Aristotle's hylomorphism, on the other hand, favored scientific observation, such as in biology. Their differences do not result in complete disagreement, however. For Aristotle, while observation of substances is necessary, such observation occurs through the use of self-evident, axiomatic first principles. Combined with the laws of logic, rational reflection on and abstraction of the forms from matter through observation make knowledge possible, allowing the knower to differentiate between a thing's unchanging essence and its distinct, changeable properties. Like Plato, Aristotle thus highly valued the use of reason because he considered humans as essentially rational animals.

Being and Knowledge in the New Testament

We now turn to another ancient epistemology as found in the New Testament. Jews lived in an interesting intellectual climate during the Second Temple period. Many Jews during this time were hellenized (i.e., influenced and shaped by Greek culture), especially due to the Jewish diaspora, which saw Jews living in various parts of the Roman Empire. This cultural syncretism (the merging of different cultural beliefs, attitudes, and practices) impacted Jewish thinking and the New Testament writers. We will explore this syncretism in Paul's speech at the Areopagus in Acts 17.

Paul's speech at the Areopagus (Acts 17:16–33) is fascinating because of Luke's multifaceted portrayal of Paul. First, Luke portrays Paul as a Socrates-like figure who engaged with anyone at the marketplace who would give him a hearing. Second, his encounter with the Epicureans and Stoics reveals the still-vibrant intellectual culture of Athens, in which Paul would not have been out of his element. As a highly educated Jew who hailed from Tarsus, one of the central cities of Stoicism in the Roman Empire, he was probably familiar with Stoicism. Some argue that Paul's writings exhibit Stoicism's influence, even proclaiming that he was "deeply influenced by Stoic philosophy, if not directly by Seneca [a Stoic philosopher]."[7] Third, not only does Paul display familiarity with Greek philosophy in quoting Greek philosophers, but he synthesizes their thoughts in seamless ways with his message.

Is Luke portraying Paul as a Hellenistic Jew? Some would say yes, but Dru Johnson disagrees, arguing that Paul's use of a Hellenistic medium does not

---

7. Emily Wilson, *The Greatest Empire: A Life of Seneca* (New York: Oxford University Press, 2014), 217. Also, see Gudrun Holtz, "Paul, the Law and Judaism: Stoification of the Jewish Approach to the Law in Paul's Letter to the Romans," *Zeitschrift für die neutestamentliche Wissenschaft und die Kunde der älteren Kirche* 109, no. 2 (2018): 185–221.

betray his thoroughly Jewish thought. According to Johnson, Jewish philosophy in the Hebrew Bible displays four convictions. First, it maintains the mysterionist conviction that the human mind cannot fully grasp truth. God reveals but also hides. Second, Hebraic thought flows from and is situated within its creationist narrative. It is thus historically rooted and presupposes that truth and knowledge are dependent on the creator. Third, truth and understanding are transdemographic and intended for everyone. Knowledge is not for the privileged few. Fourth, instruction is ritualistic—that is, knowledge does not primarily occur through lectures or mental events. The Israelites were to come to know reality by performing rites that would not only lead to knowledge and understanding but would also form them into a particular community.[8]

After analyzing and comparing Hellenistic Jewish writings with Paul's thoroughly Hebraic thought, Johnson concludes that Paul maintains the four Hebraic convictions whereas Hellenistic Jewish writings, such as those of Philo and the Wisdom of Solomon, adopt and adapt various Hellenistic convictions. For example, rather than displaying the mental humility of mysterionism, Philo and Wisdom presume the mind's ability to grasp absolute truth. Though their Jewish identity leads them to maintain their creationist conviction, they create what is effectively an epistemic caste system that is motivated by the Hellenistic preference of the mind over the body, as we saw in Plato above. Against the Hebraic ritualist conviction, which necessitates embodied involvement in the process of knowing, Hellenism denigrates the role of the body and highlights abstract reason's epistemic powers.[9] Since only those with the means can pursue the life of the mind, the mentalism of Hellenism uncovers an assumed bourgeois classism.

If Paul is not "deeply influenced by Stoic philosophy," then how can we account for his use of Hellenistic rhetoric and philosophy? The difference lies in function rather than epistemology. Paul is familiar with Hellenistic philosophy, but his overall thought is not syncretized with Hellenism. The usage of Hellenistic rhetoric and philosophy is due to Paul's strategy of tailoring the gospel message to specific audiences as a point of contact, so that he might be "all things to all people" (1 Cor. 9:22).[10] That this is merely a strategy is evident in his overall message at the Areopagus.

Paul begins his speech by noting the Athenian piety in worshiping an unknown god, whom he describes as the creator who placed people on earth so that they will reach out and find God. Yet, following the Hebraic revealed/

---

8. Dru Johnson, *Biblical Philosophy: A Hebraic Approach to the Old and New Testaments* (New York: Cambridge University Press, 2021), 92–99.

9. Johnson, *Biblical Philosophy*, 163–70.

10. Johnson, *Biblical Philosophy*, 213.

hidden schema, Paul argues that people are unable to find God through evidence in creation. Paul paints a similarly bleak picture of our epistemic powers in Romans 1:18–32, where he states that it is impossible for us to have knowledge of God when left to our own fallen and rebellious devices. Hence, the Athenians are worshiping an unknown god. God overlooked this ignorance in the past, but God now requires right knowledge of God. God has furnished evidence of God's truth and cosmic plan through the resurrection of Jesus. But since evidence in creation has already failed, knowledge of God does not come through this evidence. God has appointed the embodied ritual of repentance as the mode through which right knowledge of God occurs.[11]

The four Hebraic convictions undergird Paul's message. Looming large is the creationist narrative. We are the Creator's offspring. The message is transdemographic, as evidenced by the conversion of Dionysius and Damaris. Knowledge of God is for everyone, not just the bourgeois. Knowledge of God occurs through the ritual of repentance and is hidden from or remains a mystery to the unrepentant. The necessity of repentance reveals the important point that ignorance of God is not primarily intellectual but moral. God's hiddenness is not due to our inability to know. For not only are God's invisible qualities clear (Rom. 1:20), but we can also, in principle, know God from them.[12] This is why we are without excuse. But due to our moral idolatry, God gives us over to our sin and ignorance (repeated three times in vv. 24–28). For Paul, knowing God's truth is not merely, or even primarily, a mental act. Religious knowledge has a moral dimension that entails responding rightly to God's truth.[13] Such a moral dimension presupposes moral action, not just mental acknowledgment, and shows that coming to know God's truth is a moral struggle.

Even if Paul's thoughts are not syncretized, his use of Greek philosophy does not render it false. That we are the offspring of God, in whom we live, move, and have our being, remains faithful to Paul's creationist conviction. That such knowledge was possible in Greek philosophy is evidence of general revelation. God is the ultimate, personal reality on which all truth depends, and God also makes knowledge possible for all creatures through various forms of revelation. Therefore, what we can know (and can't know) does not begin from our own creative powers. To believe otherwise is to fall into idolatry once again. Knowledge of truth is possible because of the creator, who made the objects of knowledge. God is the transcendent epistemic condition of possibility. This creator-creature distinction maintains that we are not the absolute creators

---

11. Johnson, *Biblical Philosophy*, 171–77.

12. Ian W. Scott, *Paul's Way of Knowing: Story, Experience, and the Spirit* (Grand Rapids: Baker Academic, 2009), 19–22.

13. Scott, *Paul's Way of Knowing*, 19–20.

of truth. The Sophists were wrong. Truth and knowledge are not relative. The being of God and God's creation come before our knowledge of them. In other words, the order of being precedes the order of knowing. But lest we default to a mentalist perspective, it is important to stress the embodied aspect of knowledge. Understanding general and special revelation occurs through both embodied and cognitive faculties. For Pentecostals, the altar experience is an example of a powerful epistemic practice that engages both the mind and the body. Altar calls often act as a periodic ritual that reorients worshipers, calling them to recenter their faithfulness, to hear God's voice for Spirit-empowered living. Such embodied actions can promote a knowledge of God, of ourselves, and of the world that is not only mental but experiential.

Enlightenment Epistemology: Rationalism and Empiricism

Although we are quickly traversing a span of almost two thousand years, from the premodern New Testament era to the modern Enlightenment, it is a necessary journey because of the seismic shift that occurred in the Enlightenment. This shift reversed the order of being and the order of knowing that was presupposed throughout the premodern period. In premodernity, reality was the limiting factor and the condition of possibility for knowledge. In the Enlightenment, this priority of being over knowledge was upturned: the certainty of knowledge gained priority over being. After all, as the logic went, if we can't establish confidence in our epistemic powers, how can we even speak about reality? Thus, the Enlightenment project was the establishment of the supremacy of the mind. This ascendency of the mind can be heuristically delineated by two philosophical trajectories, rationalism and empiricism, with differing views about the foundational mode of knowing. Although they may seem like opposites, they both represent a turn toward the mental subject, creating a dualism between subject and object. Even in the creative synthesis of rationalism and empiricism in Immanuel Kant that we will see later, the mind still reigns supreme in designating the knowable from the unknowable. Before we turn to Kant, we will explore the rationalism of René Descartes and Gottfried Wilhelm Leibniz, followed by the empiricism of John Locke and David Hume.

René Descartes and Gottfried Wilhelm Leibniz

The seismic shift into the Enlightenment occurred through Descartes. Descartes was a rationalist who believed that knowledge is gained more through reason than through sense experience. Although he was a practicing Roman Catholic, Descartes was displeased with the antiscientific stance of the Roman

Catholic Church, especially its decision to put Galileo on house arrest for his heliocentrism. To avoid such irrationalism, Descartes endeavored to tear down all knowledge until he could happen upon a solid epistemic grounding, a foundation of absolute certainty upon which he could build his system of knowledge. Since he was a mathematician, his quest for certainty is unsurprising. He endeavored to doubt everything until he could doubt no longer. Gone were the formerly trustworthy sources such as sense experience and the existence of God. View any optical illusions, and we'll quickly realize that our senses can easily deceive us. We can also doubt that God is good. Perhaps God is an evil demon who intends to deceive us at every turn. Thus, Descartes's methodology of radical doubt peeled away every belief until he arrived at what he supposed was a solid foundation: his mind.

To be deceived, he had to have a mind subject to such deception. Thinking cannot be doubted. It was, in the end, doubt that led him to epistemic certainty. Hence, his famous motto "I think, therefore I am" (or, more accurately, "I doubt, therefore I am"). Although Augustine made the same argument twelve hundred years prior, Descartes's argument was radical because it sought to locate ultimacy and certainty not in God but in the human mind. In doing so, he believed he had secured knowledge that mirrored the certainty of mathematical and scientific reasoning. We again see the pre-Socratic movement from *mythos* to *logos*. Religious explanation is replaced by human reasoning—ultimate reasoning at that! Moreover, the ultimacy of abstract reason led Descartes to conclude that he is "nothing but a thinking thing."[14] Despite his Catholicism, Descartes's rationalism led him to denigrate the goodness of the body. Thus, he set the modern agenda of prioritizing the primacy of reason over everything, even over God's existence, and is appropriately considered the father of modernism.

Gottfried Leibniz came on the heels of Descartes and continued the rationalist paradigm by extending the ultimacy of the mind into ultimate reality. Leibniz argued that ultimate reality is made up of the smallest elements called "monads." These aren't like quarks as identified by modern science, however, because they aren't physical. Rather, these fundamental substances of reality are mental, psychic forces that cannot be further reducible like matter.

There exists a hierarchy of monads. Some monads become clusters that form around a dominant monad. In humans, the dominant monad develops a conscious mind. However, the mind does not control other monads because monads do not have causal relationships with one another. How is it, then,

14. René Descartes, *"Discourse on Method" and "Meditations on First Philosophy,"* trans. Donald A. Cress, 4th ed. (Indianapolis: Hackett, 1998), 65.

that the body moves according to the will of the mind? Each monad mirrors the universe. It's a passive act that doesn't cause anything. Even though they don't work together, their activities are not chaotic or random because God, the chief monad, predetermined the precise harmony of their movements. If all the clocks in a room strike 12 at the precise time, this is because their time had been programmed and not because they caused each other's movements. Divine predestination is thus the cause of this principle of pre-established harmony, and the truth of reality is foreordained by God. Divine predestination also secures the principle of sufficient reason, the idea that everything happens for a reason. Nothing is outside divine control. Nothing is purposeless. All truth is divinely ordered. Yet, while God plays a more prominent role in Leibniz than in Descartes, Leibniz's philosophy still undermines the goodness of material creation due to his overemphasis on the mental, leading to the erasure of causal relationships and the loss of genuine human interactions.

Divine predestination also has interesting implications for Leibniz's philosophy of language and truth. Leibniz distinguished between two types of propositions: analytic and synthetic. Analytic propositions are true by definition, necessary, and *a priori*. The proposition "A triangle has three sides" is true by definition; it can't be false; and its truth is dependent only on the concepts involved and not on observation. Synthetic propositions, on the other hand, are contingent, *a posteriori*, and not true by definition. Such propositions are observed, and the state of affairs they describe could have been different. For example, "The cat is on the mat" is a synthetic proposition that could have been false if the cat was on the desk. However, given God's foreordination, all sentences are *a priori*, according to Leibniz. That *this* cat would be on *this* mat at *this* time is an analytic statement given that its monads were predestined by God to be where they are. It is the essential nature of the cat to be there at that time. Therefore, such a proposition looks synthetic from our point of view, but it is analytic from God's point of view. There is sufficient reason for that cat to be on the mat (or any state of affairs). God determined it! Leibniz's rationalism thus secured truth in the transcendent reality of God's predetermination but left serious questions about human free will and evil in the world.

John Locke and David Hume

Unlike the rationalists discussed above, John Locke was a British empiricist who believed that knowledge was gained first and foremost through sense experience. He rejected the view that our minds are furnished with innate ideas of reason. The mind at birth is a blank slate, which becomes furnished through sense experience. Interestingly, however, what we come to know through sense experience are our ideas of the sense experience, not the direct objects of our experience. Knowledge occurs in the interplay between simple and complex ideas and between primary and secondary qualities. Simple ideas arise passively from the primary data of experience. They are simple because they cannot be broken down any further. For example, our encounter with the color orange creates the simple idea of orangeness, but we can't further reduce that idea. Simple ideas combine to form complex ideas through the mind's activity in drawing their various relationships together. Thus, orangeness combines with the simple ideas of tartness, sweetness, and spherical to form the complex idea of the fruit that we know as an orange.

Primary qualities are inherent within objects, and we develop ideas that reflect these qualities through our sense experience. Secondary qualities are attributes that we apply to objects but that exist only in our minds. For example, the size and shape of objects are their primary, mind-independent qualities on which our perceptions are built. Qualities such as sound and color are secondary because they are but varying air vibrations and light waves that our minds use to form simple and complex ideas. Unfortunately, then, what we can know is not the objects themselves but their representational ideas in our minds as we perceive the objects' qualities. It is as if the only world we know is the world we see depicted on television screens.

David Hume, who was also a British empiricist, radicalized Locke's representational theory. Hume used Leibniz's distinction between analytic and synthetic propositions, describing them as "relations of ideas" and "relations of fact," and considered the two as the only sources of knowledge. However, analytic statements are mere tautologies because they do not add any more information. For example, the meaning of the analytic statement that a bachelor is a single male is contained in the terms "bachelor" and "single male." Thus, analytic statements do not add relevant descriptions about the world. They are merely meaningful statements about the relationship of words. Synthetic propositions, on the other hand, describe reality through observation. Any other propositions are meaningless. For Hume, the proposition "God exists" is neither analytic nor synthetic. It is not true by definition, necessarily true, or *a priori*. It is also not synthetic because, for Hume, God's attributes cannot be observed. If someone pointed to miracles as evidence of God's existence, Hume would respond that such an incredible claim requires incredible evidence. A claim and its evidence must be proportionately balanced, and no testimony can demonstrate the plausibility of the violation of natural law. This was a critique not so much of the possibility of miracles but of the credibility of witness. Nevertheless, because the claim that God exists is neither analytic nor synthetic, Hume proclaimed, "Commit it then to the flames: for it can contain nothing but sophistry and illusion."[15]

Hume may have championed religious skepticism, but his skepticism was cast beyond religion. He also applied this analytic-synthetic schema on causality to devastating effect. Causality is fundamental to everyday function, but it is neither analytic nor synthetic. Observation of the sequence of billiard ball A hitting and moving billiard ball B creates the sense impression of the movements. However, no sense impression of causality exists. We do not observe the logical entailment of a necessary causal relationship. Rather, we expect causality from our past experiences and read it into the world. But if all knowledge arises from analytic and synthetic propositions, then we can't know much about the world since causality is integral to our experience yet is unobservable. Even if the morning sun follows the night, we can never be certain that the sun will rise again since there is no logically necessary relationship between the movement from night to day (or any seemingly causal events). We can never be certain about probabilities or that the future will be like the past. Hume thus demolished the notion of confidence in the uniformity of nature. It is not that Hume didn't believe in causality. But if "all our ideas are nothing but copies of our [sense] impressions," then his hope for "greater clearness and precision in philosophical reasonings" through his philosophy had the opposite effect.[16] Empiricism's tenet that knowledge is possible only through sense experience found its logical conclusion in Hume's skepticism.

This brief exploration not only of Hume's work but also of Descartes's, Leibniz's, and Locke's has led us to several undesirable conclusions. Descartes effectively divorced the mind from the body and replaced the authority of God with the authority of the mind. No longer will a person submit to God. God's existence is dependent on the authority of the mind. Leibniz reduced reality to minds based on divine foreordination. In addition to his difficult assertion that nothing has causal relationship with anything else, Leibniz also put forth the controversial idea that this world, with all of its sufferings, is the best of all possible worlds since God will only do what is best. Locke's turn toward the world in his empiricism might be seen as a corrective to rationalism, but it effectively divorced the world from our minds. For what we know through our observations is not the world itself but the impressions that our observations leave in our minds. Hume radicalized this idea and led us to skepticism.

---

15. David Hume, *An Enquiry concerning Human Understanding*, ed. Eric Steinberg (Indianapolis: Hackett, 1993), 114.

16. Hume, *Enquiry concerning Human Understanding*, 41.

Immanuel Kant

If Hume had had the final word, philosophical activity would have ceased. Hume himself retreated often to a game of backgammon and the presence of friends to shake off the moroseness his philosophy inspired. But soon after, a Prussian philosopher came across Hume's work and made knowledge seemingly possible again by bridging the rationalist-empiricist divide.

Immanuel Kant had been trained in the rationalism of Leibniz. But he expressed that reading Hume awoke him from his dogmatic slumber. Kant agreed with Hume that knowledge requires sense experience, which is no easy confession for a rationalist. But part of Kant's genius was modifying the analytic-synthetic distinction to overcome empiricism's skepticism. Whereas analytic propositions were seen as *a priori* and synthetic propositions as *a posteriori*, Kant argued that synthetic propositions can also be *a priori*. Recall that analytic propositions are true by definition and cannot be self-contradictory. Synthetic, *a posteriori* propositions require experience for knowing. *A priori* propositions, on the other hand, are based on their concepts and do not require experience for their knowing, even if experience can aid in knowledge.

Hume was correct that causality is neither analytic nor synthetic. It is not true by definition, necessary, or *a priori*. Even if we have always seen event B following event A in the past, it's logically possible for B to *not* follow A; this would not be self-contradictory. Causality is also not synthetic and observable through perception. But Hume was assuming that analytic and synthetic propositions were respectively *a priori* and *a posteriori*. He did not entertain the possibility that synthetic propositions could be *a priori*, that experience is understood through prior mental concepts, although the material was there for him to reach that conclusion. He saw that we infer causality in our perception rather than perceiving causality. Inference of causality is thus something we contribute to the conjunction of events A and B. Kant's overcoming of Hume's skepticism occurred through taking this "inference" as an *a priori* structure in the mind. More precisely, we do not infer causality on the events. Rather, Kant argued, we perceive experience through the intuition of causality, which is already part of our mental faculties. Without this category, experience would be a jumble of sense data that would be impossible to understand.

To understand Kant's argument, we must consider his wider epistemology. Unlike Hume (and others), who asked how knowledge is possible, Kant began with the commonsensical acceptance of the actuality of knowledge and sought the necessary preconditions that made such knowledge possible. For example, instead of asking, "Is perception possible?" or "Is causality possible?" he asked, "How is perception possible?" or "How is causality possible?" This method, called transcendental deduction, bypasses observation in deducing the necessary preconditions of knowledge.

This deduction led Kant to argue that our mental faculties comprised twelve categories of understanding that are divided into four sets of three.[17]

1. Quantity: unity, plurality, totality

2. Quality: reality, negation, limitation

3. Relation: substantiality, causality, reciprocity

4. Modality: possibility, existence, necessity

Similarly, he argued that our faculty of intuition is made up of space and time. The importance of these faculties is that they reside subjectively in our minds, not in reality. When we look at numerous marbles on a table, we understand the unity of the various marbles in their totality not because unity, plurality, and totality as concepts exist in the marbles or even in our sense impressions; rather, our sense impressions of the various marbles filter through the mental category of quantity. Our mind brings the concept of quantity into our sense experience. Similarly, we don't perceive space, time, and causality, but we project them into our sense experience. When we see event B following event A, we project the causal events of A and B as occurring within space and time.

These categories and faculties are like permanent glasses; they form the structures of the mind. Just as the world looks darker when we wear sunglasses, we see causality in the world because we see through a causal lens. What we perceive in the world is but a jumble of data. As we perceive this data through the lens of our mental structures, our mind orders it all and makes it coherent. The mind is like a processing machine that acts as the precondition of knowledge. Without it, knowledge is impossible. Therefore, empiricism is correct that sense experience is necessary for knowledge. We need data inputs from the world out there in order to begin our quest for knowledge. But the output of knowledge is impossible without the rationalist insight that our mind innately structures knowledge.

Although Kant had seemingly rescued knowledge from Hume's skepticism, his epistemology had devastating effects on the possibility of knowing ultimate reality. Again, the problem occurs within the empiricist element of his theory, although with a rationalist tinge. Kant calls ultimate reality the "noumenon," or the thing-in-itself. This world is what furnishes us with the jumble of data.

17. Immanuel Kant, *Prolegomena to Any Future Metaphysics: With Selections from the Critique of Pure Reason,* ed. and trans. Gary Hatfield, rev. ed. (New York: Cambridge University Press, 2004), 55.

No world, no data. The existence of the noumenal world is an objective precondition for knowledge. However, the noumenon is accessible to us only as jumbled data. The things of the world that we come to know through the categories of understanding are the phenomena, the world as it appears to us. The noumenon, therefore, is unknowable.[18] Although Kant sought to secure knowledge once again in the radical subjectivity of the mind, what he delivered was an epistemology that is unable to know mind-independent reality.

Furthermore, Kant considered God, soul, justice, immortality, and freedom as noumenal because they did not belong to the structures of the mind. There is no logical necessity to understanding the world through these concepts, whereas such necessity does exist for space, time, quantity, quality, relation, and modality. We cannot know the world without these structures. But Kant's view was that we *can* understand the world without such concepts as God and immortality. Was he, then, an atheist? Not so. In fact, Kant claimed that he was making room for faith by abolishing knowledge.[19] Reason can no longer critique God's existence since God remains outside the scope of reason. But this is **fideism**, a nonrational faith.

Kant sits prominently in the lineage of Enlightenment thinkers who overvalued the mind's preeminent autonomous power and authority. Even God's existence must submit to the authority of autonomous reason. And for Kant, the traditional proofs for God's existence cannot pass the high bar of reason. Even if he makes room for nonrational, blind faith, such nonrational faith is considered irrational in our post-Darwinian society. Kant may have thought he ushered in a Copernican revolution in philosophy, but like the empiricists, he cannot escape his mind into reality. Reality is an inaccessible noumenon. As rational as Kant's system may be, in the end, it cannot shed its own irrationalism. We must live *as if* God exists in order to live ethical lives since we can't *know* that God exists. This desperate attempt to salvage morality is the consequence of the Enlightenment's overvaluation of reason and the denigration of the goodness of the body.

Conclusion

What is truth, and how can we know it? The ancient periods recognized that truth and knowledge were obtainable through reason without the aid of divine revelation. Yet, reason had to conform to reality. Whether reason had to peer into the objective reality of the Forms or abstract the form-in-matter,

18. Kant, *Prolegomena to Any Future Metaphysics*, 63–67.
19. Kant, *Prolegomena to Any Future Metaphysic*, 150.

correspondence with ultimate reality made knowledge possible. The Enlightenment, however, magnified reason's power, resulting in the submission of divine revelation and reality. The result of this submission was skepticism and agnosticism about reality and the denigration of our material bodies, effectively dehumanizing us through a philosophical approach. The body became an unfortunate appendage, an unnecessary hindrance to the task of reason. In this view, we are essentially thinking things. If it were possible, we would be more human as brains in a vat than as brains in a body.

The New Testament differs in its view of truth and knowledge. Truth is personified in the *logos* who valued the material world and our bodies so much that the Son became God-incarnate-in-human-flesh. This revelational truth is the light that makes knowledge of God possible (John 1:1–18), and John wrote his Gospel in order that we may believe the truth of Jesus. But belief is not merely rational; it requires the embodied ritual of repentance. Reason must submit to the authority of God, the creator of reality, who is the revealer of truth. Although many truths are available to all, it is God's prerogative to reveal and hide. Some knowledge of truth befitting human beings is available only through submission.

A renewal worldview on truth is a retrieval of this ancient wisdom. This is fitting since to re-new is to have continuity between the old and the new. While the fuller explanation must wait until the final chapter, we argue that a renewal worldview is a return to the body and a return of authority to the divine—specifically, authority for knowledge. The Spirit is the one who reveals truth, but the Spirit does not give information for its own sake. Revelation is given so that we can participate in the life of the Spirit of truth. The body matters for truth. Truth is not a disembodied affair. Knowledge of truth occurs through the mind and body that are submitted to the revelation of God.

Study Questions

1. What is the epistemic danger of prioritizing subjective reason over objective reality?

2. How can Christians reflect Plato's rationalistic soteriology?

3. As seen in Aristotle, what is the significance of having an ultimate explanation?

4. What are some identifiable faith rituals that can inform our knowledge about God, ourselves, or the world?

11

Contemporary Christian Epistemologies

Plantinga, Zagzebski, and Lindbeck

Key Words

Basic belief: *A belief that resides in the foundation of a belief system and does not receive justification from other beliefs.*

Cognitive-propositionalism: *The theory of doctrine that considers doctrines to be timeless propositional truths that correspond to reality.*

Coherence theory of truth: *The theory that locates the ground of truth not on states of affairs but on the coherent fit of a particular belief within one's system of beliefs.*

Correspondence theory of truth: *The theory that truth obtains when a proposition accurately refers to reality.*

Cultural-linguistic theory of religion: *The theory that religion is a culturally and linguistically shaped lived-framework through which all of life and thought are given meaning.*

Experiential-expressivism: *The theory of doctrine that considers doctrines to be noninformative symbols that express our inner feelings, attitudes, or existential orientations.*

Externalism: *The theory that awareness or potential awareness of the conditions that turn belief into knowledge is unnecessary.*

Foundationalism: *An epistemological structure that divides between basic and nonbasic beliefs.*

Internalism: *The theory that justifying reason or evidence must be accessible or potentially accessible to the mind.*

Nonbasic belief: *A belief that receives justification from other beliefs and is not in the foundation.*

Warrant: *The quality or quantity that turns mere true belief into knowledge.*

I f the ancient question was "What is truth?" then the Enlightenment question was "How do we know the truth?" As we saw in the last chapter, the answer was radically subjectivized. That is, the capability of the mind was exalted as the sole and ultimate arbiter of truth. For Descartes, the mind was the absolutely certain beginning point of knowledge that cannot be doubted. Hume did much to blunt this confidence but led us into skepticism. Kant provided a synthesis that was seen as the best marriage between empiricism and rationalism and avoided Hume's radical skepticism, but it also made the external world as it is—truth of ultimate reality—unavailable to human knowledge.

Contemporary Christian philosophers and theologians have continually asked the same questions: How can we know anything? And how can we know that we know? While questions of skepticism remain and Kant's point that reality is interpreted continues in various fields, contemporary epistemologists have predominantly focused on what justifies beliefs and turns true beliefs into knowledge. These are important questions, after all. We hold many beliefs, but not all beliefs are true. Moreover, we can hold true beliefs but not know why or how they are true. For example, let's pretend that, due to the extraordinary play of Tom Brady with the Tampa Bay Buccaneers football team, I tell students that I know he will play until he's fifty years old. In the 2027–28 NFL season, Brady indeed plays, fueled in part by the salty tears of his former coach, Bill Belichick. However, did I truly know that Brady would continue playing until age fifty, or did I have mere belief that turned out to be true? We can extend this example to every area of our lives. Do I know that God exists, that it will rain tomorrow, or that the earth is round? If so, how?

The questions about how we can know and how we can know that we know have led contemporary epistemology into two camps, internalism and externalism, which we will explain below. The three contemporary Christian philosophers and theologians that we survey in this chapter, representing Reformed, Roman Catholic, and Lutheran traditions, fall along a spectrum between these two camps, and they have been chosen due to their important contributions to knowledge and truth.

The Reformed philosopher Alvin Plantinga is a pivotal figure in the history of twentieth- and twenty-first-century philosophy. Credited with playing a central role in the revitalization of Christian philosophy and with encouraging a renaissance of Christian philosophers, Plantinga was called "America's leading orthodox Protestant philosopher of God" by *Time* magazine.[1] Linda Zagzebski is a Roman Catholic philosopher who draws from virtue ethics to develop her responsibilist form of virtue epistemology. Finally, George Lindbeck is a Lutheran

---

1. Quoted by Philip Blosser, "God among the Philosophers," *New Oxford Review* 66, no. 9 (1999): 39.

postliberal theologian whose contribution was primarily to the theory of doctrine and meaning, but his postliberalism made intriguing and controversial remarks about knowledge and truth that are helpful for identifying certain markers for a renewal worldview. Before we survey these figures, we will provide a brief explanation of internalism, externalism, and two theories of truth.

An Overview of Knowledge and Truth

From the time of Plato until 1963, the standard account of propositional knowledge consisted of justified true belief (JTB). In order for a belief to be knowledge, it must be a true belief. While we can have false beliefs, we can't know what is false. I can believe that I am you, but I can't know that I am you no matter the sincerity of my belief because that belief is false. Importantly, then, we must have some justification for our true beliefs in order to claim knowledge. Such justification is provided by good evidence or arguments. But what was so significant about 1963 that the standard account no longer held in the eyes of the philosophical majority? That year, Edmund Gettier wrote a three-page paper titled "Is Justified True Belief Knowledge?" that refuted this standard account by demonstrating that JTB can be accidentally true.[2] For example, let us imagine that a clock malfunctioned right at midnight. The next afternoon, a person glimpses the clock exactly at twelve o'clock in the afternoon and comes to believe the time. Let's say that this belief is true. His belief is justified because his internal body clock usually has him checking the clock around this time as he looks forward to his lunch break. All the normal phenomena accompany his body clock: he's hungry, the sun is high in the sky, and his coworkers have begun leaving for lunch. Therefore, his belief that it's twelve o'clock is a justified true belief. Yet, he does not know the time because his JTB is accidentally true.

Contemporary epistemology is predominantly represented by the division between internalism and externalism that arose after Gettier. **Internalism** is the theory that justifying reason or evidence must be accessible or potentially accessible to the mind. If I know that God exists, it's because I have a piece of good evidence or argument for God's existence, or I at least know where to look for one. Internalists have generally taken two approaches to solve the Gettier dilemma that JTB is insufficient for knowledge. First, some doubled down and stated that the standard account still holds and that the Gettier cases merely exemplify scenarios that lack justification. In the case of the broken clock, simply looking at the clock around lunchtime does not confer justification on the resulting belief. Second, others argued that JTB is a necessary but insufficient

---

2. Edmund L. Gettier, "Is Justified True Belief Knowledge?," *Analysis* 23, no. 6 (1963): 121–23.

condition for knowledge and that some fourth requirement is necessary to obtain knowledge (that is, JTB plus some other condition C).[3]

If internalism is optimistic about JTB as at least a necessary condition for knowledge, then externalism represents a pessimistic outlook. Specifically, **externalism** rejects the view that our awareness or potential awareness of what justifies a belief is not just insufficient but also unnecessary for knowledge. A Christian externalist would claim that Christians do not need to provide or have access to good evidence or arguments for God's existence as long as their belief in God resulted from some reliable knowing process, such as a type of spiritual or mystical perception.[4] The view is called externalism because we don't need to be mentally aware of the relevant reliable mechanism at work. By rejecting this awareness requirement, externalism also replaced or reinterpreted justification. It either replaces justification because knowledge does not require it or reinterprets it externally such that justification does not require mental awareness. If our mental faculties are functioning well or properly, then the beliefs they produce are justified.[5]

Both internalism and externalism consider truth to be a necessary component of knowledge. But how is truth obtained? Surely it's not the case that merely having a belief makes it true. Moreover, what is the nature of truth? In our globalized and interconnected world, can we still say that truth is objective and stable? Hasn't our exposure to the panoply of diverse beliefs, customs, and morality proven that truth is culturally, if not also individualistically, relative?

Relativism contends that truth is dependent on the creative ability of individuals or cultures. Access to diversity through global travel and the internet has increased the popularity of relativism. Exposure to diverse beliefs and lifestyles has begun to erode our confidence in Western beliefs and ways of life. Since truth is dependent on the perspectives of individuals or cultures, the West's pronouncements of truth, whether religious, moral, or scientific, are but one perspective among a sea of perspectives and cannot claim superiority over others.[6] Even within the US, critique of others' beliefs is often considered intolerant and colonial, given the lack of a monolithic US culture.

---

3. J. P. Moreland and William Lane Craig, *Philosophical Foundations for a Christian Worldview*, 2nd ed. (Downers Grove, IL: IVP Academic, 2017), 68–70.

4. See William P. Alston, *Perceiving God: The Epistemology of Religious Experience* (Ithaca, NY: Cornell University Press, 1991). More specifically, belief in God would have *prima facie* or initial justification, which can be overcome or defeated.

5. Some, like Michael Bergmann, reinterpret justification externally. As we will see below, Alvin Plantinga replaced justification with warrant as the positive epistemic status that turns mere true belief into knowledge. See Michael Bergmann, *Justification without Awareness* (New York: Oxford University Press, 2006), 132–51.

6. The rise of relativism did not begin with globalization, however. It was present in Protagoras's claim that man is the measure of all things, and it found powerful expression in Friedrich Nietzsche,

Objectivism considers truth as discoverable and not socially constructed. New truths can come into existence, but such truths are not relative and dependent on the preferential whim of individuals or cultures. Objective truth is mind-independent and transcendental. Even if everyone sincerely believed that 2 + 2 = 5, they would be sincerely wrong since mathematical truth is not dependent on human beliefs. It transcends beliefs, and beliefs, to be true, must conform to mind-independent states of affairs. Christianity is necessarily committed to objectivism. Even if every belief about the world is relative, Christians believe that God exists independently of our minds. God has to exist prior to humans who decide to think relativistically.

Objectivism is traditionally related to the **correspondence theory of truth**, the theory that truth obtains when a proposition accurately refers to reality. Its traditional rival, the **coherence theory of truth**, is related to relativism and locates the ground of truth not on states of affairs but on the coherent fit of a particular belief within one's system of beliefs. Truth is not dependent on mind-independent reality. A coherent belief is not only justified in its coherence in relation to one's larger web of beliefs, but it obtains truth by the very fact of its justification. But we saw above that justified belief can be accidentally true, so the coherentist theory of truth (and justification) cannot deliver knowledge. Moreover, if truth is dependent merely on coherence, then mutually exclusive webs of beliefs can be justified. But this runs afoul of the law of noncontradiction—that a proposition cannot be both true and false in the same sense at the same time—and the law of excluded middle—that a proposition is either true or false. For coherentism, the Christian belief that Jesus is Lord can be coherently true to one, and the atheist belief that Jesus was merely a human being can be coherently true to another. Because coherentism is divorced from external mind-independent reality, both propositions can be true, although objectivism would claim that only one can be true.

Given its objectivism, the correspondence theory aligns better with Christianity. If God exists, then the truth of God's existence is not based on its coherent fit within one's entire set of beliefs, as if God would only exist if the belief is either coherent or part of a web of beliefs. The truth of God's existence is based solely on the mind-independent reality of God's existence. Kevin Diller thus states that Christianity is committed to a minimalist correspondence view,

---

a German philosopher and philologist, according to whom there is no pure, objective knowledge that governs all persons, whether derived from the Platonic Forms or from a transcendent God. In his famous parable of the madman, Nietzsche tells the story of the madman who proclaims the death of God, which results in the loss of an objective universal standard of truth—hence, we must create our own reality. Although the madman concludes that his message arrived too early, his message has come of age in our times. See Friedrich Nietzsche, *The Gay Science*, trans. Thomas Common (Mineola, NY: Dover, 2006), §125.

even if not to any specific correspondence theory.[7] A Christian worldview thus sees truth as a *mind-independent* transcendental. Correspondence theory encourages humility since knowledge of truth is not the product of autonomous human minds. Instead, humans must submit to the truth of reality. Inasmuch as the truth of reality is the product of God's creative work, this submission is ultimately a submission to God that acknowledges God's lordship in all reality.

The next sections exposit three significant figures in contemporary epistemology. While there are differences among them, a triperspectival renewal worldview sees these three representatives as containing amenable interrelated elements that we shall see more of in the next chapter. In fact, we'd like to remark that the strength of renewal Christianity, its global diversity, allows for continuity between seemingly different Christian traditions. The next sections act like a microcosm of this diversity that renewal Christianity takes as interrelated perspectives.

Plantinga as Representative of Externalist Reformed Epistemology

Alvin Plantinga's externalist Reformed epistemology is considered Reformed because he drew inspiration from the Reformer John Calvin, and it is externalist because Christian beliefs do not require evidence or arguments to be considered knowledge.[8] In his first books, Plantinga likened belief in God to belief in other minds. Prior to reaching that conclusion, he argued that both theistic arguments for and atheistic arguments against God's existence failed. Given his conclusion, must we all be agnostics? No, because the best argument for other minds also fails, but it is still rational to believe that other people have minds like mine even without an undefeated argument. Why can't belief in God be like belief in other minds?[9]

Plantinga, motivated by his Reformed tradition, has always viewed belief in God as the starting point of belief. According to the Reformed theologian Herman Bavinck, Christians do not believe in God on the basis of arguments,

7. Kevin Diller, *Theology's Epistemological Dilemma: How Karl Barth and Alvin Plantinga Provide a Unified Response* (Downers Grove, IL: InterVarsity, 2014), 39.

8. This does not mean that arguments for God's existence are unimportant. They are merely unnecessary for the production of faith, which Plantinga defines as "firm and certain knowledge of God." Alvin Plantinga, *Warranted Christian Belief* (New York: Oxford University Press, 2000), 206. He himself has contributed arguments for God's existence. See Alvin Plantinga, *The Nature of Necessity* (Oxford: Clarendon, 1974), 212–16; and Alvin Plantinga, "Two Dozen (or So) Theistic Arguments," in *Alvin Plantinga*, ed. Deane-Peter Baker (New York: Cambridge University Press, 2007), 203–28. For a highly technical work devoted to developing Plantinga's two dozen arguments, see Jerry L. Walls and Trent Dougherty, eds., *Two Dozen (or So) Arguments for God: The Plantinga Project* (New York: Oxford University Press, 2018).

9. See Alvin Plantinga, *God and Other Minds: A Study of the Rational Justification of Belief in God* (Ithaca, NY: Cornell University Press, 1967).

but they have the right to believe in God without arguments. More boldly, knowledge of God does not come through arguments; belief in God is like belief in the self and the external world. Likewise, Calvin argued that humans are endowed with an inward awareness of divinity that was damaged by sin (Rom. 1:18–21).[10] Since sin leads us to unbelief, it is unbelief that is the epistemically subpar state, the product of improperly functioning, sin-damaged belief-producing equipment.[11] Faith is thus not dependent on arguments since God has endowed us with an inborn disposition to believe. What is needed is the healing of this inborn disposition. Plantinga even argues against believing in God based on arguments because such belief will be unstable. We will forever look out for arguments and counterarguments to sustain our faith. Just as one does not believe in his spouse's existence based on arguments, it would be epistemically subpar to believe in God on the basis of arguments.[12]

But why is there so much social pressure to believe in God based on evidence or arguments? Plantinga believes this pressure is due to the internalist assumption that belief requires accessible justification for its rationality. Plantinga calls this the evidentialist objection to theistic belief, according to which belief in God is irrational because it lacks adequate evidence. He critiques the evidentialist objection indirectly by criticizing a form of foundationalism called classical foundationalism, which the evidentialist objection presupposes. **Foundationalism** is an epistemological structure that divides between basic and nonbasic beliefs (see fig. 11.1). Foundationalism can be likened to a pyramid made up of various beliefs. The foundation of the pyramid consists of basic beliefs. Above the foundation are nonbasic beliefs.

Figure 11.1

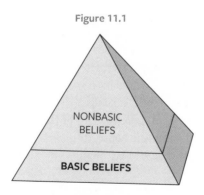

NONBASIC BELIEFS

BASIC BELIEFS

10. This damage to our mental faculties is called the noetic effects of sin. "Noetic" comes from the Greek word *nous*, which means mind.

11. Alvin Plantinga, "The Reformed Objection to Natural Theology," *Proceedings of the American Catholic Philosophical Association* 54 (1980): 50–52.

12. Plantinga, "Reformed Objection to Natural Theology," 53.

Basic beliefs are immediate beliefs. They are not the product of reflection and inference. For example, perceptual beliefs like seeing a cup in front of my desk or memories like what I had for breakfast are basic beliefs. I do not infer them from other beliefs. But not all basic beliefs are made equal. Properly basic beliefs are justified in themselves, and only they qualify as foundational beliefs. The examples above can qualify as properly basic beliefs. Some basic beliefs, however, are not self-justified even though they are immediately formed. For example, hallucinogens can create basic beliefs that are unjustified and disqualified from being foundational beliefs. Properly basic beliefs are thus basic beliefs that meet some condition that provides justification for proper basicality. A **nonbasic belief** is an inferential, reflective belief, and it receives justification from other beliefs until the chain of justification terminates on some properly basic belief. Recall the example in chapter 10 of a child who continually asks "Why?" to every explanation. As long as you can give a reason, you are probably giving a justificatory reason for a nonbasic belief. However, the chain of explanation must stop somewhere.[13] If the final explanation (if you didn't give up purely out of exhaustion) is self-justified, then you have probably reached the foundational properly basic belief that provides justification to the nonbasic belief. Nonbasic beliefs are thus the superstructure of the pyramid that requires support from the foundation of properly basic beliefs.

Classical foundationalism is a stringent form of foundationalism that specifies the conditions of properly basic beliefs as self-evidence, sense perception, or incorrigibility. That is, beliefs qualify as properly basic if they are self-evident or rationally intuitive, based on our sense experience, or psychologically undeniable. Any other beliefs are nonbasic and require evidence for their justification. The evidentialist objector assumes classical foundationalism and does not include belief in God as properly basic. It is rather a nonbasic belief that requires evidence for justification. However, Plantinga argues that classical foundationalism cannot meet its own standard. It is neither self-evident, based on the senses, or incorrigible, so it's not properly basic. Neither is there any argument that seems to justify the truth of classical foundationalism, disqualifying it as a justified nonbasic belief. By dismissing classical foundationalism, Plantinga concludes that we also dismiss the evidentialist objection that presupposes it.

Against evidentialism, Plantinga developed his proper functionalist theory of warrant. **Warrant** is what turns mere true belief into knowledge. It is a preferred term for Plantinga because he views justification as overly burdened with

13. This termination of explanation stops the infinite regress of explanations and is one of the motivations and attractions of foundationalism.

internalist demands and as unnecessary for knowledge. A necessary condition for warrant is the proper functioning of our cognitive faculties—that is, any equipment that contributes to our belief formation at any given time. If our cognitive faculties malfunction, then no amount of justification will help produce knowledge. In a rather humorous example of "the epistemically inflexible climber," Plantinga illustrates a scenario in which a mountain climber, while climbing in the Tetons, is struck by high cosmic radiation that fixes his current belief that he is climbing a mountain (an example of cognitive malfunction). Despite his friend's best efforts to get him down the mountain and snap him out of this belief by taking him to the opera, his belief remains firm that he is climbing in the Tetons. His belief is coherent within his web of beliefs, and it is justified—he is experiencing the phenomenon of mountain climbing—but he lacks warrant because his belief is the product of malfunctioning cognitive faculties.[14]

Proper function is the first of four conditions for warrant. The determination of *proper* function is set by the design plan of the cognitive faculties, the second condition. We can recognize design and its proper function for the most part. For example, we know the broad design plan of a car or heart, and we know when they are functioning properly or improperly. Design plan does not necessitate supernatural design, although Plantinga argues that supernatural design accounts for proper function better than atheism.[15] The third condition is a favorable environment for the proper functioning of the cognitive faculties for which they were designed. Our cognitive faculties are not designed to function properly under the influence of hallucinogens. Misleading situations that limit perception, such as deception and distance, are also unfavorable environments that impede warrant. In order for our cognitive faculties to function properly to form true beliefs, the epistemic environment must be favorable. Fourth, the design plan must be a good one, with high objective probability that it will produce true beliefs. Not every design plan is a good one. A cognitive faculty designed by an infantile deity will be less reliable than one designed by a perfect deity.

Based on his theory of warrant, Plantinga argues that Christian beliefs can have warrant if they are produced by properly functioning cognitive faculties operating in favorable environments according to a design plan that is successfully aimed at truth. Although our inner awareness of divinity is damaged by sin, the Holy Spirit can heal our cognitive faculties to function properly again

14. Alvin Plantinga, *Warrant: The Current Debate* (New York: Oxford University Press, 1993), 82.
15. Alvin Plantinga, *Where the Conflict Really Lies: Science, Religion, and Naturalism* (New York: Oxford University Press, 2011), 307–50.

in order to produce faith. We should expect this to happen if we are living in God's world. God has designed the environments for the type of beings we are and designed us reliably to produce true beliefs in conjunction with the activity of the Holy Spirit in us. Therefore, Christian beliefs can be warranted—that is, they can be knowledge—without justifying arguments, just as our everyday perceptual beliefs are warranted without arguments if they are produced by cognitive faculties functioning properly in a favorable environment according to a design plan that is successfully aimed at true beliefs.

Zagzebski as Representative of Catholic Virtue Epistemology

Linda Zagzebski astutely identifies internalism and externalism with the ethical theories of deontology and teleology. According to the former, morality is based on universal moral principles (think: the Ten Commandments). For the latter, morality is based on good outcomes of action, like saving more lives while sacrificing the lives of a few. Internalism is deontological because it requires the fulfillment of epistemic duties to justify beliefs (e.g., providing arguments). Externalism is teleological because the reliability of cognitive faculties is based on there being a greater number of true beliefs produced than false beliefs. Zagzebski argues that we must move beyond the internalism-externalism and deontological-teleological debate and focus instead on the role that virtuous character plays in belief formation.[16]

Zagzebski defines knowledge as "cognitive contact with reality arising from . . . 'acts of intellectual virtue.'"[17] Truth is correspondent, but knowledge of truth is not passive, as it is for Plantinga. People develop knowledge by practicing intellectual virtues. For example, I will not gain knowledge of physics by playing video games all day. I will need to be studious and practice great resolve to digest the difficult material. But such an arduous task will be greatly rewarding once I advance in my knowledge of physics. Intellectual virtue thus adds positive value to the knower and the knowledge. The knowledge is hard-earned and valuable, and the knower is to be commended for his virtuous efforts. Thus, how we go about discovering truth is as important as the knowledge of truth. For example, the value of a good espresso (knowledge) is dependent on the skill of its maker (intellectual virtue). For Zagzebski, because the knower plays no

16. Zagzebski's virtue epistemology is responsibilist or character based. The more widely known virtue epistemology is reliabilist, under which Plantinga's Reformed epistemology can also fall. See Guy Axtell, "Recent Work on Virtue Epistemology," *American Philosophical Quarterly* 34, no. 1 (1997): 3–4.

17. Linda T. Zagzebski, *Virtues of the Mind: An Inquiry into the Nature of Virtue and the Ethical Foundations of Knowledge* (Cambridge: Cambridge University Press, 1996), xv.

active role in receiving credit for knowledge, Plantinga's proper functionalism cannot explain the differences in value of true beliefs having enough warrant for knowledge when those beliefs are produced by properly versus improperly functioning faculties. A good espresso that is made by properly functioning and improperly functioning espresso machines still retains its value, while the value of the machine is not retained.[18] Intellectual virtue adds value to both the knowledge and the knower and provides a fuller picture of the epistemic process.[19] What, then, is virtue, and why is it important to knowledge?

Virtue is an enduring excellent trait or inner disposition of character that is acquired over time through habitual action.[20] It is not an act that occurs occasionally but a characteristic that identifies a person. A virtuous person can commit a wrong, but such acts are accidents of character and do not characterize her identity, such that an honest person can tell a lie in a moment of weakness, but people would not characterize her as a liar. Conversely, a habitual liar who tells the truth occasionally will not be considered an honest person. Virtue also requires having emotional motivations for certain ends and reliably succeeding in achieving that end. For example, an intellectually fair person desires to achieve fairness in the pursuit of knowledge and is reliably successful in being fair. One who lacks the motivation for fairness and is not reliably fair would not be intellectually fair. Zagzebski considers this motivational element to be internalist since we have access to our motivations.

Intellectual virtues generally are motivated by the goal of obtaining knowledge and are reliably successful in that goal. These virtues lead the knower to truth-conducive processes, which further lead her to skills that aid in the acquisition of knowledge, skills that reliably lead to knowledge. Virtue thus has a success component, which is externalist. Where a supposed intellectual virtue fails to be truth- and knowledge-conducive, it fails to be an intellectual

18. Linda T. Zagzebski, *On Epistemology* (Belmont, CA: Wadsworth Cengage Learning, 2009), 112–13.

19. Against the critique that virtue epistemology can't account for immediate beliefs that are not the product of virtuous habits, Zagzebski argues that self-trust of one's belief-forming faculties is the product of virtuous habit. See Zagzebski, *On Epistemology*, 128. Virtue responsibilism recognizes the role of reliable faculties in the production of immediate beliefs more readily than virtue reliabilism's recognition of character-based virtues in the epistemic process. See Jason Baehr, "Character, Reliability and Virtue Epistemology," *Philosophical Quarterly* 56, no. 223 (2006): 201–6.

20. Zagzebski lists some intellectual virtues as "intellectual carefulness, perseverance, humility, vigor, flexibility, courage, and thoroughness," as well as "open-mindedness, insightfulness . . . [and] intellectual integrity." Some intellectual vices are "intellectual pride, negligence, idleness, cowardice, conformity, carelessness, rigidity, prejudice, wishful thinking, closed-mindedness, insensitivity to detail, obtuseness, and lack of thoroughness." Zagzebski, *Virtues of the Mind*, 152, 155. For a curated list of virtues that are not separated between the intellectual and moral, see "The Virtues," The Virtues Project, last modified June 29, 2021, https://www.virtuesproject.com/virtues-definitions-1.

virtue. However, epistemic success need not be immediate. In certain areas of knowledge, such as the frontiers of cutting-edge knowledge, the ratio of true to false beliefs may be low. However, if the relevant intellectual virtues are necessary for advancing knowledge, then their rate of reliability is circumstance-specific and can be considered successful even if the ratio between true and false beliefs in the process of advancing knowledge is low.[21]

As habits, virtues develop through our direct control over our actions. However, does the voluntariness of action create a disanalogy between our actions and beliefs? It doesn't seem that we have direct control over our beliefs like we have over our actions. Even if someone were to grant us a lifetime of riches if we could voluntarily believe that our heads were made of cheese, such belief production would be impossible (as would our dream of a life of leisure). Even without direct control, Zagzebski argues that we can have a range of control, from indirect to no control at all.[22] Some beliefs are completely involuntary. But we can also direct our actions in certain ways to aid in belief formation. For example, motivated by curiosity and thoroughness, we can perform research on a topic to arrive at a belief that we had previously lacked. Moreover, character can involuntarily shape belief formation. Virtuous and vicious people will have tendencies for certain types of beliefs even if they are involuntary. A kind person will tend to see the best in every person, whereas a cynic will view every situation in a negative light. "It takes [good or] bad will to have certain beliefs."[23] Therefore, even involuntary beliefs can lead to a person's praise- or blameworthiness, revealing the extent to which we can be responsible for our beliefs.

Virtue epistemology calls attention to the centrality of epistemic conscientiousness in the knowing process, which highlights the agency of the knower. When the knower diligently practices the intellectual virtues, knowledge of truth is attainable. Virtue is a success concept; it entails knowledge. If a virtue is reliably unsuccessful, then it can't be a virtue. For Zagzebski, virtue epistemology avoids the Gettier problem due to this entailment. Gettier cases describe situations where failure of knowledge occurs due to some luck, but the intellectually virtuous person is motivated by knowledge and is successful in achieving her end. Gettier cases merely show instances in which intellectual virtue has not had the time to be practiced. If knowledge is cognitive contact with reality arising from intellectual virtue, then the latter part is missing; the definition of knowledge is not achieved.[24] Gettier cases reveal the reductive and atomistic issues in contemporary epistemology, which focus on a "single belief

21. Zagzebski, *Virtues of the Mind*, 182.
22. Zagzebski, *Virtues of the Mind*, 66.
23. Zagzebski, *Virtues of the Mind*, 68.
24. Zagzebski, *Virtues of the Mind*, 296–98.

of a single person at a single time" without considering the important role of embodied acts and character formation in the process of knowing.[25] While it is still possible for an intellectually virtuous person to fail to have knowledge due to luck, in the end, an intellectually virtuous person will be in a qualitatively better state than someone who is not intellectually virtuous.

Lindbeck as Representative of Postliberal Epistemology

Unlike Plantinga and Zagzebski, who are philosophers, George Lindbeck is a postliberal theologian. While he was an established scholar in his own right, he came to greater prominence due to his theory of the nature of doctrine, part of which seemed to recommend theories of truth that are separate from and equal to referential truth and that conjured up suspicions (or sometimes celebrations) of relativism.[26] Lindbeck was invested in ecumenical dialogue (dialogue between different church traditions, such as between Roman Catholics and Lutherans), and he was concerned with examining the function of doctrine in order to promote church unity in the face of doctrinal differences. Can Pentecostals and cessationists who differ on the continuing gifts of the Holy Spirit have ecumenical dialogue without forfeiting their tradition-specific doctrines, for example? To clear such doctrinal impasse, Lindbeck identified two theories of doctrine before offering his own.

The first view, **cognitive-propositionalism**, is familiar to conservative Evangelicalism. It considers doctrines to be timeless propositional truths that correspond to reality. This theory has been a classical hindrance to ecumenical dialogue. Ecumenical unity requires changes in traditions, but not at the expense of their essential traits.[27] If cognitive-propositionalism is true, then ecumenical dialogue ought to be replaced by polemical debates that seek the capitulation of one side. The second theory of doctrine, which Lindbeck attributes to modern liberal theology and calls **experiential-expressivism**, is the opposite of cognitive-propositionalism because it considers doctrines to be noninformative symbols that express our "inner feelings, attitudes, or existential orientations."[28] Doctrine is severely curtailed or even eliminated altogether since it is mere human symbols that stand in for the more important reality of

---

25. Zagzebski, *Virtues of the Mind*, 44.

26. For example, James K. A. Smith sees Lindbeck's postliberalism as a Christian relativism. See James K. A. Smith, *Who's Afraid of Relativism? Community, Contingency, and Creaturehood* (Grand Rapids: Baker Academic, 2014).

27. George Lindbeck, "The Unity We Seek: Setting the Agenda for Ecumenism," *Christian Century* 122 (2005): 28.

28. George A. Lindbeck, *The Nature of Doctrine: Religion and Theology in a Postliberal Age* (Louisville: Westminster John Knox, 1984), 16.

universal human experience and feelings of the divine. Since doctrines play no referential role, even different religions can be said to share the same faith. Contradictory doctrines are but finite, fallible human interpretations of the universal experience of divine reality. If ecumenism seeks to maintain the integrity of theological traditions, then experiential-expressivism threatens this integrity since distinctive elements are reduced to universal feelings, attitudes, or experiences.

In place of these two theories, Lindbeck offers his **cultural-linguistic theory of religion**, according to which religion is a culturally and linguistically shaped lived-framework through which all of life and thought are given meaning. As an interpretive framework, religion interprets subjective experience rather than subjective experience defining religion. To become religious is not primarily about learning propositional doctrines but about becoming socialized into religion's language and habits that develop the conceptual scheme to interpret the world anew. The core of religion is thus its culturally and linguistically derived practices and beliefs that develop into doctrines. Doctrine is not a timelessly true proposition but the explicit formalization of a tradition's beliefs and practices. The "truth" of a doctrine is thus its fidelity to the tradition's cultural-linguistic practices. For Christian orthodoxy, such practices are not derived from just any culture and language but from the narrative of Scripture. Orthodoxy is dependent on faithful expressions of scripturally driven communal practices, which derive from a tradition's cultural-linguistic understanding of Scripture's narrative world. An integrative relationship thus exists between the church's scriptural life-world, its practices, and the broader cultural-linguistic world a tradition inhabits.

Controversially, doctrine is neither universally true nor universally false. Rather, its role is regulative, like grammar. Grammar is neither true nor false. Korean grammar is not somehow truer than Spanish grammar. Grammar regulates its particular languages for their proper use. Similarly, doctrine is like different road rules. The rule about driving on the right or left side of the road is dependent on different nations/traditions. As the grammar of a theological tradition, doctrine regulates God-talk without claiming any truth about external reality, just as the rules of the road are not objectively and universally true and applicable. Doctrine merely assures that a tradition's practices and beliefs are expressed consistently.

Doctrines are thus not formed top-down, as if some magisterium chooses certain rules to lord over the church's speech. Rather, doctrines arise bottom-up, from Christian practices and beliefs that faithfully enact the narrative worldview of Scripture. Doctrines are reflections on practices and beliefs that solidify the latter into explicit formulations. Faithful worship gives the materials for doctrinal formulation, and worship consists not merely of music but also of narratives and practices that bear witness to the life-world of Scripture. It is these narratives, confessions, and practices that can be true. Doctrine's role is to act as the gatekeeper of orthodoxy, which describes and enforces the faithful enactments of the church's narrative-confessional practices.

Lindbeck illustrates this point in his famous analogy of the crusader cleaving the head of the infidel while shouting, "Christ is Lord!" While this utterance would be timelessly true for the cognitive-propositionalist, the cultural-linguist finds it false because the act does not meet the grammar of the Christian narrative of the peaceable kingdom. Context and use determine the truth of this speech. The proclamation becomes orthodox according to its fidelity to Scripture's vision of Christ's lordship, in such practices as adoration and caring for the least of the world, not in violent acts that refuse the loving of enemies.[29] Just as there is no universal language or linguistic meaning, the contextual use of language is critical for a statement's meaningfulness and truth.

Lindbeck calls this coherent fit of doctrine with biblical narrative and action intrasystematic truth. A doctrine is intrasystematically true if it coheres with the narrative world of the Bible. Moreover, the faithfulness or unfaithfulness of its enactment contributes toward its truth. Lindbeck also offers a second type of truth called categorial truth. Categories are the concepts within a religion that allow for correspondence. For example, divinity talk in atheism is both intrasystematically and categorially false because the concept of divinity does not cohere with naturalism, and naturalism does not contain a category of divinity in its worldview. The crusader's violent act and proclamation are intrasystematically and categorially false because Christianity lacks such brutality in its narrative structure.

Although doctrine isn't universally true, it can become true within context, just as the road rules of the US are contextually true within that particular place. Doctrine can achieve referential truth if it is intrasystematically and categorially true. God-speak must cohere with the narrative of the biblical drama. And inasmuch as Christianity is irreducible to mere belief, doctrinal truth is necessarily tied to faithful performance. As James 2:20 indicates, mere belief without faithful performance does not cohere with the Christian religion. Christianity does not contain categories that allow for mere belief without faithful action. This reiterates that a Christian worldview is not merely mental. Faithfully living

---

29. This view is similar to Karl Barth's doctrine of revelation, which does not hold Scripture as revelation unless it witnesses to itself through proclamation. Even the biblical authors witness beyond themselves and their words in their writing. See Karl Barth, *Church Dogmatics*, vol. I/1, *The Doctrine of the Word of God*, ed. G. W. Bromiley and T. F. Torrance, 2nd ed. (Peabody, MA: Hendrickson, 1975), 111.

into the drama of God's covenantal and redemptive involvement is critical for defining the "Christian" aspect of this worldview. Thus worldview and truth are both narratively mental and actively performative. Lindbeck's theory of truth is thus performatively correspondent.[30] That is, a possible referential truth can become false for us due to incoherence or categorial inadequacy. Postliberalism, in sum, requires more than mere belief for allegiance to God. It calls us to a faithful life.

Conclusion

The internalism-externalism debate has waged since the time of Gettier. This chapter's three figures have responded to Gettier in various ways. Plantinga squarely lands on the side of externalism. Knowledge is true belief plus the four conditions for warrant. Zagzebski employs both internalism and externalism. Responsible epistemic action is internalist, and the reliable success of virtue is externalist. Importantly, she rejects the traditional formulation of knowledge as true belief plus some other condition. Rather, she marries truth with warrant so that true belief is knowledge, and true belief is achieved by character virtues. Intellectual virtues bring about epistemic success, putting the knower in contact with reality. Finally, Lindbeck does not enter into the internalism-externalism debate, although he agrees with both Plantinga and Zagzebski that truth is ultimately referential. But how are we to understand Lindbeck's epistemology in relation to Plantinga and Zagzebski?

There are no essential contradictions between Lindbeck and Plantinga. Faithful beliefs can be knowledge if produced by properly functioning cognitive faculties. But we can broaden proper function and include embodied action as part of a relevant cognitive faculty for the knowledge of God. The crusader's actions that contribute toward belief are not functioning properly so his belief in Christ's lordship is not knowledge. Lindbeck's postliberalism has greater affinity with Zagzebski because the construction of doctrine and monitoring its regulative role requires intellectual virtue. Intellectual virtues are necessary for constructing faithful doctrines, whereas vicious motivation can hinder faithful doctrinal formulation and encourage wrong understanding of doctrine. Again, the crusader may have arrived at a different understanding of his place

---

30. Lindbeck admitted that he should have never categorized intrasystematic and categorial truths as truth. Rather, they are necessary conditions for the justification of correspondence truth. Therefore, the correspondence theory of truth is still the only truth theory that Lindbeck recognizes, although he makes achieving referential truth more stringent by adding intrasystematic and categorial conditions. See George A. Lindbeck, "George Lindbeck Replies to Avery Cardinal Dulles," *First Things* 139 (2004): 13–15.

in warfare if he had practiced intellectual courage and open-mindedness on whether he should have participated in the Crusades. Postliberalism also reminds us of the importance of good action for the obtainment of truth. Mere obtainment of referential truth could be possible even with vicious motives. But such beliefs, however ontologically true they may be, would be intrasystematically and categorially unjustified due to their vicious motives. Correspondence is (virtuously) performative.

As we move to the next chapter with its focus on the renewal perspectives on truth and knowledge, the question arises as to their continuity with the materials covered so far. Against the backdrop of the dominance of propositional truth and mentalist approaches to philosophy, it's true that renewal commitments to the importance of right belief, love of God, and faithful worship are discontinuous. However, the renewal approach does have great affinity with the embodied elements of Zagzebski and Lindbeck and with the proper functionalist epistemology of Plantinga. The primacy of embodiment will be made clear in the renewal figures of the next and final chapter, Steven Land and James K. A. Smith.

Study Questions

1. How can a Christian say that his or her belief is warranted without providing evidence or arguments?

2. How do intellectual virtues add value to the knower and knowledge?

3. Explain the regulative role of doctrine and its relationship to truth.

12

A Renewal Perspective
on Truth, Epistemology,
and Holistic Knowledge

Key Words

Narrative, affective knowledge: *A primary and irreducible knowledge that is prior to propositional knowledge and rooted in the narratives that we tell and are involved in and the affections that are elicited from those narratives.*

Spirituality: *A religious orientation toward the divine that integrates "beliefs and practices in the affections which are themselves evoked and expressed by those beliefs and practices."*[1]

What good is it to mentally know about the Spirit's power if it's lacking in our lives? We mentioned in the introduction that experience of the Spirit is the focal point of the renewal life. Theological interpretation proceeds from this pneumatological experience, which is understood through the lens of Acts 2. Not only does Scripture record past revelation that the Spirit illumines, but Scripture comes alive through the revelational experience of the Spirit in the here and now. Truth is never static or purely objective. The objective event of Scripture comes alive through the subjective event of the Spirit, such that mere objective truth does not have pride of place for Pentecostals.

---

1. Steven J. Land, *Pentecostal Spirituality: A Passion for the Kingdom* (Cleveland: CPT, 2010), 1.

In fact, the possibility of obtaining pure objective truth is seen as undesired, if not impossible. For the mere mental comprehension of truth without pneumatological encounter is the type of "cold creedalism" that North American classical Pentecostals fled at the turn of the twentieth century. It is the Spirit who leads us to truth, and such leading occurs through the Spirit's involvement in every aspect of a person's life. There is neither division among nor prominence between the head, the heart, and action. The Spirit desires to transform all three areas in order to actualize our love for God and neighbor. Mental knowledge of objective truth is deficient if the heart and action are wicked. Additionally, since the Spirit works through people situated throughout various spatiotemporal locations, human obtainment of pure objective truth becomes impossible. For just as the Spirit used the entirety of the biblical authors' cultural contexts to bring about God's revelation in Scripture, the Spirit also uses that same cultural context to bring people to the truth. Knowledge of truth, even the truth of Scripture, is thus always an interpretive event. This reality is exemplified in the diversity of beliefs and practices exhibited in the global renewal movements. However, the global movement shares the similarity of bodily encounter with the Spirit. For Pentecostals, then, truth is encountered by the mind and the body, and since the body is situated in particular places and times and the Spirit blows as the Spirit wills, truth is always possible but never fully consummated. Truth is now and not yet, actual but never absolute.

In this chapter, we will introduce two important renewal figures who have informed how Pentecostals ought to understand the knowledge of truth. With both, it is evident that the Christian life of knowing God is not primarily about having the right propositional doctrines, as important as that is. The mental life is but one part of our spirituality. To maintain the pride of place for the mental life is to turn this essential, God-given faculty to idolatry. For God cannot be captured and fully comprehended by the mind. To know God faithfully, we must know God through our affections, actions, and mind.

Steven Land's Pentecostal Spirituality

Steven Land's influential book *Pentecostal Spirituality* set forth the important thesis that Pentecostalism is a multifaceted tradition, especially regarding the relationship between reason and emotion. Land believes that there is much affinity between Pentecostals and non-Pentecostals *and* many differences between them. Although Land does not offer a renewal worldview or an explicit theory of truth or knowledge, his explanation of Pentecostalism as a spirituality describes how Pentecostals already approach the religious life as a worldview. In this way, Pentecostals primarily embody a worldview rather than thinking or believing it. This section describes Pentecostal spirituality and identifies the themes of its embedded worldview of truth.

Triperspectival, Embodied Spirituality

Land rightly describes Pentecostalism as a spirituality. It is not first and foremost a doctrinal movement as exemplified in many Protestant traditions. Unlike Protestantism, which began with Luther's doctrinal disputes with the Roman Catholic Church, modern renewal movements throughout the world began and grew through spiritual revival. First and foremost in the global renewal movements is the spiritual encounter with the living God through the Holy Spirit, who transforms not only our beliefs but also our affections and actions. Speaking from a North American classical Pentecostal perspective, Land thus argues that Pentecostalism is an affective spirituality. Shouldn't encounters with God change our affections deep in our hearts and lead us to a different vision of the world? It is this affective posture that leads Land to define **spirituality** as "the integration of beliefs and practices in the affections which are themselves evoked and expressed by those beliefs and practices."[2]

One might easily think that Pentecostalism is a counterpart to modern liberalism as an experiential-expressivist movement, in its emphasis on emotions, over against Evangelicalism's cognitive-propositionalism.[3] However, Land is quick to point out that affections, beliefs, and actions are mutually conditioning.[4] There is no hierarchy of importance between them, even if the affections act as the integrating core. For spirituality is not about the mere relationship between the affections, beliefs, and actions. Rather, it is about right beliefs (orthodoxy), right affections (orthopathos), and right practices (orthopraxis). We can't have right beliefs without right practices and affections. Nor can we have right affections without right beliefs and practices. And we can't have right practices without right beliefs and affections. The three dimensions are not separate entities that one can merely balance.[5] We can balance things without allowing the involved elements to interact with one another. Rather, practices, affections, and beliefs are perspectives within the whole. Just as a triangle can't exist if it's missing one or two angles, spirituality can't exist without this perspectival relationship among its parts. So, it is right affections about God and people that help us to live rightly and believe rightly.

2. Land, *Pentecostal Spirituality*, 1.
3. See chap. 11 on George Lindbeck's descriptions of experiential-expressivism and cognitive-propositionalism.
4. Land, *Pentecostal Spirituality*, 1.
5. Land, *Pentecostal Spirituality*, 34.

How can we have right beliefs if we hate God or people? If we say we believe God, but we hate God, we have to ask whether our belief about God is true. Relatedly, if our lives are filled with sin, can we truly say that we love God and have right beliefs? If we think we have orthodox beliefs about God but do not love God or live a life that reflects such a love, mustn't we say that our beliefs parallel the beliefs of demons? James 2:19 states that demons have right belief about God's oneness but tremble in terror rather than delight in love. They actively oppose God, indicating that mere orthodox belief is epistemically inferior to belief that accompanies right affections and practices. Pentecostalism is not primarily a doctrinal tradition. It holds "Spirit baptized living . . . as a normative model."[6] This embodied spirituality funds the imagination about our relation to truth in a renewal worldview.

The renewal life is centrally concerned with experiencing the power and presence of the Holy Spirit, which has mental and practical elements. This experience reshapes our affections, beliefs, and actions so that faith becomes a lived reality, not just some doctrine to memorize. God radically reshapes our worldview so that we are concerned not merely with ultimate questions about our origin, identity, purpose, and destiny (as important as those are) but also with how we are to live out our faith, Land says, in the "service of the people of God who are organically constituted as the body of Christ by the indwelling of the Holy Spirit."[7] Living out this faith requires imagining the world in a different way, and such imagination impacts how we feel about the world. We desire to be attuned to the world as God is attuned to the world, to love and hate what God loves and hates. Such an affective posture shapes how we participate in God's work in the world.

Worldview is dynamic and holistic. It is always reimagining the world as the domain of the Spirit, who blows as the Spirit wills (John 3:8). This surprising and unpredictable move of the Holy Spirit, who testifies to God's truth, must keep our worldview in a dynamic state because we can be surprised by how God's presence of truth manifests in the world, just as the disciples and the religious leaders were surprised by God's work in Jesus Christ that led to changes in beliefs, affections, and lives.[8] The transcendent truths of God mediated through the Holy Spirit are affective, practical, and mental. Renewal

6. L. William Oliverio, *Theological Hermeneutics in the Classical Pentecostal Tradition: A Typological Account* (Boston: Brill, 2015), 11.

7. Land, *Pentecostal Spirituality*, 21.

8. Recall the change in Peter, who started out as one who confessed right belief about Jesus but nevertheless failed to imagine Jesus's messianic call as the suffering servant and eventually became one who boldly proclaimed God's eschatological mission through Jesus and the Holy Spirit after his imagination was radically reoriented through the Spirit poured out at Pentecost.

worldview does not denigrate the mental but situates it in proper perspective and importance. It does not (or ought not) overemphasize the affective or the practical since orthopathos and orthopraxis are only possible with orthodoxy. When Pentecostals reject "man-made Creeds," they are not rejecting the importance of beliefs but saying no to "a creedalism which they believed brought disunity and rejected the new blessing that the sovereign Spirit was restoring among them."[9] Truth from a renewal perspective replaces the hegemony of propositional beliefs with an integrated, holistic understanding that arises from a triperspectival, embodied spirituality.

Theology, Prayer, and Spirit-Driven Knowledge

If theology is our reflective meditation on God, our way of pursuing the knowledge of truth, then theology too must be more than propositional. Unlike the caricatured picture of theologians debating arduously with one another on inane topics, Land describes the project of theology as an act of prayer. Indeed, this is a welcome reminder to theologians and other Christian scholars that the point of "theology is not to be identified solely or even primarily with systematic treatises, monographs, and scholarly apparatus in centers of academia. Theology begins in the prayerful response of persons to God."[10]

First, theology done merely in the "ivory towers" violates orthopraxy since knowledge of God ought to transform how we live our lives in communion with one another, especially our Christian brothers and sisters. Theology cannot merely be the plaything of intellectual elites to tickle their fancies. Second, prayer is the heart of spirituality because it is the mode of communing with the God of revelation. Land powerfully reminds us that "for Pentecostals it is impossible to know God and the things of God without prayer, because in prayer one responds to the Spirit of truth. When one ceases to be prayerfully open, even the light of truth or belief that one has becomes dark, distorted and may soon be forgotten."[11] Through prayer we address God and are addressed by God. Anselm, the medieval archbishop of Canterbury, exemplifies this prayerful theology in his work *Proslogion*. In response to Anselm's prayerful request that God reveal Godself to him, he receives a revelation of God's attribute of existence that we now understand as the ontological argument for God's existence.[12] Third, prayer reminds us that knowledge of God's truth is not the product of

---

9. Land, *Pentecostal Spirituality*, 22.

10. Land, *Pentecostal Spirituality*, 24.

11. Land, *Pentecostal Spirituality*, 24.

12. Anselm, "St. Anselm and Gaunilon, Proslogium, Preface and Chapters I–IV," in *Readings in Medieval Philosophy*, ed. Andrew B. Schoedinger (New York: Oxford University Press, 1996), 37–40.

our own rational powers but a gift from God, who makes God's truth accessible to our feeble minds and hearts. We don't accomplish the baptism or infilling of the Holy Spirit by our own holiness but rely on the sovereign work of the Holy Spirit. In the same way, Land reminds us that our knowledge of God is a divine gift made possible through prayer. Importantly, then, our epistemic authority of truth is not our own experience of the Spirit, as popularly understood. Rather, our authority is the agent behind the experience: the Holy Spirit.[13]

Land recognizes that this view might seem to contradict the authority of Scripture in the eyes of some, so he addresses this issue by arguing for a perspectival view of authority. The Spirit does not subjugate Scripture, as some might imagine, by simply allowing any "private revelations" to somehow violate the parameters of Scripture's truths. Likewise, Scripture does not subjugate the Spirit by relegating the work of the Spirit only to its illumination. The epistemic authority of the Spirit is due to the Spirit's mission in continuing the work of Christ that intends to gift and guide God's people who are formed through Scripture.[14]

This gift of the Spirit of truth presupposes that knowledge of God and God's truth is the result of right relation with God. Such right relation further presupposes an obedient life since the Spirit-filled life is made possible by and perpetuates the sanctified life. Therefore, Land argues that mere belief of truth that is not accompanied by obedience to that truth is a contradiction and a lie.[15] The Spirit-filled life that integrates orthodoxy and orthopraxis through orthopathos also unifies knowledge, truth, and ethics.[16] We must be committed to and know God's truth and ethically live it out.

Is Orthopathos the First among Equals?

Although orthodoxy, orthopraxis, and orthopathos are integrated, Land identifies orthopathos as the integrating center of Pentecostal spirituality. Does this mean that there is somehow a subtle hierarchy between affections, beliefs, and actions? After all, Land does not state that orthodoxy or orthopraxy are integrating centers. Has Land opened the door again to the emotion-reason dichotomy? Although Land applies the term "integrating center" only on orthopathos, his explanation provides equal integrity to the other elements. First, Pentecostal affections are shaped by biblical narratives, especially Acts 2. When the disciples were gathered in the upper room at Pentecost, they were already

13. Land, *Pentecostal Spirituality*, 27.
14. Land, *Pentecostal Spirituality*, 28.
15. Land, *Pentecostal Spirituality*, 26.
16. Land, *Pentecostal Spirituality*, 31.

caught up in the narrative of expectation. Jesus's command to his disciples in Acts 1:4–5 to wait for the baptism of the Holy Spirit in Jerusalem for the purpose of gospel witness located them in the drama of God's mission that propelled them in eager and prayerful expectation. Upon receiving the Spirit, Peter preached to the amazed crowd that gathered at the sight and sound of the great commotion, but his sermon was not a propositional, three-point sermon. It was a recounting of the divine eschatological (that is, end-times) drama that Peter wove through the Old Testament and the life, death, resurrection, ascension, and glorification of Jesus, who bestowed them with the promised Holy Spirit. It was this eschatological narrative that cut their hearts to the core and prompted them to ask, "Brothers, what should we do?" (Acts 2:37). This affective response prompted by the eschatological drama led to a devoted life that perpetuated the growth of the early church.

Second, biblical narratives are incorporated within Pentecostal narratives, which are eschatologically oriented in picturing Pentecostal renewal as God's involvement in the last days to restore the people of God before his final judgment. A particularly formative Pentecostal narrative structure, one that is central to the Pentecostal story, is the latter-rain motif, which provided the eschatological structure for understanding one's identity, purpose, and affective fervor. The early and latter rain represent the Palestinian weather cycle. Pentecostals applied this motif to God's involvement in the world, viewing the first Pentecostal outpouring on the early church as representing the early rain and the modern Pentecostal revivals as the latter rain that was to prepare the world for the imminent return of Jesus. Pentecostals used this narrative motif to locate themselves in God's drama, which acted as the worldview filter through which they understood the flow of reality.[17] It was through Pentecostal renewal that God was reestablishing the "apostolic faith . . . , power, authority, *pathos*, and practice."[18] This narrative thus provided the eschatological identity of Pentecostalism as an end-times movement, the eschatological purpose of mission, and the eschatological affections for missiological fervor and hopeful longing. As we will see later with James K. A. Smith, narrative and affection are intricately intertwined. Narratives evoke emotions, and emotions are embedded in narratives. The most powerful narratives are those that engage and shape our emotions, framing and directing our imagination and beliefs. Beliefs shape the affections, but they are narrative rather than propositional beliefs.

17. Kenneth Archer, *The Gospel Revisited: Towards a Pentecostal Theology of Worship and Witness* (Eugene, OR: Pickwick, 2011), 27–32.
18. Archer, *Gospel Revisited*, 50.

Third, the Wesleyan-Holiness theological background that made North American classical Pentecostalism possible insisted on a holy life of sanctification that must precede the baptism of the Holy Spirit. Even non-Wesleyan streams of Pentecostalism became "Wesleyanized" in agreeing that orthopraxy, the obedient life of holiness, precedes Spirit baptism. African American spirituality, a prominent source of classical Pentecostalism, expressed its theology through narratives, dreams, and visions and afforded maximal participation in church worship and life.[19] These various embodied means of theologizing denote a perspectival relationship between beliefs, affections, and practices.

Contributions toward a Renewal Worldview

Although Land does not offer a renewal worldview on truth, it is implicitly present in his writings. Truth is determined by God and God's divine drama. Our knowledge of truth can occur through theological reflection, but such reflection is made possible through Pentecostal spirituality, which integrates right affections, right actions, and right beliefs. Theoretical beliefs are important, but orthodox beliefs can only occur through these other means. Worldviews can and should provide propositional answers to ultimate questions, but a renewal worldview developed through a living spirituality indicates that truth is primarily felt, imagined through stories, and lived out. It is unsurprising that many renewal Christians throughout the globe have eschewed formal theological study given that living out God's calling is not primarily done through theoretical beliefs. While this has fostered anti-intellectualism in certain circles, it is a testimony to the importance of an embodied spirituality. And despite the prejudice against academic theology, Pentecostals have always participated in reflective theology. But such reflection is never divorced from right affections and actions. Our goal, then, is to show that the divide between mind and body and between belief and Spirit is actually a betrayal of our worldview. A renewal worldview on truth includes room for propositional truth, but truth is more than that.

To choose either the life of the mind or an impassioned, Spirit-driven life is an aberration to our worldview. Pentecostals have *always* theologized. We have always believed, even if much of our theologizing came through prayers and stories. Our Spirit-driven emotions and experiences drive us toward belief and action. The Spirit interacts with us in our pursuit of God's mission and continually reforms and deepens our beliefs and emotions. What Land helps us discover is that this spirituality is itself a description of our worldview. A

19. Land, *Pentecostal Spirituality*, 38–43. For a study on the background of classical Pentecostalism, see Donald W. Dayton, *Theological Roots of Pentecostalism* (Metuchen, NJ: Scarecrow, 2004).

renewal worldview on truth is that truth is not merely something outside our minds that we must believe but something we must also desire and live. Truth is a relationship. It is something we must embody in our everyday lives with each other and with God.

James K. A. Smith's Pentecostal Epistemology

Within renewal scholarship, James K. A. Smith has done more to highlight the epistemic power of narratives and affections than any other renewal figure. Since we covered some of the relevant information in the introduction and chapter 4, in this section we will briefly cover Smith's epistemology and then move to address how it relates to truth.

Tell Us a Story

Calling his theory "Pentecostal epistemology," Smith argues that stories and emotions are themselves forms of knowledge that are more primary than propositional knowledge. **Narrative, affective knowledge** comes before propositional knowledge and is irreducible to it. It is "the heart and affections [that act] as the *basis* for a rational, intellectual engagement with and interpretation of the world."[20] We can't reduce narrative, affective knowledge to something else without losing a central aspect of its nature. For example, if we explain in propositional form how a particular narrative and the affections it elicits act as knowledge, we lose something essential to our understanding of it. Some knowledge can only come through the medium. It's like explaining a joke. We can explain a joke to someone who doesn't understand it, and we can transmit the meaning to the level of the person's understanding, even realizing some level of humor. However, the essence of the joke and full force of its humor gets lost in translation. In this way, narrative, affective knowledge is irreducible.

We may have heard that right beliefs are central to the Christian faith. We are to "take every thought captive to obey Christ" (2 Cor. 10:5) and seek transformation through "the renewing of [our] minds" (Rom. 12:2). One of the central focal points of many Evangelical churches is the sermon, with emphasis placed on the New Testament letters. Such worldviews assume the preeminence of propositional knowledge. Such assumption can be traced to the Enlightenment, which raised the profile and power of human reason to an absolute state. Reason defines the essence of humanity and leads us to universal truth.[21]

20. James K. A. Smith, *Thinking in Tongues: Pentecostal Contributions to Christian Philosophy* (Grand Rapids: Eerdmans, 2010), 59.
21. Smith, *Thinking in Tongues*, 54–55.

This modernistic view, however, betrays the fullness of human being as both mental and embodied. Not only do we believe, but we also feel and act, and we do so through our interactions with eliciting contexts. Narratives and affections cannot avoid the particularities of different perspectives. Stories are told from a perspective. There is no universal, absolute story that is told outside of a perspective. Hence, Smith explains that metanarratives (that is, supposed perspective-less grand stories that claim universal truth) are self-deluded myths that haven't recognized their own rootedness in particular stories.[22] The same goes for affections: "Our passional orientation to the world is reflective of the particularities of our embodiment."[23] There is no universal emotion or mood that rules them all. They arise as responses to our specific involvement with our world. Even a universal story like the divine redemptive story becomes contextual as we place ourselves within it and ask where we fit. Divine truth is not merely propositional but also narrative and affective, and it involves us in the divine drama.

Our involvement in stories creates attendant emotions and meaning in our lives. Narratives create connections between events in order to make meaningful sense of the world.[24] How we understand the meaning of a tragic event can vary depending on our worldview. A nihilist who imagines all events as meaningless chaos will be resigned to understand the tragedy as but another meaningless event. A Christian, however, can find cosmic meaning and hope despite seemingly senseless tragedy due to the narrative belief that God works all things out for good (Rom. 8:28), resting on the evidence of God's goodness in her life story, which strengthens the hope elicited by Romans 8:28 and other passages throughout Scripture. These two accounts show how narratives provide meaning for reality and elicit emotions. Propositional beliefs are part of this process of meaning-making, but they are not often the primary mode.

In fact, our beliefs operate predominantly in narratives rather than in propositions. Think about our theology of God and God's involvement in our lives. We don't primarily rely on propositional doctrines. Rather, we tell stories about God's involvement in our lives and use the stories as the basis for our doctrines as they testify to the narratives of Scripture. Thus, we testify to God's goodness in our walk. We talk about how God redeemed us from our sinful rebellion and destitution. We talk about the dry valley and our thirst for God's presence. Pentecostalism has always taken this spiritual holism seriously. Not just the mind but the body engages in relational worship. We don't just stay in our pews, but

22. James K. A. Smith, *Who's Afraid of Postmodernism? Taking Derrida, Lyotard, and Foucault to Church* (Grand Rapids: Baker Academic, 2006), 67.

23. Smith, *Thinking in Tongues*, 59.

24. Smith, *Thinking in Tongues*, 69–70.

we physically move to the altar to pray and be prayed for, even dancing and falling on the floor in the Spirit. We give testimonies and share about God's mighty and merciful acts to each other. Such bodily involvements grasp our (pneumatological) imagination and shape our views about God, ourselves, and the world.[25] As Smith states, "This is a kind of Spirit-induced paradigm shift."[26] Our worldview is dependent on narratives and affections because we are embodied beings that participate in narratives that engage the emotions. We are not, as Descartes argued, merely thinking things.

We Are Not Just a Mind

The problem with Descartes's influence on Enlightenment philosophy is that it idolized human reason as absolute and supreme. If humans are essentially thinking things, then the body is unimportant and secondary. Because reason can transcend the particularities of space-time, it is seen as universal, neutral, and timeless. It was in this cultural context that secularism arose and discriminated against religion as being biased since it represented the particularities of embodiment.[27] This privileging of human reason deifies it and is therefore idolatrous. Smith incisively critiques this view, stating that

> what was often touted as "rational" turned out to be what white European males thought would be a good idea. In other words, the lineaments and conclusions of universal reason are . . . only one particular perspective writ large as if it were not a perspective but "just the way things really are." So what claimed to be a universal, neutral, God's-eye-view of the world turns out to be only the elevation and deification of one particular perspective pretending and parading as if it were not a "perspective" at all. And what is hailed as "knowledge" and "rationality" is one particular mode or register of calculation and perception—one particular way of "processing" the world according to the rubric of a particular logic.[28]

Yet Christianity hasn't been immune to this Enlightenment assumption insofar as some traditions have viewed beliefs as central to the faith. Despite their opposing viewpoints, and as strange as it may seem, rationalistic Christianity and secularism are bedfellows.

Against this propositional-truth mania, Pentecostals have emphasized the experiential, heartfelt encounter with the Holy Spirit. Religion is not a system of beliefs and doctrines but "a constellation of practices, rituals, and embodied

25. Smith, *Thinking in Tongues*, 80.
26. Smith, *Thinking in Tongues*, 69.
27. Smith, *Thinking in Tongues*, 55–56.
28. Smith, *Thinking in Tongues*, 57.

habits that 'carry' a story and an understanding."[29] For Pentecostals, this constellation begins and ends with the Spirit. It is this centrality of encounter with the Spirit not just in persons but in all creation that acts as the "heartbeat of the development of doctrine."[30] Belief arises from our involvement with the Spirit and the world within the divine drama. Smith identifies this spiritual holism and the importance of embodiment in Land's definition of Pentecostalism as a spirituality and not in Pentecostalism as a set of core doctrines.[31] Emphasis is placed on pneumatological encounter that elicits emotive rituals such as testimonials, ecstatic worship, laying on of hands for healing, and dancing, thereby avoiding the centrality of beliefs, which so easily divides and reduces religion to a system of beliefs.

By pinpointing Pentecostalism's radical openness to the Spirit's work in the world, Smith is able to avoid the fracturing that easily occurs when highest emphasis is placed on beliefs. Despite the divergences of beliefs and doctrines within global Pentecostalism, the experiential evidence of Spirit-inspired renewal makes it difficult to deny that God accepts "in every nation anyone who fears him and does what is right" (Acts 10:35). Evidence of renewal is not mere renewal in belief. It is rather the renewal of the whole person's life through encounter with the Holy Spirit.

Desire for the Good Life

Necessarily, narratives and affections are interpretive. There is no *absolute* narrative or affection. Even with Scripture, different emotions can be drawn from the same passages based on one's theological commitments. This is because emotions are related to their objects as they relate to our concerns and values, and we can project our emotions onto the object.[32] Hence, people can have vastly different attitudes and emotions toward "objects of wrath" (Rom. 9:21–23) depending on their theological views. How can we then rightly adjudicate between wrong narratives and affections, on the one hand, and true narratives and affections, on the other?[33] For Smith, the answer lies in the direction of desire.

29. Smith, *Thinking in Tongues*, 112.

30. Wolfgang Vondey, *Pentecostalism: A Guide for the Perplexed* (New York: Bloomsbury T&T Clark, 2013), 88.

31. Smith, *Thinking in Tongues*, xix–xx.

32. Katherine M. Hockey, *The Role of Emotion in 1 Peter* (New York: Cambridge University Press, 2019), 27.

33. Technically, wrong belief cannot be knowledge since truth is a precondition for knowledge that differentiates it from mere opinion. For a prescriptive account of how to determine when narrative, affective interpretation can qualify as knowledge, see Yoon Shin, *Pentecostalism, Postmodernism, and Reformed Epistemology: James K. A. Smith and the Contours of a Postmodern Christian Epistemology* (Lanham, MD: Lexington Books, 2022).

Smith argues that our hearts are primed toward an end. We are fundamentally desiring beings whose hearts are aimed toward the vision of the good life, however construed. This vision is part of the story we tell and in which we involve ourselves. Our human condition further demonstrates that we are not primarily thinking things.[34] An example of a static thinking being is Aristotle's Godlike Prime Mover, a perfect being who contains no dynamic motion and whose perfect act is thinking itself. As the first cause of everything, it causes motion and change in the world without being moved itself. In fact, it does not cause movement by directly involving itself in the moving process as an efficient cause, such as ball A moving to hit ball B to cause the latter's movement. Rather, it causes movement and change in others by drawing them to itself as an object of desire, just as an electric zapper draws insects to its mesmerizing blue light.[35]

We are not a static mind, a pure thought, like the Prime Mover. As embodied beings, we are involved in the world in dynamic ways. Take a moment to reflect on your day. Most likely, your primary mode of operation was through the "muscle memory" of the heart rather than through reflection. We don't think about every step we take. We don't analyze every plot point and every bit of dialogue as we watch a movie. We don't intentionally focus on the placement of our fingers on each key as we play an instrument, lest we fumble our way through the music. Importantly, our involvement in the world is primarily directed by our desires, by what we ultimately love.

Perhaps you are pursuing an education or a career that you desire. Even if you haven't yet decided the path you most want to follow, you are likely seeking an education that will fulfill your desires, if only the generalized desire to discover what you truly love. This is what it means to be aimed toward the vision of the good life. This vision captures our imagination and primes our heart to act. These actions turn into habits over time, habits that in turn begin to solidify our character. Our habits help define who we are: our default, prereflective mode of being.[36] A person who tells a lie in a moment of weakness differs from a habitual liar. A charitable person is known by his or her regular giving, compared to a miser who occasionally gives to satisfy a public image. Our habituated character is thus more foundational than our beliefs.

The affective vision of the good life is a narrative that we find ourselves in. However, not all visions of the good life and their attendant desires are right or correct. Like the descriptive explanation of narrative, affective knowledge, acknowledging that our actions are primed by our desires and vision of the

34. James K. A. Smith, *Desiring the Kingdom: Worship, Worldview, and Cultural Formation* (Grand Rapids: Baker Academic, 2009), 52.

35. Bertrand Russell, *The History of Western Philosophy* (New York: Touchstone, 1945), 168–69.

36. Smith, *Desiring the Kingdom*, 54–56.

good life is a descriptive statement that does not differentiate between right and wrong visions. For Smith, our desires cannot be aimed at and motivated by just any narrative of the good life; they must be rightly ordered and not misdirected.[37] This view presupposes that not all narratives that structure and describe the good life have equal validity.

For Christians, the affective vision of the good life must be anchored in the narrative outlined by the triune God in the world, ourselves, and Scripture. The good life is one that anchors us in the mission of God to redeem and reconcile the world. This story is a transcendent story because it is rooted in God's cosmic purposes. But it is a story told from a perspective. It is not some neutral narrative that is deductively or inductively proven by "objective" knowers.[38] Interpretation is true if our narratives are aimed toward God's story and our affections are rightly ordered. We can (externally) know that they align with God's mission because they reflect the interpreted values of Scripture and because of the testimony of the Holy Spirit in our hearts and lives. These are dynamic criteria, more like rules of thumb. They require trust and are not for those seeking deductive certainty. But much of our knowledge is not based on such certainty. We are guided by trust in those who testify to truth even as we use our critical thinking skills to examine their testimonies. Developing a rightly ordered vision of the good life that is anchored in the cosmic divine narrative requires this same trust and critical examination.

Developing this trust requires hearing and obeying the voice of the Spirit. Participating in God's story through obedience is the only way to prime our hearts and develop the necessary faculties for correctly interpreting the good life. Developing discernment, therefore, is a circular, nonlinear process. We must perceive, listen to, and obey the voice of the Spirit in the world, ourselves, and Scripture in order to develop our discernment. Discernment is an en-graced habit. As such, loving the good life is made possible by participating in the cosmic divine drama of loving God and loving others. As we are Spirit baptized into the love of God, we will gain the affective vision to discern the God-enacted good life.

Contributions toward a Renewal Worldview

If you recall from the introduction, we considered Smith's five-point outline of a renewal worldview. In this chapter on truth and knowledge, we have focused on the fourth point—narrative, affective knowledge—which flows from

37. Smith, *Desiring the Kingdom*, 52.
38. Even without proof, there are rational means, such as through deductive, inductive, and abductive logic, to determine whether a narrative is truer than not. We can also have warranted beliefs without evidence or arguments. Recall the section on Alvin Plantinga in chap. 11.

the affirmation of embodiment, Smith's third point. Truth is really out there. Truth can be known propositionally through correspondence from a perspective. Our knowledge of truth is an interpretation of reality from a particular perspective. Christians should not be afraid to claim their "biased" reading of reality since all knowledge is interpretive.

As important as propositional truth is, knowledge of truth is not primarily propositional, but narrative and affective. Propositional claims to truth arise from our location within the overarching divine story that provides their context and rationale. As we locate ourselves in this story, our hearts become primed toward its end: the vision of the good life according to the gospel of Jesus Christ. Through our participation in this story, our hearts begin to desire what God desires. However, our hearts are also pulled by other narratives that seek to capture our desires. While we want to live a just life, we can be drawn toward revenge against someone who deeply hurt us. We know that the riches of this world cannot satisfy our deepest longings, but the latest products tug at our hearts. The success of staying the course does not occur by merely doubling down on our beliefs. Belief is important, but it is impotent without attendant emotions and actions. We prime our hearts by habituating ourselves within the stories we desire, developing a consistent character that faithfully participates in the particular story. That story, for Christians, is God's cosmic mission in the world. In this mission, we don't merely believe correct doctrines. We must believe, act, and feel faithfully as we integrate our story within God's cosmic drama.

There is much compatibility between this renewal worldview and the ideas of Plantinga, Zagzebski, and Lindbeck. As in Plantinga, narrative, affective knowledge is most compatible with externalism. The question about narrative, affective knowledge's correct interpretation of the world cannot be resolved by providing evidence or argument to no end. Our everyday participation in God's mission is rarely theoretical. In obedience, we seek to live out God's purposes. How do we know that our understanding of God's mission is true? We know based on our reading of Scripture, the testimony of the Spirit in our hearts, and the wisdom of others. We see our participation in God's mission as continuing the scriptural narrative of God's involvement in the world. The Spirit has spoken and acted upon the Spirit-anointed community. Through sanctification, our spirits are renewed, made holy, and healed from spiritual dysfunction. The anointing of the Holy Spirit makes knowledge possible, even the hidden depths of God and the secrets of persons, without logical and evidential demonstration. In the end, we know God's story is true not because of some undefeated evidence or argument but because the Holy Spirit testifies to its truth in our hearts, through Scripture and through the world, and heals and sanctifies us from the corrupting effects of sin. It's not that the Spirit merely gives us new epistemic content, which does happen. But, more importantly, the Spirit brings about a new paradigm or worldview shift that helps us to see what we couldn't see before. This access can turn what used to be available only through inference into the level of proper basicality. With the help of a (pneumatological) guide, we can begin to see easily what we couldn't see before even with great effort.

Sanctification, then, is an important means to knowledge. The paradigm shifts and healing of our epistemic faculties and processes must occur through the aid of the Spirit if we are to know reality truly. Moreover, sanctification is the theological equivalent to virtue formation. Since part of becoming like Jesus and knowing him occurs through the development of our virtues, the virtues are essential for knowledge. But because the virtues are intellectual *and* moral, virtues also cultivate our character. Therefore, together with the Holy Spirit, we are able to develop the virtues that allow us to live, know, and feel faithfully. Whether in the Sermon on the Mount or in the list of the fruit of the Spirit or elsewhere, Christians are often commanded to develop virtues and avoid vices, for our sanctification is God's will, and this command is tied to the ministry of the Spirit (1 Thess. 4:3–8). As part of the Spirit's work, virtue formation is a way toward being changed into the image of Christ (2 Cor. 3:18).

To use Zagzebski's language, sanctification regarding knowledge requires our continual development of the intellectual virtues through habit formation. While Plantinga is correct that some beliefs are warranted without any reflection, other beliefs must be reflectively discerned. In certain circumstances, such as when someone effectively challenges our beliefs in a way that raises doubts, it's important to develop reasons for why our beliefs are true. The work of pursuing these reasons is only made possible through the use of various intellectual virtues. In fact, we may not even take the steps toward reflection unless we display virtues such as open-mindedness, love of truth, and intellectual courage. The virtues thus help in our reflections and in directing our affections. In this way, a person of virtue and a person of vice will holistically know the world differently because they will develop their knowledge in antithetical ways. In fact, a person of virtue will know the world more fully and in better ways than a person of vice since the attainment of knowledge through sanctification is a Spirit-inspired activity. The sanctified person will be attuned to the revelation of the Spirit, who leads God's people into truth (John 16:13).

Finally, Lindbeck's theory that religion is a cultural-linguistic lived framework that provides meaning describes how Pentecostals worldwide are identifiable despite having different beliefs and practices. The shared renewal is Spirit-focused, and it develops with distinct local flavors. Global Pentecostalism does not share some essential doctrines. Doctrines arise bottom-up from the worshipful practices and beliefs of local communities as they seek to faithfully live out the narratives of Scripture in their own lives. Therefore, religion is primarily performative rather than mental. Lindbeck's performative correspondence theory describes how Pentecostals understand participating in truth. Pentecostals reject the importance of mere belief in truth. To believe rightly requires loving and doing the truth, to be enraptured in the presence of God and to be transformed into the sanctified life. Pentecostals may not espouse a developed theory of truth, but they implicitly affirm a performative theory of truth that is affective, mental, and active.

Conclusion

Upon examining Pentecostalism as a lived spirituality rather than a doctrinal movement, it becomes clear that a renewal commitment to truth is more stringent than the more common notion of truth as absolute, objective, and propositional. The latter places belief as the primary indicator of fidelity. This view is recognizable in Christian traditions that emphasize "biblical" teaching and doctrines as the means to return to orthodox, faithful Christianity. Pentecostals, on the other hand, implicitly understand that the transcendent truth of God is not something to merely believe. What is the point of believing if there is no renewal in our lives? Truth must be present deep in our bones. Truth is something to which we assent *and* in which we participate as the object of our love. We must experience and live out the truth because truth is personified in the Spirit of God, who has been poured out on all flesh. This is why a renewal worldview is not primarily about giving answers to ultimate questions. Ultimate beliefs are part of a renewal worldview, but Pentecostals believe within the nexus of worship and love. Living out God's mission by participating in God's cosmic narrative transforms minds, hearts, and actions, which forms the holistic lens through which we interpret reality. Therefore, truth is not either subjective or objective. The subject must participate in the object to be united with the truth. For God is truth, and to be in union with truth is to be in union with God.

Study Questions

1. Explain the relationship between right belief (orthodoxy), right affection (orthopathos), and right action (orthopraxis).

2. Explain how narrative, affective knowledge differs from propositional knowledge.

3. How are trust and discernment related to determining the correct picture of the good life?

EPILOGUE

Living Renewed in a Pluralistic World

In the introduction, we mentioned that the Spirit ultimately guides us to the triune life through the experience of beauty, goodness, and truth. Since God is Beauty, Goodness, and Truth as such, knowing, desiring, and participating in them is to know, desire, and participate in God. Beauty, goodness, and truth are transcendental because they represent who God is; God is beautiful, good, and true. They are not transcendental because they merely exist mind-independently and transcend our subjective beliefs. They are properly transcendental because of their relation to God's being. A renewal worldview on beauty, goodness, and truth begins from this experiential confession that God stands behind them as their living reality.

A Pneumatological Approach

Although the triune God is presupposed, a renewal worldview approaches the transcendentals from a pneumatological perspective. By this, we are not making the prescriptive claim that pneumatology is the only or most accurate approach for any worldview. Triperspectivally speaking, this is but one perspective, and worldviews can be developed paterologically or christologically. But since renewal occurs through the Spirit, renewal worldview most appropriately develops pneumatologically.

Many approaches frame worldviews propositionally, whether by thinking or believing. We surmise that this approach is primarily christological, with its connection to *logos* or Word (John 1:1). The connection between Christ, on the one hand, and belief and confession, on the other, has long been established.

213

In common parlance, we speak of believing in the Lord Jesus Christ or making every thought captive to Christ (Rom. 10:9; 2 Cor. 10:5). However, we are not raising the question of whether this connection between Christology and propositional beliefs is appropriate. Our position is merely that a renewal worldview should be primarily framed pneumatologically rather than christologically without eliminating the latter. Belief and thinking impact worldviews, but that impact is secondary as worldviews are primarily formed experientially and narratively.

The ministry of the Holy Spirit fits the experiential picture better than the ministry of Christ, which is now primarily as high priest and Spirit baptizer. Pentecostals view their relationship with the Spirit as an everyday experiential interaction. They do not merely or even primarily think about their relationship with the Spirit. Rather, they are open to the Spirit's leading and voice for their everyday existence. Unlike mental beliefs, this posture toward the Spirit engages both the human spirit—in its openness to and discernment of the spiritual world—and the human body—in living obediently to the leading of the Spirit—and presupposes a holism between body and soul. It's an everyday posture that frames how we understand and navigate reality. Renewal worldview is something Pentecostals imagine, feel, and inhabit more than what they believe or think, and we stressed throughout the book that a renewal worldview develops from an embodied spirituality.

Nevertheless, triperspectivally speaking, we do believe and think, and there are instances in which our beliefs and reflections can have great influence on our worldview. When I (Yoon) became a new Christian as a young adult, I had a wooden picture of God's revelation in Scripture. I took every story of the Bible literally and projected that picture onto God. Part of this was due to my social locations, especially the formative time I served in the US Navy. All official communications were direct and to the point.[1] I spent four years receiving and repeating orders; there was *no room* for considering the *broader* meanings of words.[2] My worldview about God and revelation was directly impacted by my everyday immersion in the life of a sailor. But this changed when I encountered philosophy and theology as an undergraduate student. Learning about the depth of God and revelation led to a worldview shift about the different possibilities of God's action in the world.

While our emotions and actions most frequently inform and perpetuate our worldview, beliefs and reflections can have infrequent but powerful impact on

---

1. This was prior to my understanding that much of human communication is metaphorical.

2. Do you see how metaphors *snuck in* this sentence so easily? You probably wouldn't have even *batted an eye* if I didn't point it out. On the metaphorical usage of language, see George Lakoff and Mark Johnson, *Metaphors We Live By* (Chicago: University of Chicago Press, 1980).

its form. Worldview materials that provide propositional information about God and the world are still important. That is why this book also consists primarily of propositional information, although our stylistic decision had more to do with our lack of skill in storytelling than with the value of propositional information. One could have implicitly picked up some of our content by reading spiritual or theological biographies (not to mention the Bible!). Pentecostals have been immersed in the renewal worldview through their daily Spirit-filled lives. We have merely attempted to make explicit what is implicit in our lives.

One Renewal Worldview to Rule Them All?

Making explicit what is implicit in a global renewal movement is a daunting, and perhaps impossible, task. Christian renewal occurs across denominational and confessional lines. Could we adequately capture the renewal worldview of Roman Catholicism, Presbyterianism, and nondenominational neo-Pentecostalism across the globe? The answer is a resounding no!

Even a propositional approach cannot achieve a singular worldview, given that communities have differing views on worldview topics such as the relationship between God and creation (e.g., theism and panentheism), the body-soul relationship and its implications for death and the afterlife (e.g., substance dualism and Christian materialism), humanity's relationship to evil (e.g., the fall of Adam and Eve and theistic evolutionism), and our core commitment to the kingdom of God (e.g., the gospel of forensic justification and the gospel of just righteousness).[3] Given that these various views are contested within Christian communities, it is misleading to proclaim that one view is the definite Christian worldview. For example, in the famous worldview text *The Universe Next Door*, James Sire argues that a core worldview commitment is "to glorify God and enjoy him forever."[4] Yet, that statement comes from the Westminster Catechism, a distinctly Reformed confession, which asks, "What is the chief end of man?" Given that the Westminster Catechism is not an ecumenical confession, it cannot act as a *definitive* part of a Christian or biblical worldview.[5] The lack of an absolute doctrinal agreement gives us a clue that there is no single Christian or biblical worldview.

3. Due to space constraints, we cannot describe the various views mentioned here, but we encourage our readers to research them. The topics are inspired by James W. Sire's *The Universe Next Door: A Basic Worldview Catalog*, 5th ed. (Downers Grove, IL: IVP Academic, 2009).

4. Sire, *Universe Next Door*, 44.

5. Sire is careful to note that this statement can be personalized in various ways, but allowing so many qualifications risks departing from the Westminster Catechism's understanding, such as qualified by the second question and answer in the Westminster Shorter Catechism.

We shouldn't be afraid of lacking uniformity since unity does not require it. Even in its early history, Christianity exhibited this diversity, as the first ecumenical confession on the Trinity quickly led to disagreement between the churches of the East and West. Unity does not require absolute agreement in affection, action, or doctrine. While greater agreement is possible on the most general pronouncements, how those pronouncements are nuanced creates greater differences. For example, Christians agree that they are to love God and neighbor, but how they are to love is disputable in terms of feeling, acting, and believing. We are not, however, advocating relativism. The choices are not simply absolute truth or relativism. Even without absolutely clear lines between "orthodox" and "nonorthodox" worldviews, we can use rational means to question the faithfulness of a worldview since revelation can only provide a finite range of meaning. Proclaiming that Jesus is Lord requires understanding Jesus as someone greater than ourselves, submitting to him, and loving him. How these proclamations are understood and practiced may diverge, but such divergences cannot accommodate seeing Jesus advocate for, say, slavery or hatred. Revelation (and all of objective reality) provides only a finite range of faithful understanding that encourages unity through diversity while precluding relativism.

The renewal worldview we have offered works within the logic of unity through diversity. We cannot capture all the nuanced differences between each renewal community's worldviews. However, we have sought to capture (at a general level) objective resemblances provided by the commonality of pneumatological renewal, which affects the whole person. While there is not one renewal worldview to rule them all, we have provided a picture of a renewal worldview on beauty, goodness, and truth that is grounded in the Spirit and a picture of embodiment that is faithful to our affections, practices, and beliefs. We encourage readers to build on and modify *this* worldview in light of their own renewal communities.

We have emphasized embodiment and its necessary social locationality. Our social locations provide strengths and weaknesses for our understanding of a renewal worldview. As Pentecostals affiliated with classical Pentecostal denominations, we have firsthand knowledge and understanding of the renewal life and of renewal studies. Our context also blinds us to some of the differences in other renewal traditions. We hope to have mitigated some of those limitations with our diverse backgrounds. Steven was long affiliated with the Christian and Missionary Alliance Church and the United Methodist Church. Yoon has served in Korean American churches with the Presbyterian Church of America and the Southern Baptist Convention and has always maintained ties with the Reformed tradition. Our life experiences have been cross-cultural.

Steven is of mixed ethnic heritage (Puerto Rican and German) and grew up outside the US. Yoon was a child immigrant from South Korea. We are also interdisciplinarians, traversing between philosophy, systematic theology, and biblical theology. Our diverse backgrounds have aided a broader understanding of a renewal worldview. We also encourage Pentecostals to better understand their renewal worldview by seeking diverse life experiences and interdisciplinary studies in order to recognize the diversity of the renewal life and worldview.

SCRIPTURE INDEX

SUBJECT INDEX